PLOTTING THE GOLDEN WEST

PLOTTING
THE
GOLDEN WEST

American literature and
the rhetoric of
the California Trail

STEPHEN FENDER

Lecturer in English and American Literature
University College London

CAMBRIDGE UNIVERSITY PRESS

CAMBRIDGE

LONDON NEW YORK NEW ROCHELLE

MELBOURNE SYDNEY

Published by the Press Syndicate of the University of Cambridge
The Pitt Building, Trumpington Street, Cambridge CB2 1RP
32 East 57th Street, New York, NY 10022, USA
296 Beaconsfield Parade, Middle Park, Melbourne 3206, Australia

First published 1981

Printed in United States of America by Vail-Ballou Press, Inc., of
Binghamton, N.Y.

Library of Congress catalogue card number 81–6077

British Library Cataloguing in Publication Data
Fender, Stephen
Plotting the Golden West.
1. Gold mines and mining – California – social
life and customs
I. Title
979.4'04   F865
ISBN 0–521–23924–9

CONTENTS

ILLUSTRATIONS

ACKNOWLEDGEMENTS

It is a great pleasure to recall the generous help given by institutions and individuals at various stages of the preparation of this book. I am particularly grateful to the Huntington Library for a fellowship to enable me to examine their holdings of forty-niners' diaries and other materials relating to the California Gold Rush, and to Ray Billington and Virginia Renner for helping me to make the best use of it when I got there. My own employers, University College London, made two grants of travel money from the Dean's Fund, Faculty of Arts, and several from the Chambers Fund to meet typing and copying costs – and this during a period of prolonged austerity in British universities. In Berkeley the late Fred Anderson, head of the Mark Twain Papers in the Bancroft Library, spent many hours of his precious (and, as it turned out, tragically curtailed) time taking me through his files of letters and early sketches of Mark Twain, explaining references, filling in lacunae and generally providing the context that made them live. He also read, and offered many valuable suggestions for improving, an early version of chapter 6. Two San Francisco novelists and historians, Kevin Starr and my cousin Richard Reinhardt, have provided unfailing encouragement and expertise – the latter with particular respect to chapter 3, and the former in a more general sense, ever since we first met in 1974. The Palo Alto artist Jane Kamine and the Berkeley novelist and critic David Littlejohn provided advice and practical help with the illustrations.

Hennig Cohen, of the University of Pennsylvania, took time off on a visit to London to instruct me in the sublime and beautiful as these terms have been applied to the American landscape, and James Cox, of Dartmouth, read and offered valuable suggestions for chapters 1 through 6. Among my colleagues at UCL who must be relieved to see this thing at last in print, I would like to mention

Karl Miller and John Sutherland, whose suggestions and encouragement lived up to their reputations as editor and critic, and Susan Oldacre, who typed the manuscript and warned me when it was getting boring. Finally Buffy Fender, a fearsome detector of trendiness, caused me to revise every chapter at least once in favor of reater comprehensibility and was particularly insistent that I should delete the word 'recuperate' whenever possible.

A version of Chapter 6 first appeared in *The Modern Language Review,* vol. 71, no. 4 (October 1976), pp. 737–56, and appears here by kind permission of the Editors and the Modern Humanities Research Association.

I would like to thank the Bancroft Library, University of California, Berkeley, and the Huntington Library, San Marino, California, for permission to quote from manuscript material in their possession. Previously unpublished material of Samuel L. Clemens is Copyright 1981 by Thomas G. Chamberlain and Manufacturers Hanover Trust Company as trustees under the will of Clara Clemens Samossoud.

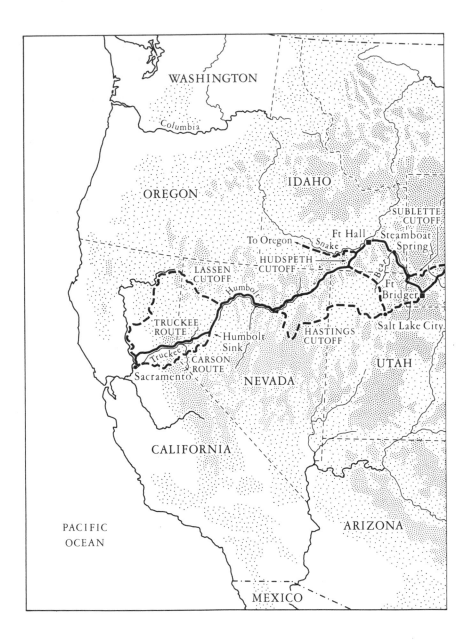

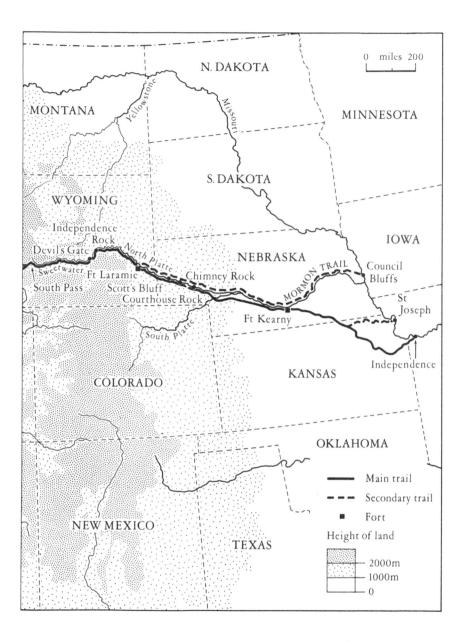

INTRODUCTION

Someone once said that America was the only country to pass directly from barbarism to decadence without an intervening period of civilization. And certainly, insofar as American novelists have ever been satirists, they have addressed themselves to these two extremes. The persistent, if apparently contradictory, critique of American life is both that it lacks what Washington Irving called 'association' (by which he meant the relationship of present to past as well as of things to people in a landscape), and also that it is stiflingly, even obsessively overplotted. Henry James was not the only novelist, nor the first, to utter a long list of titles and prerogatives missing from the American scene. The famous negative catalogue in his book on Hawthorne was anticipated by over fifty years by James Fenimore Cooper's *Notions of the Americans:*

There are no annals for the historian; no follies . . . for the satirist; no manners for the dramatist, no obscure fictions for the writer of romance; . . . no costume for the peasant, (there is scarcely a peasant at all), no wig for the judge, no baton for the general, no diadem for the chief magistrate.[1]

Mark Twain in *Huckleberry Finn* gets a good deal of fun out of the confusion of styles in the Grangerfords' parlor — the crockery dog, the wild-turkey-wing fans, the copy of *Friendship's Offering* on the oilcloth table cover; all overlooked by the gloomy romanticism of Emmeline's pictures. But when the more stable and comprehensible culture of St Petersburg overtakes Huck at the end of the novel, and when Tom Sawyer articulates Jim's escape according to the stale conventions of schoolboy romance, Huck has to make his own, authentic escape into Oklahoma Territory, one of the last of those magical tracts of the American West to become a state of the Federal Union. In *The Great Gatsby* Fitzgerald's Nick Carraway is amused at Meyer Wolfsheim's reference to 'Oggsford College,' and at the multiplicity of detached signifiers in the names and occupations of Gatsby's guests, but what he escapes from is the established wealth and rooted privilege of an East now grown corrupt in its antiquity. 'I see now that this has been a story of the West, after all,' he writes at the end of his tale, and Gatsby emerges as the novel's hero by virtue of the very rootlessness of his background; though, paradoxically, and unlike Tom Buchanan, he really has spent some time as a student at Oxford. Thomas Pynchon's *The Crying of Lot 49* begins as a typical easterner's satire on California life, with its hectic uprooting and eclectic consumption of a dozen

diverse cultures, ancient and modern, European and Oriental. Oedipa Maas goes to the supermarket in *downtown* Kinneret-Among-
The-Pines to buy ricotta, where she hears a Muzak recording of the
Fort Wayne Settecento Ensemble playing the Vivaldi Kazoo Con-
certo, returns home to read the book reviews in the latest *Scientific
American,* make dinner, mix the whisky sours and get the news
from Huntley and Brinkley. Yet at the end of the book she looks
around desperately for an escape from an America replete with plots
– plots of building land as well as of schemes and stories – at about
the same time the reader begins to look for a way out of Pynchon's
overplotted novel. For escape Oedipa looks, not to the West
(because by now the restless advance of American civilization has
reached the shores of the Pacific and well beyond) but eastwards; to
the white spaces in the American text, the empty tracts not seized
by real-estate developers, and the waste products of American technology:

She thought of other, immobilized freight cars, where the kids sat on the floor
planking and sang back, happy as fat, whatever came over the mother's pocket
radio; of other squatters who stretched canvas for lean-tos behind smiling bill-
boards along all the highways or slept in junkyards in the stripped shells of
wrecked Plymouths, or even, daring, spent the night up some pole in a lineman's
tent like caterpillars, swung among a web of telephone wires, living in the very
copper rigging and secular miracle of communication, untroubled by the dumb
voltages flickering their miles, the night long, in the thousands of unheard messages.

This is the most attractive scene in the novel, not only because it
is the most concrete, but also because here, if only here, the messages no longer get through to a protagonist already burdened with
a surplus of information. But like any paradisal vision, it is unat-
tainable, except as a gesture or a rhetorical flourish. It is, in other
words, like dropping out, or like Thoreau's 'Economy' in *Walden,*
which fails to account for the cost of labor and machines to cut and
mill the lumber he stripped from the Irish shanty, or like Mark
Twain's idea of the territories, for which he himself had once lit out
from the Civil War in a fantastic search for silver, over twenty years
before completing *Huckleberry Finn.*
  Yet the critique of American culture is only apparently contradictory. Writers, like pioneers, experience these opposing feelings
in turn, not simultaneously. The author, looking at the expanse of

white paper that confronts him at the beginning of his task, may be appalled at its emptiness; while towards the end, his boredom and disgust at a surfeit of plots may prompt him to look for a means of escape from his book. The pioneer may be uneasy at his first sight of the wilderness, but just as anxious to light out again when civilization catches him up. If this connection between writing and geography is no more than fortuitous or rhetorical, it has, at least, a long history in American criticism. As seen from the East, the unsettled West was a natural backdrop on which the still unfulfilled hopes of American society could be projected. 'It presents a fruitful theme of anxious contemplation . . . as the destined theatre of future events and exhibitions of human character,' according to the long notice in the *North American Review* of Timothy Flint's *Recollections of the Last Ten Years, passed . . . in the Valley of the Mississippi,* published in 1826. 'In that region it is to be determined whether . . . our intellectual and moral progress will be adequate to maintain our republican forms of government.'

But first the slate had to be cleaned, or the stage emptied. 'Until the cession of Louisiana to the American government, under the administration of Mr Jefferson,' the reviewer continued, '. . . Chateaubriand had peopled it with beings of his own creation, and had pictured it to our imagination, as the region of romance.' Once the illusions of European, aristocratic romance were banished, the republican traveler from the American States could document the West in all its commonplace actuality. The reviewer allowed that Flint might have 'been more minute, and filled up more completely some of his outlines,' but he praised his delineation of the various types to be found in the West:

The scene is changed, and we are introduced to the rough, but frank and hospitable *backwoodsman,* with his rifle in his hand, his dogs at his heels, 'all girt for the chase,' receiving his visitant with little appearance, but with all the reality, of a cordial welcome. The preachers, the lawyers, the great and little men of the West, the Indian, the negro, the fanatic, the venerable chronicler of 'the olden time,' the fresh and lovely 'rose of the prairie,' successively pass in review before us.[2]

So two years before the publication of *Notions of the Americans,* someone had already produced a positive catalogue of types to be discerned, even in that sparsely cultivated part of the American continent. They were not the figment of a romantic imagination, but really there. Though not labeled by title and uniform as in a traditional hierarchy, they could form the basis for fiction; even here they are aesthetically framed, imaged as passing on parade or across a stage. Emerson, who was twenty-three when this review appeared, and who can hardly have missed it, was later to base his program for the whole of American literature on a similar list. 'The meaner the type by which a law is expressed, the more pungent it is, and the more lasting in the memories of men,' he wrote in 'The Poet,' probably in 1842. 'Bare lists of words are found suggestive to an imaginative and excited mind . . .':

Banks and tariffs, the newspaper and caucus, Methodism and Unitarianism, are flat and dull to dull people, but rest on the same foundations of wonder as the town of Troy and the Temple of Delphi, and are as swiftly passing away. Our log-rolling, our stumps and their politics, our fisheries, our Negroes and Indians, our boats and our repudiations, the wrath of rogues and the pusillanimity of honest men, the northern trade, the southern planting, the western clearing, Oregon and Texas, are yet unsung. Yet America is a poem in our eyes; its ample geography dazzles the imagination, and it will not wait long for meters.[3]

Quite right. As de Tocqueville had predicted, 'Amongst a democratic people, poetry will not be fed with legends or the memorials of old traditions. The poet will not attempt to people the universe with supernatural beings, in whom his readers and his own fancy have ceased to believe.'[4] And if this was to be true of American literature as opposed to European, it was to be doubly true of writing in, or set in, the American West. Whitman took up Emerson's challenge to put the 'poem in our eyes' straight down on paper, to utter 'bare lists of words' without the mediating formalities of European meter diction or conventional figures. He too saw the western plains, in their 'superb monotony' and 'unbounded scale' as 'the home both of what I would call America's distinctive ideas and distinctive realities.'[5]

Even before Whitman wrote that, W. D. Howells, himself a westerner who saw the West as a likely source for the new realism in American letters, had begun to use his position as editor of *The Atlantic* to promote young writers, like Mark Twain, Edward Eggleston and Hamlin Garland, whom he considered western in origin. In Mark Twain's work, thought Howells, there was 'something curiously, not very definably . . . Western.' Mark Twain was western because of his very lack of association:

The West, when it began to put itself into literature, could do so without the sense, or the apparent sense, of any older or politer world outside of it; whereas the East was always looking fearfully over its shoulder at Europe, and anxious to account for itself as well as represent itself. No such anxiety as this entered Mark Twain's mind, and it is not claiming too much for the Western influence upon American literature to say that the final liberation of the East from this anxiety is due to the West, and to its ignorant courage or its indifference to its difference from the rest of the world.[6]

In fact, Mark Twain and Hamlin Garland (not to mention Howells himself) came from what we now call the Midwest, not the Far West, and their best writing was set in the towns and farms that had been settled for some fifty years after the frontier had passed their way. The fiction of the Midwest was the gritty realism* of *Main-Travelled Roads* and the social satire of *Huckleberry Finn*. For Howells achievements like these were enough to signal 'the final liberation' of American writing from its European origins. For Garland, however, the Far West of the pioneers might yield a further stage in native realism. In *Crumbling Idols,* his collection of essays published three years after *Main-Travelled Roads,* the flare of prophecy burns as bright as ever it did in Emerson or Whitman. Even at the end of the century, the true American novel was still trembling to be born:

We have had the figures, the dates, the bare history, the dime-novel statement of pioneer life, but how few real novels! How few accurate studies of speech and life! There it lies, ready to be put into the novel and the drama, and upon canvas; and it must be done by those born into it. . . . . All over the West young people are coming on who see that every literature in the past was at its best creative and not imitative. . . . . They are reading the most modern literature, and their

---

* I should say that I am using the problematic term 'realism' here in the sense in which it was used by Howells and his contemporaries (though Garland preferred 'veritism'): that is, a form of fiction attending to the details of commonplace life, including the way people actually speak and the rather shapeless plots of actual events. The distinction between the romance and the realistic novel has been a commonplace of Anglo-Saxon literary criticism since Clara Reeve's *The Progress of Romance* (1785): 'The Romance in lofty and elevated language, describes what never happened nor is likely to happen. – The Novel gives a familiar relation of such things, as pass every day before our eyes . . .' (vol. I, Evening vii). Other uses of 'realism' not relevant here include Zola's *réalisme* (Americans called it 'naturalism') and Lukács's socialist realism, both of which imply fidelity to objective natural or historical processes. Thus, for Lukács, Scott and Cooper are 'realistic' authors, despite their inattention, so deplored by Mark Twain, to the details of ordinary life and speech, because their fiction focussed on crucial moments in the class struggle.

6

judgements are not dependent upon New York or London, though they find themselves in full harmony with progressive artists everywhere.[7]

The hope of the West, then, for writing no less than for the general prosperity of the country, lay in its material resources. Had American literature failed, so far, to attend to the facts of American life and landscape? Had the authors of New England and the Atlantic States already lost their nerve and fallen back on the comforting props of Old-World cultural conventions? Never mind, the West would redeem the promise. Its splendid variety of ordinary things, its rich profusion of minerals, mountains, rivers, trees and wild animals, of big-hearted men with their novel occupations and earthy vernacular – all this would at last become so vivid (or, as Whitman would say, the monotonous would become so superb) that the most fantastic romance borrowed from conventional fiction would retreat before it as an embarrassed ghost in the light of day.

Of course, the prophecy could never have been fulfilled literally. This side of the millennium there are no places waiting to leap onto paper, canvas, or even photographic emulsion without the mediation of the artist, and there are no neutral receptors ready to transcribe the experience without infecting it with the prejudices and predilections brought from another place. Everyone, no matter how unsophisticated, has a culture. The American Far West could never have expressed itself for itself; it was described by easterners for other easterners who stayed at home. This truism requires some emphasis if only because, as chapter 7 will show, a number of historians and literary critics are still looking at the American West from the standpoint of the nineteenth-century positivists – as though it consisted of things and events in history and not those things and events as represented by people with their own inescapable stereotypes of reality.

Even so, any mediation between terms is bound to be unbalanced in favor of one or the other extreme, and it must be an occasion for some surprise that the writing of the Far West turned out to be so much more formal than material. Paradoxically, the frontier seems to have attracted more antique literary conventions, to have been more heavily plotted, than any of the more settled regions of the continent. Travelers wrote about it in terms of the sublime or picturesque. Novelists, authors of pulp fiction and screenwriters have set it repeatedly in the frame of epic or pastoral romance. Cooper mined 'obscure fiction for the writer of romance' from the (much refined) tales about the old mountain men, and synthesized, in his hierarchies of hair color, complexion, dress and levels of speech, a set of codes to replace the missing costume, wig, baton and diadem. Garland's abhorred Dime Novelists did not give way to a new breed of realists but to yet another wave of romance – this time about cowboys – characterized by Emerson Hough's *The Girl at the Half-way House* (1900), *Bransford in Arcadia* (1913) by Eugene Manlove Rhodes, and – best known of all, because it set the pattern for thousands of western movies – Owen Wister's *The Virginian* (1902). Mark Twain lost his cultural bearings in Nevada, and his styles of life and prose show the signs of that strain. Even Garland, the great 'veritist' himself, defected to romance when he began to travel widely in the Far West in the 1890s. His *The Captain of the Grey Horse Troop* (1902) and *Cavanaugh, Forest Ranger* (1910) exploited the situational melodrama of cowboys struggling with Indians and federal agents trying to manage the wilderness. In *They of the High Trails* (1916) he further inflated his diction and elaborated his syntax to glamorize what he saw as types of the West ('The Grubstaker,' 'The Cow Boss,' 'The Outlaw') as stock figures in the epic or pastoral. Howells's response to all this was mild enough, considering the disappointment he must have felt in seeing his protégé relax his attention to the minutiae of social behavior. 'If [Mr Garland's] work seems to lose at times in closeness of texture on its westering way, it gains in breadth,' he wrote in 1912.[8] By the time he came to supply a preface to *They of the High Trails*, he had to admit that he had 'enjoyed the level footing more and got [his] breath better in the lower altitudes of Main-Travelled Roads.'[9]

So the more plotless the landscape, the more plotted the writing. The paradox is easily explained by reference to that well-known anxiety which so often accompanies the exhilaration at escaping the constraints of home, the growing awareness that foreigners are dirty, dishonest and unkind to animals. The traveler's concern at leaving behind what he takes to be his cultural center prompts a more-than-ever rigorous observance of whatever forms he thinks distinguishes him from the foreign culture in which he finds himself. And these outward conventions must not be covert, subtle and recognized by only a small elite within his society; they must be the lowest common denominator of Englishness, or Americanness, or whatever nationality they represent — so much so that they have become almost music-hall jokes by the time they are employed.

If the journey is taken a stage further, beyond the borders of civilization itself rather than outside one's own country, both the paranoia and the corresponding reaction may become more extreme. One fears not smells and brusqueness, but perhaps death itself; one longs not for chips, hamburgers or a good cup of tea, but for more dramatic evidence of human control. Those who have spent more than a day or two in a real wilderness may know the urge to hunt, or to clear away some of the slovenly growth that encloses the camp. At home we would act differently — perhaps even support conservation laws.

This association of distance and melodrama is neatly outlined in *Northanger Abbey,* Jane Austen's critique of the gothic romance. When Catherine Morland is finally disabused of her suspicion that General Tilney has secretly done away with his wife, her 'visions of romance' fall away. Later she reflects:

Charming as were all Mrs Radcliffe's works, and charming even as were the works of all her imitators, it was not in them perhaps that human nature, at least in the Midland counties of England, was to be looked for. Of the Alps and Pyrenees, with their pine forests and their vices, they might give a faithful delineation; and Italy, Switzerland, and the south of France might be as fruitful in horrors as they were there represented. Catherine dared not doubt beyond her own country, and even of that, if hard pressed, would have yielded the northern and western extremities. But in the central part of England there was surely some security for the existence even of a wife not beloved, in the laws of the land, and the manners of the age. Murder was not tolerated, servants were not slaves, and neither poison nor sleeping potions to be procured, like rhubarb, from every druggist. Among the Alps and Pyrenees, perhaps, there were no mixed characters. There, such as were not as spotless as an angel might have the dispositions of a fiend. But in England it was not so; among the English, she believed, in their hearts and habits, there was a general though unequal mixture of good and bad.

The same effect on authors, especially on writers of fiction, may be a reversion to the old, familiar formulae of romance: the high plotting of improbable action, the comforting simplicity of character. To the Harvard-educated grandson of Fanny Kemble, brought up in the East, the American equivalent of the Alps and the Pyrenees was the Far West. On one of his trips to Wyoming Owen Wister entered in his journal a description of one Henry

Smith, 'the only unabridged "bad man" I have had a chance to know,' who spent his time 'stealing cattle or, more likely mavericking':

He is not a half-way man. Not the Bret Harte villain with the heart of a woman. Not the mixed dish of Cambric tea so dear to modern novelists. He is just bad through and through, without a scruple and without an affection. His face is entirely cruel, and you hear cruelty in his voice. How do I know all this? Because I know something of his past and present, and I have heard him speak for himself. He has attended to scores of men and women in his talk and never to one without a corrosive sneer. When I come to my Castle in Spain – my book about Wyoming – I shall strain my muscles to catch Smith. I'm getting to believe mixed characters are not the only ones in the world. [10]

He could, of course, be reporting what he found. Doubtless Smith was unpleasant. But the question is whether, set in the familiar scale of the home environment, he would have been described anything more than that – or noted anything at all. Wister's own question would indicate some doubt, at least, some hint that only on this blank canvas would Smith appear so unequivocally and dramatically evil. And there is more than a hint that the appropriate form for dealing with the phenomenon will be an antique fable, a 'Castle in Spain' rather than a modern novel of the kind Wister had written before, and would write after, *The Virginian*.

Even the English novel may be thought to have exhibited some of this association between remoteness and romance. Novelists who found themselves traveling, for business or pleasure, to the furthest reaches of the Empire and beyond, had greater need for conventional fictions the further they moved from their metropolitan center. In *Heart of Darkness,* until his confrontation with Kurtz, Conrad's Marlow presents darkest Africa with a closely observed verisimilitude wholly convincing in its lack of glamor. The reality of the Congo was in slovenliness and inefficiency, rather than boundless cruelty and inexpressible evil, in rusting piles of unused rivets rather than jungle drums. But in the heart of darkness itself the reader meets 'exalted and incredible degradation,' 'weird incantations' (twice), 'inconceivable mystery' and a statuesque female savage whose 'face had a tragic and fierce aspect of wild sorrow and of dumb pain mingled with the fear of some struggling, half-shaped resolve.' The novels of Graham Greene and Evelyn Waugh, two inveterate travelers fascinated by the border between civilization

and barbarism, look curiously formal in the context of the twentieth-century English novel, with its shapeless plots, its mixed
characters, its concern for the minutiae of ordinary life. *Black Mis-
chief, The Heart of the Matter, A Handful of Dust* and *The Power and
the Glory* are plotted comparatively heavily and structured by sym-
bolic references to timing and naming, and other instances of
human organization of chaos. Waugh's characters even have names
like labels that function, on occasion, as humors in Ben Jonson.

On the other hand, it is hard to see how the perennial prophecies
about the literature of the American West could have been fulfilled
by any kind of conventional fiction. Consider some of the major
desiderata: (from de Tocqueville) 'The destinies of mankind — man
himself, taken aloof from his country and his age, and standing in
the presence of Nature and of God, with his passions, his doubts,
his rare prosperities and inconceivable wretchedness — will become
the chief, if not the sole, theme of poetry amongst these nations.'[11]
That lets out the fiction of social interaction, or most of the subject
matter of the English novel. Or (from de Tocqueville again):
'Amongst a democratic people, poetry will not be fed with legends
or the memorials of old traditions. The poet will not attempt to
people the universe with supernatural beings, in whom his readers
and his own fancy have ceased to believe.' This forbids romance
fiction — or a good proportion of it, anyway. And what about (from
Garland): 'There it lies, ready to be put into the novel,' and (from
Emerson) 'Bare lists of words are found suggestive'? With the
materiality of the West so ready to leap onto the page without
mediation, what becomes of the writer? Why, he withers away, of
course, like the state or the priest in other apocalypses. So no realism, no romance, no professional author.

Again, it could never happen literally. But recast the prophecy
in the more familiar terminology of a much less familiar prediction
of Emerson's than his famous promise in 'The Poet,' and it begins
to look more probable. There will come a time, he wrote in his
journal, when 'novels will give way, by and by, to diaries and autobiographies; — captivating books, if only a man knew how to choose
among what he calls his experience that which is really his experience, and how to record truth truly!'[12]

Of course, that is it: diaries, journals, autobiographies; man
alone against nature, no author in the conventional, professional

sense, no fiction. And that, at least, did happen – and in the West too. The great trek of 1849–50 to the gold fields of California has long been recognized as crucial in the long series of events that characterizes American demographic history, but it is odd that an age so interested in American autobiography should have paid so little attention to its importance for American *writing*. What happened was an explosion of vernacular autobiography – letters, journals, diaries and travel accounts – about countless individual experiences of crossing the plains, mountains and deserts to the West Coast. More Americans than ever before, and a higher proportion of those going West in the years either before or after the Gold Rush, felt compelled, whatever the difficulties, to record for their posterity their participation in a great adventure. And the problems of writing about the experience must have been formidable. Not only were most of these people unaccustomed to writing about great events, even in their own lives, but they had to cope with the fear, the physical strain and the cultural agoraphobia of traversing an unplotted wilderness.

An additional anxiety for the forty-niners was the uncertainty of their role. They were not travelers on a scheduled transport service – the trip to California could not yet be planned from a timetable – yet they were not explorers or natural scientists, or pioneers. The trail had been blazed and described by mountain men and emigrant parties to Utah, Oregon and California. Lewis and Clark – and latterly and more colorfully, John Charles Frémont – had produced scientific accounts of the topography, geology and natural history of the overland route. They were not even emigrants themselves, for the most part. The majority went in the first instance without wives and families in circumstances bearing some (at least) striking resemblances to a holiday. Yet they were on business, or professed to be – the business of speculating for gold to free themselves and their families from the drudgery they left behind.

In other words, for once the twin polarities of American unease, the fear of underplotting and the surfeit of overplotting, were experienced not in turn but simultaneously. The wilderness was manifestly devoid of 'culture' in any sense: empty, unplanted, largely uninhabited; yet it had been described, even inscribed, and there were ample texts, from widely circulated books to names carved on lonely, distant rocks to attest to that inescapable fact.

It is not just from the vantage point of the late twentieth century, and it was never just for sophisticated professional authors, that experience of this kind looks so acutely ambiguous. Anxieties about plotting in the West, about how to inscribe the experience of transcontinental travel, are present in the journals, diaries and letters of the forty-niners: problems of how to write, about the efficacy of writing — and especially its more risky strategies such as metaphor and other figurative excursions — about how to make an epic out of an experience so commonplace as to be replicated by thousands of other parties so visibly travelling the same route at the same time. In such an extreme setting, from which the physical signs of culture had fallen away, what hope was there for the verbal culture even of the vernacular autobiography?

The chief sign of this strain was a double style — not the famous *alternative* styles of American prose, the international genteel as opposed to the regional vernacular, or (in Philip Rahv's terms) the paleface versus the redskin, but a fissure within a single narrative between descriptive templates held up, as it were, to the landscape. Elaborate formality would collapse into elaborate factual description. Many parties of forty-niners started their journey with complicated sets of rules worked out on the model of the American constitution. They described the bizarre shapes of the western topography in terms of fanciful comparisons with artifacts left behind them — courthouses, capitol buildings — even with cathedrals and castles and other testimonies to an older civilization which most of them had only heard about. But when this desperate descriptive project failed, and when the imagination stood revealed as fancy (as of course it must in a landscape so apparently devoid of the reassuring signs of human habitation) they subsided into the rhetoric of scientific description, the nomenclature of animals, plants and minerals, the statistics of altitude, temperature, latitude and longitude. The rhetoric, not the primary fact of science; for the forty-niners were not 'real' scientists really contributing to knowledge, and they had little scientific training. The language of science was a lowest common denominator of what could be communicated to those at home or still unborn, when the language of the fancy had failed. One kind of figure gave way to another.

That is why the core of this book is the experience of the California Gold Rush of 1849–59; not what happened (that subject has been amply explored) but how people of various levels of sophistication wrote about it. The forty-niners are set in the context both of the books they read, like Frémont's *Report on an Exploration of the Country . . . Between the Missouri River and the Rocky Mountains* (1843) and Edwin Bryant's *What I Saw in California* (1848), and also the more polished accounts of the California scene written by professional journalists covering the Gold Rush. A chapter on the letters and diaries of the few women who went with husbands and fathers to California at the same time serves to contrast the forty-niners' writing with the more secure discourse of dependent or contingent members of a family unit, in which the anxieties of western travel were somewhat naturalized by the familial setting. An earlier chapter shows how the fissure between picturesque and scientific rhetoric may have originated even among literary men in the West, and how it spread into Frémont's prose.

The last two chapters draw the significance of all this for an understanding of the classic writers of American prose, the authors 'every schoolboy knows.' An examination of Mark Twain in the Nevada silver boom shows the extent to which his early style was infected by the same kind of cultural anxiety as the forty-niners experienced, not least that of reliving and rewriting their experiences and those of the Gold Rush journalists, while avoiding the more pressing adventure of the Civil War. Finally the forty-niners' 'double style' is set in the context of their better-known contemporaries, Hawthorne, Thoreau and Melville, whose prose also exhibits (though more designedly and much more famously) the strategic fracture between fantasy and documentary fact. The problem of plotting the West was, after all, only the distillation of the challenge, already recognized and accepted by the great mid-century American authors, of plotting new fiction in a new country. And the strategy of the double style was to become a peculiarly American recourse, one with unexpected reverberations extending down even to the present day.

1

THE WEST AND THE MAN OF LETTERS: CONFIDENCE AND ANXIETY

The act of metaphor then was a thrust at truth and a lie, depending on where you were: inside, safe, or outside, lost.

The Crying of Lot 49

In the autumn of 1960 the American historian Daniel Boorstin was sent an illustrated brochure advertising a new car. The picture showed the vehicle parked at the edge of the Grand Canyon. Inside a man was about to look through a small viewer at three-dimensional scenes of natural beauty. Outside stood his wife and three small children, of whom the eldest was preparing to photograph her father. No one was looking at the Grand Canyon.

'Here, if ever,' wrote Professor Boorstin in *The Image,* his classic study of the American technology of self-absorption that put the phrase 'pseudo event' into the language, 'is a parable of twentieth-century America':

All the ingenuity of General Motors, Eastman Kodak, generations of Fords, Firestones, and Edisons, the accumulated skills of fifty years of automotive engineering, of production know-how and industrial design, all the imagination and techniques of full-color printing, of junior and senior executives, and the whole gargantuan paraphernalia of the American economy have brought us to this. An opportunity . . . to be impressed by the image of a man (with the Grand Canyon at his elbow) looking at an image, and being photographed as he does it![1]

But in one sense the advertisement conveys a truth, and not just about twentieth-century American society. People confronted by unfamiliar landscapes have often needed the reassurance of frames or focussing devices, whether physical or conceptual, brought along from their own cultural base. In the eighteenth century even aristocratic travelers on the grand tour were accustomed to describing landscape according to set canons of the sublime, the beautiful and the picturesque. The formula for picturesque description demanded verbal composition and contrast between near and far, light and dark, present and past (the latter expressed by mention of a ruin, perhaps), natural and artificial, wild and cultivated, and so forth. The idea was to represent the scene as it might have been painted, and travelers often compared the landscape to the work of European artists.

On their part, painters and sketchers, whether professional or amateur, sometimes carried a device called a Claude glass, a small, plano-convex mirror on a black foil, rather like a dark rear-view mirror in a car. It was designed to compose the scene in the sombre tones and subdued contrasts so characteristic of eighteenth-century landscape painting. The artist turned his back to the scene and viewed its reflection as a ready-made painting by Claude de Lorraine.[2]

At this time the American countryside was not thought to be particularly rich in picturesque scenery, because it could provide little of the contrast that contributed to the composition of the landscape. There was little cultivated ground, still fewer ancient cypresses and yews surrounding peasant cottages and country chapels, to set against primeval forests and steep escarpments. There were no ruined castles or temples to inspire meditations on the past glories from which the present vernacular scene had fallen. American writers and artists felt this lack particularly acutely. 'The Author's Account of Himself' introducing Washington Irving's *The Sketch Book* (1820) is only the best known of many laments for the thinness of cultural deposits on American soil; another is Hawthorne's preface to *The Marble Faun* (1860), and the negative catalogues of Cooper and James must also be counted within the genre.* Europe's advantage over America, according to Irving, was in its 'charms of storied and poetical association. There were to be seen the masterpieces of art, the refinements of highly cultivated society, the quaint peculiarities of ancient and local custom.' In Europe the 'very ruins told of times gone by,' and one could 'loiter about the ruined castle' or 'meditate on the falling tower' until one had escaped 'the commonplace realities of the present' into 'the shadowy grandeurs of the past.'

Of course, there were things to be said in favor of the American natural scene, and Irving said some of them in this place. The American countryside made up in profusion what it lacked in proportion. If Europe inspired meditations on the past, America prompted hope for the future. 'My native country was full of youthful promise,' Irving allowed; its 'mighty lakes,' its 'valleys, teeming with wild fertility,' its 'tremendous cataracts' and 'boundless plains' were a reminder that 'never need an American look beyond his own country for the sublime and beautiful of natural scenery.' This seems to have been a fairly standard defense even as late as 1840,

---

* For a fuller discussion of negative and positive catalogues in descriptions of America, see below, pp. 215–19.

when the American poet, essayist and travel writer N. P. Willis published his two-volume collection of commentaries on sketches by W. H. Bartlett, called *American Scenery*. In America, wrote Willis in his preface, the traveler finds 'a lavish and large-featured sublimity . . . quite dissimilar to the picturesque of all other countries.' Nature in America aroused astonishment at its vast scale more than it pleased with its proportion. In fact, most of the scenes included in Willis ('View of the Capitol at Washington,' 'Rail-road Scene, Little Falls,' 'Faneuil Hall, from the Water') are compositions of natural and artificial objects, so might properly be called picturesque. But an observer seeking pleasant or instructive associations in such scenes would need to draw on thoughts of the future, not the past:

The picturesque views of the United States suggest a train of thought directly opposite to that of similar objects of interest in other lands. There, the soul and centre of attraction in every picture is some ruin of the past . . . which history or antiquity has hallowed. The traveller visits each spot in the same spirit — ridding himself, as far as possible, of common and present associations, to feed his mind of the historical and legendary. . . . The American . . . is perpetually reaching forward. Instead of looking through a valley . . . in which live lords and tenants, whose hearths have been surrounded by the same names through ages of tranquil descent, and whose fields have never changed landmarks or modes of culture since the memory of man, he sees a valley laden down like a harvest waggon with a virgin vegetation, untrodden and luxurient; and his first thought is of the villages that will soon sparkle on the hill-sides, the axes that will ring from the woodlands, and the mills, bridges, canals, and railroads, that will span and border the stream that now runs through sedges and wild flowers. . . . He looks upon all external objects as exponents of the future.[3]

But for Irving, though he granted its power to inspire awe, America remained for seventeen years a place neither to be lived in nor written about. Instead he explored the possibilities of Europe, turning its folklore, legend and historiography into collections of tales and popular history, like *The Sketch Book* (1819–20), *Tales of the Alhambra* (1832) and the *History of the Life and Voyages of Christopher Columbus* (1828). When he returned to New York in 1832, he came home not only as a successful government official (he had represented the United States in Madrid and London) but also as the first American author to be widely read and accepted by European literary society. America loved him for it, and he responded warmly to their gratitude. In an emotional speech at a formal dinner given in his honor soon after his arrival in New York, he expatiated warmly, if a trifle hectically, on his willingness to return:

It has been asked, 'Can I be content to live in this country?' Whoever asks that question must have but an inadequate idea of its blessings and delights. What sacrifice of enjoyments have I to reconcile myself to? I come from gloomier climes to one of brilliant sunshine and inspiring purity. I come from countries lowering with doubt and danger, where the rich man trembles and the poor man frowns – where all repine at the present and dread the future. . . . Is this not a land in which one may be happy to fix his destiny, and ambition – if possible to found a name? [A burst of applause, when Mr Irving quickly resumed] – I am asked how long I mean to remain here? They know but little of my heart or my feelings who can ask me this question. I answer, as long as I live.[4]

Why did he return? More to the point, why did he start, once again, to write about his country? The two questions are connected. Irving's biographer says that he had resolved to return to America every New Year's Day since 1815, and that 'there was really no better reason for this belated action [in 1832] than ten years earlier.'[5] Even so, two factors may have contributed to his decision. Political changes at the top of the American Legation in London meant that he would probably have to take a post outside England in the near future. He also may have sensed that he was fast exhausting his European material. The Columbus book led to work on a volume about the travels and discoveries of Columbus's companions, and *Tales of the Alhambra* looked like yielding a few leftovers for a life of the Prophet. His English publisher, John Murray, had lost money on *Columbus* and on Irving's history of the conquest of Granada, and thinking that Irving had written himself out, he finally accepted only the sequel to *Columbus,* and that with the greatest reluctance.

If the matter of Europe was played out, what about the matter of America? Cooper had already transferred Scott's romance of the disappearing tribe from the borders of Scotland to the American frontier. Irving had exploited the romance of the vanished Moors. Might he also work the Indian vein?

By the time Cooper had completed the first three of the *Leather-Stocking* books, the Indians had all but vanished from that part of New York State in which all but one of the stories are set. Their disappearance added to their attractiveness as objects of popular sentiment, just as the near genocide of the Highlanders led the British royal family, within two generations, to stop hunting them down and start affecting the kilt. The Indians were soon to be pushed much further West, and in greater numbers. In 1830, two years before Irving's return to the United States, the American Government passed the 'Indian Removal Bill' inviting the Choctaws, Creeks, Chicksaws, Cherokees and Seminoles to leave their homelands in the southeastern quarter of the continent, to make room for white settlers in Florida, Alabama, Georgia and the Carolinas. From that date all Indians would be strongly encouraged to live west of a line drawn from Lake Michigan, across Wisconsin to the Mississippi river, down to the northern boundary of Missouri, west to the Missouri river, down the present western borders of Missouri and Arkansas to the Red river. The Indians were to be removed, in other words, from what was then thought to be the arable part of the North American continent, and instead granted territory in a climate in which few of them would know how to survive. The Army would superintend their removal and help them on their way; commissioners representing the War Department would accompany the soldiers and mark out the boundaries of the new Indian territories.

Washington Irving rightly surmised that the Indian Removal Bill meant the end of the Indian culture in the eastern half of the United States. In the *Sketch Book* he had written two essays defending the Indians against the depredations and slanders of the European settlers; now a chance meeting with one of the Indian commissioners, a Henry Ellsworth, gave him the chance to see the Indians close up and make a first-hand assessment of their motives and behavior. When Ellsworth invited him to accompany one of the parties moving West late in 1832, Irving jumped at the idea. 'The offer was too tempting to be resisted,' he wrote his brother in a widely published letter. 'I should have an opportunity of seeing the remnants of those great Indian tribes, which are now about to disappear as independent nations, or to be amalgamated under some new form of government.'[6] The Indians, in other words, were about to pass into history. At last Irving had found the 'storied and poetical association' for which he had looked so long in America. He was ready to write about his country. Only five months after his return to America he set off, together with two European friends, for the West.

The result was *A Tour on the Prairies,* the most frankly and uni-vocally exotic account of the American West to be written by an American. Once he had decided that an aspect of the American scene could provide the kind of romantic associations he had found in Europe, Irving spared nothing to bring his new material within the various European conventions with which he was familiar: pic-turesque travel accounts, allusions to literature and classical history, the pastoral. Almost nothing in the New World is seen outside the framework of one or more social or aesthetic models drawn from the Old. The landscape reminded him of the more cultivated country-side of Europe:

Beyond the [Arkansas] River, the eye wandered over a beautiful champaign coun-try, of flowery plains and sloping uplands, diversified by groves and clumps of trees, and long screens of woodland; the whole wearing the aspect of complete, and even ornamental cultivation, instead of native wilderness.   (*Tour,* 36)

Elsewhere European architecture came to mind:

We were overshadowed by lofty trees, with straight, smooth trunks, like stately columns; and as the glancing rays of the sun shone through the transparent leaves, tinted with the many-colored hues of autumn, I was reminded of the effect of sunshine among the stained windows and clustering columns of a Gothic cathedral. Indeed there is a grandeur and a solemnity in our spacious forests of the West, that awaken in me the same feeling I have experienced in those vast and venerable piles, and the sound of the wind sweeping through them supplies occasionally the deep breathings of the organ.   (*Tour,* 41)

Yet another scene, inevitably, had 'the golden tone of one of the landscapes of Claude Lorraine' (*Tour,* 73).

The Indians, too, slipped easily into a frame of classical reference or hypothesized art form. A group of Osages were 'stately fellows,' 'stern and simple in aspect,' without ornament. Their hair was cut short, 'excepting a bristling ridge on the top, like the crest of a helmet.' 'They had fine Roman countenances,' 'wore their blankets wrapped around their loins, so as to leave the bust and arms bare,' and 'looked like so many noble bronze figures' (*Tour,* 21–2). They were not only like the Romans; they were, in a sense, better. Their 'helmets' were organic, part both of themselves and of nature. Like those triumphal arches of laurel under which Washington marched on his way from Mt Vernon to New York to be inaugurated as the country's first President, they perennially recreated and improved upon their model, just as America itself was thought to have superceded the prototypical Republic of Rome. To Irving the Indians embodied a purity of type – drawing as they did on both classical and natural sources – unmatched by the rest of the frontier population.

Even his traveling companions, to compare Irving's account of them with other sources, were tailored to fit literary convention. Two of them Irving had met on the steamer between Le Havre and New York, the British traveler Charles Latrobe, who wrote his own account of the tour, and the Swiss Count de Pourtalès. The third was a French Creole guide from St Louis, called Antoine Deshetres. Irving describes Latrobe as 'a botanist, a geologist, a hunter of beetles and butterflies, a musical amateur, a sketcher of no mean pretensions, in short, a complete virtuoso' (*Tour*, 12). Pourtalès had accompanied Latrobe from Europe 'and travelled with him as his Telemachus; being apt, like his prototype, to give occasional perplexity and disquiet to his Mentor' (*Tour*, 13). Finally, there was:

a personage of inferior rank, but of all-pervading and prevalent importance the squire, the groom, the cook, the tent man, in a word, the factotum, and, I may add, the universal meddler and marplot of our party. This was a little swarthy, meagre, French creole named Antoine, but familiarly dubbed Tonish; a kind of Gil Blas of the frontiers, who had passed a scrambling life, sometimes among white men, sometimes among Indians; sometimes in the employ of traders, missionaries, and Indian agents; sometimes mingling with the Osage hunters. We picked him up at St Louis, near which he has a small farm, an Indian wife, and a brood of half-blood children . . . he was without morals, without caste, without creed, without country, and even without language; for he spoke a jargon of mingled French, English, and Osage.   (*Tour*, 13–14)

This is to say, the travelers are defined by their approximation to European literary types. Pourtalès steps out of the *Iliad;* Latrobe out of *The Faerie Queene* or any other renaissance pastoral in which a knight's civil accomplishments prove useful even in a remote country setting, and 'Tonish,' of course, is the antimasque to these, the comic servant with none of the gifts of nature or fortune, except a sly cunning and the ability to survive.

The tour itself was recuperated as a pastoral idyll. When a meal on the prairie could exploit 'no less than twenty bee-trees . . . cut down in the vicinity' and a 'surrounding country . . . [that] abounded in game,' then 'every one revelled in luxury' (*Tour*, 57).

Whatever was not immediately palatable, was soon rendered so by the circumstances of camping out with the hunters:

The cooking was conducted in hunters' style: the meat was stuck upon tapering spits of dogwood, which were thrust perpendicularly into the ground, so as to sustain the joint before the fire, where it was roasted or broiled with all its juices retained in it in a manner that would have tickled the palate of the most experienced gourmand. As much could not be said in favor of the bread. It was little more than a paste made of flour and water, and fried like fritters in lard; though some adopted a ruder style, twisting it round the ends of sticks, and thus roasting it before the fire. In either way, I have found it extremely palatable on the prairies. No one knows the true relish of food until he has a hunter's appetite.

(*Tour*, 58)

The codes of cooking and eating are important signs of human culture, and this is why pastoral romances, those famous fictional test-beds of the value of culture, often include meals in the country – away from the court – so as to examine what, if any, civility remains after the table manners are taken away (or what manners remain after the table is taken away). For the same reason pastoral romancers often manipulate events so as to include an outdoor dance. In *As You Like It* the dialogue between Orlando and Duke Senior about the nature of true civility takes place over – literally above as well as about – a meal being eaten in the Forest of Arden. Orlando's lesson in manners is only part, though perhaps the most important part, of his growth into manhood. He must leave the court for the country to test for himself what remains of courtly values when they are unsupported by authoritarian conventions, but only so he may reenter courtly life at the end of his period of initiation.

Irving describes himself as enacting a similar rite of passage. Shortly after the meal described above he willingly undergoes a further, formalized, withdrawal from 'civilized' comforts, when he decides to 'abandon the shelter of the tent and henceforth to bivouac like the rangers [hired by the Indian Agency to accompany the Osages]. A bear-skin spread at the foot of a tree was my bed, with a pair of saddle-bags for a pillow. . . . I stretched myself on this hunter's couch, and soon fell into a sound and sweet sleep, from which I did not awake until the bugle sounded at daybreak' (61-2).

Nor does he fail to generalize the lesson:

23

I can scarcely conceive a kind of life more calculated to put both mind and body in a healthful tone. A morning's ride of several hours diversified by hunting incidents; an encampment in the afternoon under some noble grove on the borders of a stream; an evening banquet of venison, fresh killed, roasted, or broiled on the coals; turkeys just from the thickets, and wild honey from the trees; and all relished with an appetite unknown to the gourmets of the cities. And at night – such sweet sleeping in the open air, or waking and gazing at the moon and stars, shining between the trees! (85)

He makes no attempt to disguise all this as real hunting, or real exploring, really 'roughing it' or really carrying on any business. One would expect (and not be disappointed in that expectation – see chapter 7 below) to find this journey described quite differently by one of the professionals who accompanied Irving and his friends – say, Ellsworth or one of the rangers. To Irving, on the other hand, these are diverse 'incidents' whose interest lies in their recreative effect on the health and character of the easterner who will soon be returning to his habitat:

We send our youth abroad to grow luxurious and effiminate in Europe; it appears to me that a previous tour on the prairies would be more likely to produce that manliness, simplicity, and self-dependence, most in union with our political institutions. (55)

There may be some personal feeling behind this program, which so clearly reverses the order of his own experience, but it is also the most wide-ranging generalization in the book. Not only Irving himself, but also a whole American generation (at least those whose families have the means to send them on grand tours) are invited to partake of a pastoral initiation to fit them to take a responsible part in the governance of the society from which they are to absent themselves only temporarily. The fact that the government they will enter is a democratic republic and not a feudal hierarchy makes no difference to the thematic import of the pastoral action.* In the renaissance pastoral, it was the princes who were to receive the education, the princes who would return to govern. In Irving's pas-

---

* The narrator of Owen Wister's *The Virginian*, shortly after meeting the cowboy hero of the book, reflects that, 'It was through the Declaration of Independence that we abolished a cut-and-dried aristocracy. We had seen little men artificially held up in high places, and great men artificially held down in low places, and our own peaceloving hearts abhorred this violence to human nature. Therefore, we decreed that everyman should thenceforth have equal liberty to find his own level. . . . That is true democracy. And true democracy and true aristocracy are one and the same thing.'

toral, every man (again, subject to the financial test mentioned above) is invited, because in the home of universal male suffrage, every man was a prince.

The *North American Review* for July, 1835, devoted 27½ pages to Irving's *Tour,* quoting from it at considerable length. At last America had found its voice; not for the first time, and certainly not for the last, that voice was heard on the frontier:

For ourselves, we wish for nothing so ardently, as that the literature of the country should be the indigenous growth of the soil. . . . We are proud of Mr. Irving's sketches of English life, proud of the gorgeous canvass upon which he has gathered in so much of the glowing imagery of Moorish times. We behold with delight his easy and triumphant march over these beaten fields; but we glow with rapture as we see him coming back from the Prairies, laden with the poetical treasures of the primitive wilderness, — rich with spoil from the uninhabited desert. We thank him for turning these poor barbarous *steppes* into classical land.[7]

Above all other literary journals, The *North American Review* had been anxious to refute the charge commonly made by English visitors that the American cultural soil was too thin to support fiction, history or verbal sketches of local life. Now here was a Daniel come to judgement, an American who could not only beat the Europeans at their own game but also redeem the promise of the barren wilderness.

It was a different matter with Irving's contemporaries Timothy Flint and James Hall. Irving's praise of the West, backed as it was by the specie of his European reputation, counted for something. Theirs, coming from two men actually living in the West and determined to defend it against the scepticism of eastern intellectuals, was more uncertain in both tone and effect. Irving might have had the confidence unblushingly to apply European models to his description of the West. They were determined to draw on more native materials. Though well educated, Flint and Hall had no European experience, had made no grand tours. For them the West was not an adventure, but the place in which they lived and worked. Flint, a Congregational minister from Massachusetts, was a missionary in various frontier settlements in the Mississippi valley between 1816 and 1822, and Hall, trained as a lawyer, emigrated to frontier Illinois in 1820, where he later became a circuit judge and State Treasurer. Both saw themselves as experts and propagandists countering eastern fantasies about the West and both edited 'western' journals to convey information eastwards and to encourage western literary talent.* Flint even became an exponent of the doctrine that it was the Americans' 'Manifest Destiny' to occupy the North American continent from coast to coast. Yet it was they, not Irving, who also turned their experiences into highly colored romance fiction heavily derivative from Scott and Cooper. It seems that their confidence in the vigor of their native materials was not consistent. The symptoms of this uncertainty can be found in their non-fictional accounts of their experience in the West, Flint's *Recollections of the Last Ten Years* (1826), during which he and his family lived in the Mississippi valley, and Hall's *Sketches of History, Life and Manners of the West* (1835) and *Notes on the Western States* (1838).†

A sense of their insecurity, and a hint of the reason underlying it, can be gathered from this instance taken from Hall's *Notes:*

The gayety of the prairie, its embellishments, and the absence of the gloom and savage wildness of the forest, all contribute to dispel the feeling of lonesomeness, which usually creeps over the mind of the solitary traveler in the wilderness. . . . The groves and clumps of trees appear to have been scattered over the lawn to beautify the landscape, and it is not easy to avoid the illusion of the fancy, which persuades the beholder, that such scenery has been created to gratify the refined taste of civilized man. Europeans are often reminded of the resemblance of this scenery to that of the extensive parks of noblemen, which they have been accustomed to admire, in the old world; the lawn, the avenue, the grove, the copse, which are there produced by art, are here prepared by nature; a splendid specimen of massy architecture, and the distant view of villages, are alone wanting to render the similitude complete. *(Notes,* 74)

---

* Hall edited the *Illinois Gazette* and the *Illinois Intelligencer* between 1820 and 1832, and founded the first literary periodical west of Ohio, the *Illinois Monthly Magazine,* in 1833. Upon the death of his first wife in that year, he went to Cincinnati and founded the *Western Monthly Magazine.* It survived until 1836, when it lost most of its subscribers after Hall had defended Roman Catholics against Lyman Beecher's *A Plea for the West* (1835).

    Flint returned to Cincinnati, after the success of his romance, *Francis Berrian; or, the Mexican Patriot* (1826). Mrs Trollope considered him the one exception to her general condemnation of American boorishness. He edited the *Western Monthly Review* from 1827 until its collapse in 1830.

† One should also mention Hall's first book of this kind, *Letters from the West,* parts of which were published in the *Illinois Gazette* and the *Port Folio* between 1820 and 1825. The book appeared in London in 1828 and was not published in the United States until 1967, when Scholar's Facsimiles and Reprints, Gainesville, Florida, brought out a reprint of the English edition, edited by John T. Flanagan.

At first glance this passage, with its comparisons between culture and nature, resembles one of Irving's essays in picturesque description. The difference is hard to summarize, but it is profound. It is not that Irving was immune to the feelings of loneliness and tedium that sometimes sweep over the traveler in a wilderness; indeed the formality of his descriptive conventions are very probably a reaction to feelings of that kind, only occasionally admitted in the *Tour* itself. The difference between them is that Hall analyzes the feelings minutely and explicitly — the loneliness and the corresponding desire for human artifacts to fill the void. He goes further than that. He all but says that the lawn and the avenue are a cruel delusion. The problem is that the 'massy' architecture (perhaps a castle or a cathedral) and the villages *are* missing, and therefore the similitude is incomplete. But if they were there, and it was complete, it would no longer be a similitude. What the traveler in the wilderness longs for is not just the illusion of civilization, but civilization itself. In this instance the incomplete metaphor is not merely a figure of speech wanting the final burst of invention or twist or rhetoric to bring it off, but a mirage; not a fiction but a lie. That is why Hall applies words like 'illusion' and 'fancy' (the latter a pejorative word elsewhere in this book, as in others) to the impression of cultivated landscape. He senses the tension in the process of his self-conscious figuring of what he knows to be untrue. Only twelve years later Hawthorne would claim that his novels inhabited a world midway between reality and gothic romance; the familiar setting seen in the moonlight, where the author could pretend that impossible things were happening. Like Hawthorne, Hall felt the need, in the absence of culture, to confect his own artifacts out of thin air. Like him too, he sensed the precariousness of the project.

In Hall, then, the West brought out a deep unease about the validity of metaphors. And given his tendency to analyze his problems, it should hardly come as a surprise to find him discussing the difficulty of writing in, and about, the West. 'Books we have had in abundance,' he writes in the Preface to the *Sketches*; 'travels, gazetteers, and geographies inundate the land; but few of them are distinguished by literary merit or accurate information' (*Sketches*, I, 13). Hall had his own version of Irving's feeling that America lacked association, one he applied more specifically to the frontier. The great handicap of the western writer was the absence of a framework of accumulated knowledge about his subject on which to build and to which his readers could be referred. The European historian or novelist 'but fills an outline previously sketched out in the seclusion of his closet, and the design itself is but a copy' (*Sketches*, I, 13–14). But the traveler on the Ohio river:

leaves behind him every object which has been consecrated by the pen of genius. He beholds the beauties of nature in rich luxuriance, but he sees no work of art which has existed beyond the memory of man, except a few faint and shapeless traces of a former race, whose name and character are beyond the reach even of conjecture. Every creation of human skill which he beholds is the work of his contemporaries. All is new, the fertile soil abounds in vegetation. The forest is bright, and rich, and luxuriant, as it came from the hands of the Creator. The hundred rivers . . . present grand and imposing spectacles to the eye, while they fill the mind with visions of the future wealth and greatness of the lands through which they roll. But they are nameless to the poet and historian; neither song nor chivalry has consecrated their shores.

The inhabitants are all emigrants from other countries; they have no ruins, no traditions, nothing romantic or incredible, with which to regale the traveler's ear. They can tell of their own weary pilgrimage from the land of their fathers . . . but they have no traditions that run back to an illustrious antiquity.

(*Sketches*, I, 14–15)

Unlike Irving, who merely mentioned it as part of his excuse for not writing about America, Hall seems ready to proceed on the basis of the argument from profusion. The American writer's advantage was that he could write about his country as it was, unencumbered by stale copies and pallid outlines. What more appropriate celebration of the New Creation than a new creation, drawing on nothing more than the profuse factuality lying around waiting to be catalogued? Or, as Hall would put it, 'To acquire an adequate knowledge of such a country, requires extensive personal observation. It is necessary to examine things instead of books . . .' (*Sketches*, I, 16).

Hall's trouble was that he could not let the argument rest there. Just in case the westerner still wants 'storied and poetical association,' he may like to reflect that:

The valley of the Mississippi has been the theatre of hardy exploit and curious adventure. . . . If we trace the solitary path of the fearless Boone; if we pursue the steps of Shelby, of Clarke, of Logan, and of Scott, we find them beset with dangers so terrible, adventures so wild, and achievements so wonderful, as to startle credulity. (*Sketches*, I, 17)

So having condemned the stale unreality of the traditional forms available to the European writer, having praised the freshness and plentitude of the raw environment open to the American, he posits a new melodrama to satisfy the most avid thirster after the incredible. Like the lady in Wallace Stevens's 'Sunday Morning,' he still feels the need of some imperishable bliss. But words like 'theatre' and 'curious adventure' betray his ambivalent feeling about the project.

Flint goes through exactly the same mental process in *Recollections of the Last Ten Years,* in reflecting on the Indian burial mounds on the Cahokia prairie, Illinois:

The English, when they sneer at our country, speak of it as sterile in moral interest. It has, they say, no monuments, no ruins, none of the massive remains of former ages; no castles, no mouldering abbeys, no baronial towers and dungeons, nothing to connect the imagination and the heart with the past, no recollections of former ages to associate the past with the future. But I have been attempting sketches of the largest and most fertile valley in the world, larger, in fact, than half of Europe, all its remotest points being brought into proximity by a stream, which runs the length of that continent, and to which all but two or three of the rivers of Europe are but rivulets. Its forests make a respectable figure, even placed beside Blenheim park. We have lakes which could find a place for the Cumberland Lakes in the hollow of one of their islands. We have prairies, which have struck me as among the sublimest propsects in nature. . . . In the most pleasing positions of these prairies, we have our Indian mounds, which proudly rise above the plain. At first the eye mistakes them for hills; but when it catches the regularity of their breastworks and ditches, it discovers at once that they are the labours of art and of men. . . . Is there no scope beside these mounds for imagination, and for contemplation of the past? The men, their joys, their sorrows, their bones, are all buried together. . . . Unfortunate, as men view the thing, they must have been. Innocent and peaceful they probably were; for had they been reared amidst wars and quarrels, like the present Indians, they would doubtless have maintained their ground, and their posterity would have remained to this day. Beside them, moulder the huge bones of their contemporary beasts, which must have been of thrice the size of the elephant. I cannot judge of the recollections excited by castles and towers that I have not seen. But I have seen all of grandeur, which our cities can display. I have seen, too, these lonely tombs of the desert, − seen them rise from these boundless and unpeopled plains. My imagination had been filled, and my heart has been full.   (*Recollections,* 124–5)

As in Hall, the argument changes direction. To the accusation of no tradition, the *size* of the rivers, valleys and lakes of the West is no proper answer. Yet its refusal to engage the accusation gives the proposition of size a certain strength — as if to say, with all this natural profusion, who needs tradition? But then a curious shift occurs in the rhetoric. The reader expects the 'size' argument to culminate in the mention of prairies, since the term 'prairie' comes at the end of a series for which increasingly ambitious figures have been found to suggest enormousness (and anyway, the prairies were famously America's biggest geographical feature). Instead, Flint alters course, predicating of 'prairies' the stilted phrase 'among the sublimest prospects,' and from there starts to build tension towards the real (or is it the false?) climax of his argument: that the Indian burial mounds are sufficient cultural artifacts to match against European castles; that we westerners, too, have our history to meditate. The argument from nature shifts to the argument from culture, just for good measure.

This uncertainty about where lie the sources of strength in the western landscape is reflected in Flint's and Hall's uneasy rhetoric of landscape description. All too often they impale themselves on the stock phrases of European travel accounts. Flint's prairies that are 'among the sublimest prospects in nature' is an example. So is Hall's disastrous figure of a 'hundred rivers . . . present[ing] grand and imposing spectacles to the eye.' Yet these fossils are present in strata of rhetoric more appropriate to the subject being celebrated:

Approaching towards Cincinnati [along the Ohio river] the scenery becomes still more monotonous. . . . But the woodland is arrayed in a splendor of beauty, which renders it the chief object of attraction. Nothing can be more beautiful than the first appearance of the vegetation in the spring, when the woods are seen rapidly discarding the dark and dusky habiliments of winter, and assuming their vernal robes. The gum tree is clad in the richest green; the dogwood and red-bud are laden with flowers of the purest white and deepest scarlet; the buckeye bends under the weight of its exuberant blossoms. The oak, the elm, the walnut, the sycamore, the beech, the hickory, and the maple, which here tower to a great height, have yielded to the sunbeams, and display their bursting buds, and expanding flowers. The tulip tree waves its long branches, and its yellow flowers high in the air. The wild rose, the sweet-briar, and the vine, are shooting into verdure; and clinging to their sturdy neighbors, modestly prefer their claims to admiration, while they afford delightful promise of fruit and fragrance.
(*Notes*, 24)

Again, the monotony of the wilderness prompts the desire for a formal gesture, an assertion of culture. Hall's rhetoric rises to the occasion. But the information conveyed here is not that formally set

out by the syntax and rhetoric. The sentence 'But the woodland
. . . object of attraction' is not only ponderous but nearly tautolog-
ical. The long series of elegant variations on the theme of blossom-
ing trees ('vernal robes . . . exuberant blossoms . . . bursting buds,
and expanding flowers') is no news to Hall's readers, whose own
trees go through approximately the same process in springtime.
The interest and energy, once again, comes from the sense of natural
profusion conveyed by the catalogue of names, many of them common and vernacular, like dogwood, red-bud and sweet-briar.
Through the 'dusky habiliments' of Hall's old-fashioned rhetoric, a
crowd of ordinary things burst forth irresistibly to be recognized
and given a native name.

It is to the simple list of ordinary things, then, to which Flint
and Hall find themselves returning again and again as a way of
describing their West, even though they rarely felt happy with it
for long. The catalogue, after all, was an answer to the fear (in
themselves) or the criticism (in eastern and European journals) that
its absence of traditional forms made the West impossible to work
into literature. Quantity and variety could make up for lack of quality. The catalogue would become Whitman's chief tactic in his cel-
ebrations of America, but Whitman would develop the invention
by greatly simplifying his syntax and rhetoric to the point at which
it became as common as the things he was naming.

But there was one method of description with which Flint and
Hall always seemed confident, both in their ability to deploy it and
in their faith that it would convey useful information to their eastern readers. This was the scientific account of aspects in the West.
This, too, frequently took the form of a catalogue, and was another
pretext for uttering a profusion of concrete things. But over the
simple list the scientific catalogue had the advantage of a certain
'scholarly' respectability and of communicability in terms recognized by the eastern literary establishment. It was a way of expressing the 'things' that Hall determined to examine, without abandon-
ing the 'form' apparently so important to the eastern reader. In
Notes on the Western States Hall's more descriptive passages are interspersed with tables showing elevations, areas, types of trees, and so
forth. The chapter headings of the *Notes* suggest that subjectively
assessed qualities will be buttressed by the more objective facts of
geography and natural history: 'The Western plain – its limits – its

topography — the general character of its formation'; 'The River Ohio — its etymology — scenery — timber — low water — floods — the great flood of 1832 — impediments to navigation — proposed improvements.'

The claim to scientific accuracy is part of the strenuous dialogue in which Hall encountered exaggerated eastern notions of the western environment:

The same course of reasoning may be applied to the alledged variability, and the reputed unhealthiness, of our climate. Facts of such grave importance should not be considered as settled, by that common rumor, whose want of veracity is so notorious. The results of patient and careful investigation, by competent men of science, will hereafter decide these points, and will, in our opinion, shew that the current reports in relation to these matters, have been in direct opposition to the truth. . . . The climate differs but little from that of corresponding parallels of latitude, in the United States. So far as health is concerned, we suppose the advantage to lie on our side of the mountains, while in reference to vegitation, there is no observable difference. (*Notes*, 19)

This is not scientific writing, of course (he even dissociates himself from 'competent men of science,' to come later), but rather the rhetoric of science used in persuasion. Though he is not a scientist, his language ('alledged variability,' 'corresponding parallels of latitude,' 'no *observable* difference') puts him in that rank of professionals who observe the facts and reason dispassionately from them. But from the elaborate gesture of scientific neutrality grows, first, a partisan appeal, and then an excited projection into the future:

Neither is there any supernatural fertility in our soil, which yields its rich returns only under the operation of careful and laborious tillage. . . . It is the accumulation within one wide and connected plain, of the most vast resources of agriculture and commercial wealth . . . and bringing into combined action the energies of millions of industrious human beings, on which are based the broad foundations of our greatness. . . . With the breadth of an empire, we have all the facilities for intercourse and trade, which could be enjoyed within more limited boundaries. Our natural wealth is not weakened by extension, nor our vigor impaired by division. (*Notes*, 19–20)

At this point Hall goes on to list the mineral resources of the region: coal, iron, copper, lead, salt, chalybeate (mineral water) and sulphur. This naked boosterism is among Hall's best writing; here, at least, the rhetoric is put to a purpose in which Hall believes totally. It may be worth remembering, too, that his apparently fanciful projection turned out to be literally true in every respect. But the confidence that produces efficiently deployed rhetoric out of such unlikely prospects grows out of the scientific pose, reinforced by tabulated data. Like the future of the West itself, Hall's prose here is based on solid, material facts.

But science, or the pretense of it, could also come to the aid of the less official, more personal narrative of western travel. Flint's first view of the prairies inspired him, as it did most travelers, to self-consciously romantic musings about the future:

> 'Here,' said I to my companion who guided me, 'here shall by my farm, and here I will end my days!' In effect, take it all in all, I have not seen, before nor since, a landscape which united, in an equal degree, the grand, the beautiful, and fertile. It is not necessary in seeing it to be very young or very romantic, in order to have dreams steal over the mind, of spending an Arcadian life in these remote plains, which just begin to be vexed by the plough, far removed from the haunts wealth and fashion, in the midst of rustic plenty, and of this beautiful nature.
>
> (*Recollections*, 90–1)

Yet immediately after this passage, as though to ballast his flight of fancy, Flint provides a scientific account of the same prairie, a concrete, factual description that leads, nevertheless, to the same optimistic projection for the future:

> I will only add, that it is intersected with two or three canals, apparently the former beds of the river; that the soil is mellow, friable, and of an inky blackness; that it immediately absorbs the rain, and affords a road, always dry and beautiful, to Portage des Sioux. It yields generally forty bushels of wheat, and seventy of corn to the acre. The vegetable soil has a depth of forty feet. and earth thrown from the bottom of the wells, is as fertile as that on the surface. At a depth of forty feet are found logs, leaves, pieces of pit-coal, and a stratum of sand and pebbles, bearing evident marks of the former attrition of running waters. Here are a hundred thousand acres of land of this description, fit for the plough.
>
> (*Recollections*, 91)

Even Flint's rhapsody on the Indian burial mounds is finally underpinned with data dispassionately recorded. From various accounts, he says, 'it appears . . . that the graves were numerous, that the coffins were of stone, that the bones in some instances were nearly entire.' As for the pottery, 'it is evident, from slight departures from regularity in the surface, that it was moulded by hand. . . . The composition, when fractured, shows many white floccules in the clay, that resemble fine snow, and this I judge to be pulverized shells' (*Recollections*, 126–7).

33

There is no doubt that Hall and Flint felt the same impulse as did Irving to supply formal structures to the chaos of the western wilderness. But Irving was an international man, a traveler, a diplomat, a writer with wide readership in both the Old and the New Worlds. The Americans, far from resenting his popularity in Europe, were flattered by it; they approved his European experience because the Europeans approved of him. Made bold by this approval, Irving could allude to, and borrow, European literary conventions with the confidence that they would be understood and admired by his large, literate audience. But Hall and Flint, the embattled partisans, saw themselves as defending the West against a hostile, or at least uncomprehending, readership of eastern Americans who, they felt, were a little too beholden to European conventions. However they may have longed for castles, cathedrals or an accumulation of descriptive conventions, they could not fancy or dally with such consolations for long, without threatening their polemical stance against such outworn models. What they could offer, with confidence, was the lowest common denominator of formal description; the simplest verifiable discourse that they shared with their readers in the East; the readiest token of their common culture.

And in this process, of course, they were drawing on a source of authentication already exploited, perhaps even by the 'books we have had in abundance' of which Hall complained in his preface to the *Sketches*. The frontier scientist was already a sufficiently typical character by 1827 to be lightly satirized in the person of Dr Battius in Cooper's *The Prairie*. Perhaps the best known of these learned wanderers was William Bartram, whose *Travels through North and South Carolina, Georgia, East and West Florida* (1791) 'views science as the servant of piety,' in the words of a recent study of early discoverers and explorers of America.[8] European authors, too, especially those writing descriptions of feelings of sublimity at seeing mountains, frequently naturalized those unruly and confused excrescences of nature (as they were thought to be) within a triadic formula of (1) expressions of awe, (2) comparisons with architectural forms of other aesthetic framing devices, and (3) scientific description. Gary Wills, in his fascinating book on the philosophical ideas behind Thomas Jefferson's draft of the Declaration of Independence, shows how this tradition of 'sublime' description was applied to features of American landscape too, such as the Natural Bridge in Virginia, described very similarly by both the Chevalier de Chastellux and Jefferson himself, in the *Notes on the State of Virginia* (1784).[9]

Indeed, that book may be read, cover to cover, as Jefferson's attempt to authenticate his region. Ostensibly his answer to 'certain queries' put to him by the Marquis de Barbé-Marbois, Secretary to the French Legation in Philadelphia, about the geography and politics of his native state, *Notes on Virginia* is also a defense of the New World against the charge made by the Comte de Buffon and the Abbé Raynal that animals and men transplanted to America (as all had been, of course, if the Bible was right) invariably declined in size, fertility and strength, whether physical or mental. From the outset of the book, Virginia is established – placed, in more senses than one – with unchallengeable data. It is 'bounded on the east by the Atlantic' and 'on the north by a line of latitude crossing the eastern shore through Watkin's Point, being about 37° 57′ north latitude . . . on the west by the Ohio and Mississippi, to latitude 36° 37′ north',* and so on. Supported by technical notes, diagrams and statistical tables, *Notes on Virginia* is, to paraphrase two of Jefferson's modern editors, a major contribution to American scientific writing that formulated principles of scientific geography later developed by the German explorer and physical geographer Baron von Humboldt.[10] But that its scientific unimpeachability was at least in part a response to Buffon and Raynal, is suggested by the especially meticulous care taken by Jefferson to establish the fossil remains of the mammoth as suggesting a contemporary native species distinct from (and much larger than) the elephant, and by what happens to his prose when he draws the necessary conclusion:

[The mammoth] should have sufficed to have rescued the earth it inhabited, and the atmosphere it breathed, from the imputation of impotence in the conception and nourishment of animal life on a large scale; to have stifled, in its birth, the opinion of [Buffon] . . . that nature is less active, less energetic on one side of the globe than she is on the other. As if both sides were not warmed by the same genial sun; as if a soil of the same chemical composition was less capable of elaboration into animal nutriment; as if the fruits and grains from that soil and

---

* Of course, he was referring to the original colony of Virginia, plus its western territories as far as what was to become the Louisiana Purchase; that is, present-day Virginia, West Virginia, Kentucky, and the southern halves of Ohio, Indiana and Illinois.

sun yielded a less rich chyle, gave less extension to the solids and fluids of the body, or produced sooner in the cartilages, membranes, and fibres, that rigidity which retains all further extension, and terminates animal growth. The truth is, that a pigmy and a Patagonian, a mouse and a mammoth, derive their dimensions from the same nutritive juices.   (*Virginia,* 205–6)

The argument derives much of its strength from traditional rhetorical devices – from syntactical parallelism, antithesis, alliteration – but the technical vocabulary authenticates the impassioned plea; converting it from a matter of opinion into an objective (and – more to the point – *universal*) natural process. It was a species of rhetoric, one especially well suited to describing situations for which subjective responses, however eloquently articulated, were felt to be insufficiently persuasive. Whether borrowed or rediscovered many times over, this new rhetoric was to become the recourse not only of Flint and Hall, but of the thousands of amateur and professional travelers on the Overland Trail to California – and even, as a later chapter will attempt to show, of some writers better known to the student of literature.

2

FRÉMONT AND THE HUMBLE BEE

BOTANY *Plate II.*

Actomieon Californicum

By the early 1840s Hall's 'theatre of . . . curious adventure' had shifted from the Mississippi valley to the great transcontinental trails being used by increasing numbers of emigrants to Oregon and California. A demand began to grow for travel accounts, journals of western exploration, or anything else that might provide information, however impressionistic, about the climate, terrain, pasture and water of the Overland Trails. By the end of the decade a number of shorter, more straightforward handbooks had appeared, the best of them based on experience gained by the Mormons in their great trek to Utah in 1847. These gave tables of distances, rough sketches of routes and helpful tips of what to take and how to travel. Slight as they were on topographical detail (not to mention subjective impressions of the scenery by the way), they were no doubt welcome on the wagon trains and saved many emigrant lives. Yet the guidebooks apparently preferred — or at least most frequently cited — by the men who swarmed across the country in search of California gold in 1849 and 1850 were the more profuse, more subjective accounts of exploration and adventure.

Of these the most frequently mentioned in forty-niners' diaries are Captain John Charles Frémont's *Report of the Exploring Expedition to the Rocky Mountains in the Year 1842 and to Oregon and North California in the Years 1843–44*, published by the U.S. Government in 1845, and Edwin Bryant's *What I Saw in California* (1848), reprinted many times under the not inappropriate title of *Rocky Mountain Adventures*. Bryant's book includes a table of distances at the end of his account of crossing the plains, and enough detail of the trail to provide the occasional cross-reference to the forty-niners' own experiences, but as a guide it must have been of little use. As far as what is now Wyoming it followed the route already well established by emigrant parties moving West to Oregon and California, and beyond that, Bryant's party took the Hastings Cutoff straight across the deserts of Utah and Nevada, a route known by 1849 to be hazardous for wagon trains. Even Frémont's *Report*, based on journeys made up to four years before Bryant's, followed the well-known route from Missouri to the South Pass in the Rocky Mountains, via the Platte valley (now in Nebraska) and Fort Laramie (Wyoming). His expedition in 1843 followed the emigrant's trail to Oregon, headed south into what is now Nevada, then crossed the Sierra Nevada range *in the middle of winter* into California. From the Rockies onwards, his steps would hardly have been dogged by even the hardiest seeker of California gold; east of the Rockies, his route was common knowledge to emigrants well before 1849.

What kind of books were these, then, and why were they taken on the trail along with the cheaper and more pointed guidebooks? Bryant's *What I Saw* is a work of personal reflection and analysis – in fact, a description of western travel not unlike Flint's *Recollections*. Like Flint too, Bryant was a former editor (of the Louisville, Kentucky, *Courier*) promoting western settlement and the doctrine of Manifest Destiny. While heightening the pleasures, excitement and occasional danger of the journey overland, he did not fail to mention the favorable climate and potential fertility of California, nor how underpopulated and undercultivated the area was under the former Mexican administration.

Frémont was even more directly involved than Bryant in the American conquest of California. Married to the striking and intelligent daughter of Senator Thomas Hart Benton, he had come a long way for a humble officer in the U.S. Army Corps of Topographical Engineers, and naturally allied himself with the interest in western expansion and the rights of frontier settlers so fervently espoused by his father in law. Frémont was active in the 'Bear Flag' revolt, the serio-comic uprising of American settlers against the Mexican Government. Before the local skirmishes were swept up into the more sombre events of the Mexican–American War of 1846, Frémont had formed and led in California a battalion of mounted volunteers that included Bryant himself. After the war resulted in the United States Government formally claiming and occupying California, the Frémonts settled there, where they got on as well with the remaining Old Californians as with their new Anglo-Saxon masters.

But Frémont's *Report,* though free with its praise of California's climate, the variety of its vegetation and landscape, and the paradisal surroundings of its mission settlements, was set out as a much more serious affair than Bryant's *What I Saw.* It was loaded with tables of distances, altitudes, latitudes, longitudes and temperatures taken at their various encampments; maps, views of notable topographical features; a catalogue of plants; botanical sketches; drawings of fossil bearing rocks – everything, in short, befitting a report made by a Captain of the Army Engineer Corps to his superior officer, and subsequently ordered by the Congress to be widely published.*

The question is whether this elaborate display actually contributed to the store of scientific knowledge about the West, or merely set out Frémont's experience in a way that seemed unassailably objective. Perhaps even to ask this question is to impose on the subject a dissociation more appropriate to twentieth-century American western exploration. After all, who can say whether, when Thomas Jefferson commissioned Lewis and Clark to make the first expedition across North America in 1804–6, he was motivated most by scientific curiosity, imperialistic designs on the continent, the compulsion to authenticate America in the eyes of sceptical Europeans, or simply a boyish enthusiasm for the unknown? One thing that can be said is that the Lewis and Clark expedition included hunters, scouts, a black slave, and an Indian woman and her half-breed baby, but not one scientist, natural or otherwise. Everyone of military rank was allowed to call himself 'Captain,' the only distinction remaining that the real officers were ordered to keep journals of their experience, and the enlisted men only encouraged to. Yet despite this official preference of prose description over tabulated observations, the expedition managed to collect botanical, zoological and even anthropological specimens; to assemble notes on Indian vocabularies; and to draw numerous maps, later to be improved by Clark when he was Indian Superintendent at St Louis. They discovered not only new species of plant, but two new *genera* as well, suitably named Lewisia and Clarkia.

In any case, it would seem that even the sternest account of western discovery could range over as many different levels of style as could descriptions of amateur travel. Sometimes this could be explained by the process of composition, as when Washington Irving rewrote the journals of Captain Benjamin Bonneville as *The Rocky Mountains* (two vols, Philadelphia, 1837), later (and often) reprinted under the even more promising title, *The Adventures of Captain Bonneville, U.S.A.[rmy]*. In Bonneville's case the question of how original were his discoveries raises itself more sharply than

---

* It would also have included photographs, if Frémont had managed to use successfully the cumbersome daguerreotype cameras carried on the first two western expeditions.

in Frémont's, because there is some doubt whether Bonneville was seriously engaged in exploration at all, or merely prospecting for beaver.* It did not matter much, because his adventures, as Irving put it himself, were eventually 'given a tone and coloring drawn from my own observation, during an excursion into the Indian country beyond the bounds of civilization' (*Bonneville*, 6).

Irving's *Tour* had sold so well in Europe and America that he must have felt there was still a bit more to exploit of the western theme. A year after his *Tour* appeared, he published *Astoria*, a history of the fur trade based on the papers of John Jacob Astor, and a year after that his version of Bonneville's journal. The capital raised by Irving's one-month visit to the frontier was still paying dividends; the style of *Bonneville* maintained, almost unflaggingly, the high exoticism of the *Tour*:

It is difficult to do justice to the courage, fortitude, and perseverence of the pioneers of the fur trade. . . . Accustomed to live in tents, or to bivouac in the open air, [the trapper] despises the comforts and is impatient of the confinements of the log house. If his meal is not ready in season, he takes his rifle, hies to the forest or prairie, shoots his own game, lights his fire, and cooks his repast. With his horse and his rifle, he is independent of the world and spurns at all its restraints.   (*Bonneville*, 8–12)

Well, not so difficult, perhaps. Certainly, despite his inability *topos*, Irving found it easy enough to work what he called the 'wild chivalry of the mountains' (*ibid.*) into his accustomed comparison with life in the East:

It is not easy to do justice to the exulting feelings of the worthy captain, at finding himself at the head of a stout band of hunters, trappers, and woodmen; fairly launched on the broad prairies, with his face to the boundless West. The tamest inhabitant of cities, the veriest spoiled child of civilization, feels his heart dilate and his pulse beat high, on finding himself on horseback in the glorious wilderness; what then must be the excitement of one whose imagination had been stimulated by a residence on the frontier, and to whom the wilderness was a region of romance!   (*Bonneville*, 14)

---

* Bonneville himself claimed only one original discovery: that the Great Salt Lake had no outlet. For this feat Irving named the lake after him, but contemporary historians soon disallowed even that. For Bonneville's statement had a discussion of its validity, see Lieut. G. K. Warren, 'Memoir', *Pacific Railroad Reports*, XI [1861], 33. Now the only lake named after Bonneville is the postulated prehistoric original of the remaining salt lakes in Utah. He has also given his name to the salt flats in Utah on which car speed records are established.

Bonneville's route to California followed almost exactly that of the forty-niners, at least as far as the Humboldt Sink in Nevada, reached by one of Bonneville's scouts in 1833 (for more on the history of the trails West, see below, pp. 213–15). The book also describes a number of landmarks that they would encounter and describe for themselves. Although it is doubtful if enough detail of the route sifted through Irving's presentation to recommend *Bonneville* as a guide, there seems little doubt that many of the forty-niners knew the book, or its reputation. By 1849 it had reached twenty-six foreign and domestic editions or reprints. Frémont seems to have known and used it as a model for the reports of his own expeditions.

For, contrary to what might be inferred from the outline of his career, Frémont was anything but a cold-blooded imperialist. With a French father and a Virginian mother, and trained by the French naturalist Joseph Nicolas Nicollet, he was as open to the more romantic and picturesque associations of landscape as he was to the need to measure and document the wilderness. His companions on the first expedition were, as he wrote, 'principally Creole and Canadian *voyageurs*' with splendidly appropriate names like J. B. L'Esperance, J. B. Lefèvre and Basil Lajeunesse, as well as the German topographical surveyor, Charles Preuss, and two young men, one of them his brother in law, who 'accompanied me for the development of mind and body which such an expedition would give' (*Report,* 170). They were guided by none other than Kit Carson himself, perhaps the most famous of all the old frontier trappers, who had accompanied one of the first overland expeditions to California in 1829–31.

At times, Frémont's imaginative associations were like Irving's. The sight of some Indian spears and shields 'reminded [him] of the days of feudal chivalry' (*Report,* 201), and the Platte valley 'resembled a garden in the splendor of fields of varied flowers, which filled the air with fragrance' (*Report,* 205). Meals on the prairie, too, could be rich with exoticism. This one celebrated the Fourth of July:

The kindness of our friends at St. Louis had provided us with a large supply of excellent preserves and rich fruit cake; and when these were added to a macaroni soup, and variously prepared dishes of the choicest buffalo meat, crowned with a cup of coffee, and enjoyed with prairie appetite, we felt, as we sat in barbaric luxury around our smoking supper on the grass, a greater sensation of enjoyment than the Roman epicure at his perfumed feast.   (*Report*, 192)

In places the account seems to assume an almost European sense of landscape as picturesque composition:

On the opposite side, a little below the spring, is a lofty limestone escarpment, partially shaded by a grove of large trees, whose green foliage, in contrast with the whiteness of the rock, renders this a picturesque locality.   (*Report*, 231)

But something odd happens here. The description moves along well until the last five words, at which it seems to freeze into the jargon of a Baedeker. Why was Frémont unable to maintain the momentum of this sentence, to predicate something interesting about his description? It is almost as though he were embarrassed, as though his nerve had failed him suddenly. An answer to that question is suggested by the change in manner that comes over the account immediately following this passage:

The rock is fossiliferous, and, so far as I was able to determine the character of the fossils, belongs to the carboniferous limestone of the Missouri river, and is probably the western limit of that formation. Beyond this point I met with no fossils of any description.   (*ibid.*)

Frémont's first *Report* is full of disjunctions of this kind. Again and again a picturesque description will be followed by a scientific account of the same setting, as though he had caught himself daydreaming. Sometimes the oscillation between the two modes is nervously rapid, and the sense of guilt made almost explicit:

Like the whole country, the scenery of the river had undergone an entire change, and was in this place the most beautiful I have ever seen. The breadth of the stream, generally near that of its valley, was from two to three hundred feet, with a swift current, occasionally broken by rapids, and the water perfectly clear. On either side rose the red precipices, vertical, and sometimes overhanging, two and four hundred feet in height, crowned with green summits, on which were scattered a few pines. At the foot of the rocks was the usual detritus, formed of masses fallen from above. Among the pines that grew here, and on the occasional banks, were the cherry, (*cerasus virginiana*), currants, and grains de boeuf (*shepherdia argentea*). Viewed in the sunshine of a pleasant morning, the scenery was of a most striking and romantic beauty, which arose from the picturesque disposition of the objects, and the vivid contrast of colors. I thought with much pleasure of our approaching descent in the canoe through such interesting places; and, in the expectation of being able at that time to give them a full examination, did not now dwell so much as might have been desirable upon the geological formations along the line of the river, where they are developed with great clearness. The upper portion of the red strata consists of very compact clay, in which are occasionally seen imbedded large pebbles. Below was a stratum of compact red sandstone, changing a little above the river into a very hard siliceous limestone.

(Report, 232)

So it is not only from a twentieth-century point of view that Frémont's dissociation between the description and the measurement of landscape becomes visible. The tension between the two modes is there in the text, in the warfare between the pleasures of pictorial composition and the business of surveying. Although the freshness and enthusiasm of his responses make of Frémont's prose a more fitting celebration of the wilderness than almost anything written by Flint or Hall, like them he seems to have felt uncertain as to what stylistic grid to impose on his material.

Nor can this stylistic oscillation be explained by the old canard that Jessie Frémont ghost-wrote the first *Report*. This misconception may be so widespread among historians of American life and letters because it conforms to subterranean patterns of belief about the West (the possibility is considered briefly in chapter 7), but its efficient cause is undoubtedly the persuasive prose of Jessie Frémont herself and a misreading of the lively narrative style of Frémont's biographer, the distinguished historian Allan Nevins. 'With Jessie Frémont's help, for she possessed high literary gifts, he composed a report which gave him a wide popular reputation. . . . Modelled on Irving's *Adventures of Captain Bonneville,* it showed a zest for adventure and a descriptive sparkle which appealed to the fast-growing interest in Oregon settlement.' So goes Nevins's entry in the *Dictionary of American Biography* (vol. VII, 20). His full-scale study of Frémont elaborates the argument (Frémont 'had a natural command of graphic English [but] he lacked elegance'[1]) and cites Jessie's own account of how she became her husband's collaborator: 'After a series of hemorrages from the nose and head had convinced him he must give up trying to write his report, I was let to try, and thus slid into my most happy life work!'[2]

Whether a wife's claim to have aided a famous husband is a surer proof of her indispensability to his success than are nose-bleeds of authorial ineptitude, will have to be left to later historical judgement. If they did collaborate, it was not a case of his supplying the rough factuality and her putting on the twiddly bits. There is more than enough in Frémont's background – his education by the classical scholar trained at Edinburgh University, Dr Charles Robertson, his association with the French naturalist Nicollet – to explain his sensitivity to rhetorical nuance and scientific detail alike, and to distinguish it from what the admittedly talented Jessie would have imbibed at her native spring. 'That she helped him, no one can deny,' writes Frémont's latest biographer. 'But her aid in putting together his narrative was no more than that of any good editor with an ear for the cadence and sweep of prose that brought to life an epic in exploration.' In the main, 'He expressed what he thought, felt and saw in his own prose style,' which 'differed considerably from Jessie's.'[3]

With the first *Report,* at least, she may have had even less to do than that. The only documentary remains of their cooperation on that work is the manuscript in the National Archives (DNA-77), of which the first nineteen sheets are in Jessie's hand, and the rest in John's, with subsequent alterations and corrections by Jessie. These changes, noted in the modern edition, seem neither frequent nor substantial, and serve to remove literary allusions and other sophisticated associations at least as often as to add them.[4]

The rivalry in Frémont's first *Report* between the picturesque and scientific modes comes to a head over the matter of the Rocky Mountains. The chief object of the expedition was to determine the altitude of their highest point. But for Frémont the Rockies were also the theater of an older battle, the Americans' struggle to have their landscape esteemed by European travelers. As far as Frémont could tell, the American West was a match for any of the more celebrated natural features of Europe, but how could he be sure? Unlike Irving, he had never been to Europe, and no great writer had validated with his praise the American scene west of the Mississippi river. Surely the Rocky Mountains, at least, would claim their place in landscape description. 'Though these snow mountains were not the Alps,' wrote Frémont, 'they have their own character of grandeur and magnificence, and will doubtless find pens and pencils to do them justice' (*Report,* 255).

What made the comparison between the Alps and the Rockies especially embarrassing for Americans was that it ran against the usual defense that their landscape made up in sublimity what it lacked in the picturesque. The Alps were the commonplace from which European travel accounts took their idea of the sublime. By contrast the Rockies were something of a disappointment. Though almost as high as the Alps (at 14,431 feet, Mount Elbert in Colorado is not much more than a thousand feet short of Mont Blanc), they are, from most approaches and with a few exceptions like the Grand Tetons, a rather unexciting collection of hills and peaks. On the route traveled by Frémont, and by most of the forty-niners, the ascent to the summit is so gradual that the sense of a distinct mountain range is lost.

At any rate, Frémont's curmudgeonly German cartographer, Charles Preuss, was not impressed. In a passage later deleted from his manuscript draft, Frémont records Preuss's disappointment with his first sight of the Wind River Mountains in the Rockies chain:

As we had been drawing nearer to the mountains, Mr. Preuss had kept constantly before his mind the moment in which he had first seen the Alps; when turning a corner of the Jura between Basle and Tololburn, the whole ridge, from Mt. Blanc to the Tyrolese Alps, burst upon his view in the glory of a bright sunshine, and his disappointment was proportionately great.[5]

How pleased Frémont must have been, then, to find himself capable of applying his own pen to the task of describing the Rocky Mountains, especially after affirming that it could only be done in the future.

With nothing between us and their feet to lessen the effect of the whole height, a grand bed of snow-capped mountains rose before us, pile upon pile, glowing in the bright light of an August day. Immediately below them lay the lake between two ridges covered with dark pines, which swept down from the main chain to the spot where we stood. Here, where the lake glittered in the open sunlight, its banks of yellow sand and the light foliage of aspen groves contrasted well with the gloomy pines. 'Never before,' said Mr Preuss, 'in this country or in Europe, have I seen such magnificent, grand rocks.' I was so much pleased with the beauty of the place, that I determined to make the main camp here.   (Report, 255–6)

If the Rockies did not answer to the canons of the sublime, they could, at least, be recuperated as picturesque. And no doubt Preuss's assent to this project contributed to Frémont's pleasure. This European opinion, at least, he could print.

But to scale the Rockies with fine words was one thing; Frémont's business was to measure their height. And if their altitude looked less dramatic than it was, all the more reason to get it right, in verifiable data. At this point something happened to make that object very difficult. In crossing a river they broke their one remaining barometer. Since atmospheric pressure decreases at a known rate the higher one goes, the barometer was an essential instrument for measuring the altitude of the mountains. The only other method available to them was to take the temperature of boiling water, since the higher the altitude, the lower the temperature at which water boils. But the thermometer was broken too. Frémont was desolate:

A great part of the interest of the journey for me was in the exploration of these mountains, of which so much had been said that was doubtful and contradictory; and now their snowy peaks rose majestically before me, and the only means of giving them authentically to science, the object of my anxious solicitude by night and day, was destroyed. We had brought this barometer in safety a thousand miles, and broke it almost among the snow of the mountains.   (*Report*, 256)

Fortunately, the mercury of the broken barometer had been preserved. If only they could find another receptacle, and somehow manage to calibrate it accurately, they might still proceed as they had planned. Frémont's detailed, concrete account of his attempts to remedy the accident is an excellent piece of technical writing, among the best prose in the first *Report*. Clearly his imagination and intelligence were engaged in this task as in few others on the journey. First he found a few glass vials among his equipment and tried to cut these to the required length, 'but, as my instrument was a very rough file, I invariably broke them.' Then he tried what seems now a most unlikely solution:

Among the powder horns in the camp, I found one which was very transparent, so that its contents could be almost as plainly seen as through glass. This I boiled, and stretched on a piece of wood to the requisite diameter, and scraped it very thin, in order to increase to the utmost its transparency. I then secured it firmly in its place on the instrument with strong glue, made from a buffalo, and filled it with mercury, properly heated. A piece of skin, which had covered one of the vials, furnished a good pocket, which was well secured with strong thread and glue, and then the brass cover was screwed to its place.   (*Report*, 257)

It seemed to work, though without the thermometer with which to run the other test, they could not be sure. Finally they managed to climb the highest of the peaks, going up most of the way by mule, and climbing the rest on foot. Frémont put on a light pair of moccasins, so that he could grip with his toes. At the top they 'mounted the barometer in the snow . . . and, fixing a ramrod in a crevice, unfurled the national flag to wave in the breeze where never flag was waved before.' At last they had achieved their ambition. Then, as they sat in their ease, something happened that seems to emblemize the stylistic struggle going on in the book:

while we were sitting on the rock a solitary bee (*bromus, the humble bee*)* came winging his flight from the eastern valley, and lit on the knee of one of the men.

It was a strange place, the icy rock and the highest peak of the Rocky mountains, for a lover of warm sunshine and flowers, and we pleased ourselves with the idea that he was the first of his species to cross the mountain barrier, a solitary pioneer to fortell the advance of civilization. I believe that a moment's thought would have made us let him continue his way unharmed, but we carried out the law of this country, where all animated nature seems at war; and, seizing him immediately, put him in at least a fit place, in the leaves of a large book, among the flowers we had collected on our way. The barometer stood at 18.293, the attached thermometer at 44°, giving for the elevation of this summit 13,570 feet above the Gulf of Mexico, which may be called the highest flight of the bee. It is certainly the highest known flight of that insect.   (*Report*, 270)

This is a fitting climax to the first *Report*, with John Charles Frémont at the height of his achievement as of his exploration, clapping a bee in a book along with his other specimens. There is no need even to ask which of the two descriptive modes — the picturesque or the scientific — he finally preferred, or to which he more readily applied the adjective 'authentic.' Whereas in Flint and Hall the stylistic debate never resolves itself, in Frémont the rivalry becomes an issue, almost a plot, whose exciting conclusion is felt out, and spelt out, through the hard experience of travel in, and writing about, the West. Breaking and repairing the barometer seems to have concentrated Frémont's mind, brought him back to his proper business. Or at least that is how he tells the story. It certainly focusses the narrative; and the story of the bee, so artfully placed as light relief, reinforces the resolution of the conflict between pictures and numbers. Now the values are clearly assigned: thoughts about the bee as a tenuous link between civilization and the wilderness were what we 'pleased ourselves' with for the moment; inevitably our duty, to our mission for the country as to

* Frémont's modern editors correct this to the modern *bumble bee*, while pointing out (p. 270n) that the species is really named *Bombus*. I have kept the *humble bee* of the original *Report of the Exploring Expedition to the Rocky Mountains in . . . 1842 and to . . . North California in . . . 1843–44* (1845).

48

the 'law of this country,' was to put an end to idle fancies, make the bee a specimen, and take our readings. Frémont the frontier dreamer awoke into Frémont the patriotic surveyor. He had found his métier and his proper style.

After the bumble bee, the first *Report* is all downhill and dénouement. In the ten remaining pages (fifteen in the modern edition) there is only one further reference to the landscape, and that is severely circumscribed, by a not-altogether-rhetorical *occupatio* at the beginning, and a summarizing sentence at the end:

It is needless to attempt any further description of the country; the portion over which we travelled this morning was rough as imagination could picture it, and to us seemed equally beautiful. A concourse of lakes and rushing waters, mountains of rocks naked and destitute of vegetable earth, dells and ravines of the most exquisite beauty, all kept green and fresh by the great moisture in the air, and sown with brilliant flowers, and everywhere thrown around all the glory of the most magnificent scenes; these constitute the features of the place, and impress themselves vividly on the mind of the traveller. (*Report*, 272–3)

In his second *Report,* of the expedition to Oregon and California, published with the first in the same volume, Frémont would never again allow a description of scenery to stand on its own long enough to draw attention from his narrative of travel and discovery. The few references to scenery in the second *Report* (about ten in over 300 pages of the modern edition) are short and subordinated to the main discourse. Either they are related to the practical affairs of the expedition, as when mountains 'luminously white' 'from summit to foot' portend an early winter (*Report,* 522); or they appear as punctuation to the narrative, as in the case of the brief references to the various colors of Mount Hood seen in different lights as Frémont's party moved down into California. When the scenery is allowed slightly more space than this, it is related to the mood of the observer; either as a foil, as when their Indian guide deserts them shortly before they attempt the summit of the California Sierra in winter:

Scenery and weather, combined, must render these mountains beautiful in summer; the purity and deep-blue color of the sky are singularly beautiful; the days are sunny and bright, and even warm in the noon hours; and if we could be free from the many anxieties that oppress us, even now we would be delighted here;
(*Report,* 632)

or as a way of relaxing after an achievement, as when they cross the Sierra Pass almost two weeks later:

49

February 21 [1844]. – We now considered ourselves victorious over the mountain. . . . We enjoyed this morning a scene, at sunrise, which even here was unusually glorious and beautiful. Immediately above the eastern mountains was repeated a cloud-formed mass of purple ranges, bordered with bright yellow gold; the peaks shot up into a narrow line of crimson cloud, above which the air was filled with a greenish orange; and over all was the singular beauty of the blue sky.   *(Report,* 638–9)

What has happened here is that landscape as scenery has ceased to exist as an objective fact different from and sufficiently powerful to rival the scientific mode. Instead it has become subjective, human, a reflection of feelings, a device of the narrative.

3

THE FORTY-NINERS: THE STYLISTIC PATHOLOGY OF THE OVERLAND TRAIL

In 1847 John Sutter, the Swiss immigrant who had established a large ranch near what is now Sacramento, California, decided to go into the lumber business and began to build a sawmill on the American river near Coloma. Early the next year one of his employees saw signs of free-standing gold in the new tailrace below the water wheel. Sutter's wishes to the contrary, there was no hope of keeping the secret. For one thing, his ranch was a regular stopping off place for emigrant trains coming down from the Sierra Nevada. (Frémont had stayed there too). For another, only nine days after the discovery, the treaty of Guadalupe Hidalgo ended the Mexican War and ceded the whole of California to the United States. Though the American military occupation of California had been consolidated over a year before, the new territory had to be made American in population as well as in law, and a gold rush was an ideal way of attracting United States citizens to the area. So when people began to spread rumors and the newspapers picked up the news, the military governor of the new territory wasted no time in getting off an official letter to Washington. He did not exactly play down the golden promise:

I have seen the written statement of the work of one man for sixteen days, which averaged twenty-five dollars ($25) per day; others have, with a shovel and pan, or wooden bowl, washed out ten to even fifty dollars a day. There are now some men yet washing, who have five hundred to one thousand dollars. As they have to stand two feet deep in the river, they work but a few hours in the day, and not every day of the week.[1]

It was not long before the news was substantiated in the balustraded prose of President Polk himself. His last Annual Message to Congress, on 5 December, 1848, was largely taken up with his satisfaction at the acquisition of California, from where 'the accounts of the abundance of gold . . . are of such an extraordinary character as would scarcely command belief were they not corroborated by the authentic reports of officers in the public service.'[2] After that, no one needed to write books praising the climate of the region and its opportunities for agricultural development. The Gold Rush did for California what a million copies of *What I Saw* could never have done — enlarged its population by over seven times in just under two years, from 14,000 in 1848 to about 100,000 in late 1849.

The Americans came to California by three main routes: by ship around Cape Horn; by ship to Chagres on the Atlantic side of the Isthmus of Panama, thence across the Isthmus to Panama City and by sea again to San Francisco; and straight across the country, for the most part by the California Trail made famous, if not exactly defined, by Irving's *Bonneville,* by Bryant and by Frémont's first expedition. The trail started near the old line set by the Indian Removal Bill which Irving had toured in 1832, and which could now be reached by the relatively 'public' transport of train, stage coach or river steamer. Independence and St Joseph, both in Missouri, were the most popular gathering places for the overland parties. From there they went, by horse, mule, or wagon train, northwest across the prairies to the shallow valley of the Platte river, which they followed for almost 500 miles, past Fort Laramie (about 80 miles northeast of the present Laramie, Wyoming) to Independence Rock. By this point they were in the valley of the Sweetwater, which formed a providential gap in the Rocky Mountains leading to the South Pass. Here, at the continental divide, the forty-niners were 8,000 feet up and could see the snow-capped Wind River chain of the Rockies to their right, but the pass itself was more like a broad plain. Once over the pass they could choose to take Soublette's Cutoff straight for the Green river and Bear river valley, or choose to go down to Fort Bridger, in what is now the southwest corner of Wyoming. Either way, they had eventually to turn north, following the Bear river valley to Fort Hall, now in southeastern Idaho, unless they elected to take the hazardous Hastings Cutoff from Fort Bridger straight into Utah and south of the Great Salt Lake. At Fort Hall the wagons could at last head south and west for Utah, to the head of the Humboldt river, which they would follow for almost three weeks and about 350 miles to where it simply vanished, at the Humboldt Sink, in the alkali desert of western Nevada. At the Sink they needed to store up water and grass, because they had to cross fifty miles of desert before reaching the Truckee river. This ran down out of the Sierra and could be followed up past what is now Reno to where it turns south to Lake Tahoe. From there to the Donner Pass 7,000 feet up in the Sierra, was the hardest climbing of all. The Sierra range tilts, presenting to the east an awesome, wall-like face, and to the west the anticlimax of a gradual descent through seemingly endless foothills. When the forty-niners finally pulled into Sutter's Fort, they had come almost 2,000 miles across prairie, desert and mountain. Others took an even longer route, heading north from the Humboldt river to Goose Lake, almost in Oregon, coming down past Mount Lassen into the Sacramento valley. Others again went south from the Humboldt Sink to pick up the Carson river and to cross the Sierra south of the Donner Pass. This route saved the arduous, repeated fording imposed upon travelers up the Truckee.

Considering that all this had to be achieved between the beginning of May (when the grass on the central prairie had grown high enough to provide food for the animals) and the end of October (when the first snows begin to settle in the Sierra), one can understand the comment of the California author who made the journey that 'Any man who makes a trip by land to California deserves to find a fortune.'[3]

By contrast, the route around the Horn was comparatively safe and easy on the constitution, though the fatigue of boredom, frustration and seasickness cannot be discounted. Forty-niners on this journey were essentially gentlemen and passengers, and a high proportion of those who went West to service the needs of the miners, as shopkeepers and other entrepreneurs, appear to have gone that way. The route across the Isthmus was the fastest, the most expensive (as much as $1,000, *steerage,* for the earliest passages, though the price soon settled to around $600), and more perilous than a trip around the Horn, offering at least the adventure of working one's way up the Chagres river by dugout canoe and possibly catching malaria in the process. The overland way was the cheapest of all, of course. $200 to $300 would buy a share of wagon, food and equipment sufficient for the whole journey, and if you had your own gear (as many farmers did), the trip could be made for less. A knowledge of how to drive a team, repair a wagon and handle firearms would be a strong recommendation. One would have expected this route to appeal most to farmers without a great deal of disposable cash, especially if they lived in one of the settled western states, like Ohio, Illinois or Missouri, and were thus starting from a point up to a third of the way across the country towards the West Coast. So more people went to California during 1849 and 1850 over the cheaper cross-country trails than took the ship around the Horn or via the Isthmus — perhaps half again as many* — and in 1849, at least, about half of the overlanders came from the American states north of the Ohio river and west of Pennsylvania, including Iowa.[4]

For those crossing the country, the hazards were almost as dramatic as the statistics. Not that the Indians gave them much trouble. The Sioux were then friendly to the whites, and spent a good part of their time fighting the Arapahoes, Cheyennes and Pawnees. The last of these had been ravaged by smallpox and cholera, and in 1848 their crops had failed almost entirely because of drought. Apart from some thieving and occasional violence on the part of the Paiutes of the middle Humboldt, the forty-niners seem to have encountered the Indians mainly in small groups of traders or beggars. Cholera was another matter. It was not a danger peculiar to the West; in fact an epidemic of cholera had reached such proportions in the States by the middle of 1849 that President Taylor called for a national day of 'fasting, humiliation, and prayer.' But the crowded, unsanitary conditions at the points of assembly in Missouri helped to spread the bacteria, with the result that many men died on the first hundred miles or so of the trail, and many even before setting off. The difficulty for historians is that the same conditions also encouraged other, less dangerous illnesses of which diarrhoea was the initial symptom, such as salmonella, amoebae and simply a change of diet; the victims, unable to distinguish between these, tended to record all instances of diarrhoea as more or less

---

* Exact figures for the numbers of forty-niners traveling by the various routes to California are unavailable. Historians have reached some measure of agreement on the figures for those going via the Horn and Panama. John Caughey, author of the standard history of California, gives 40,000 as a total for these routes in 1849–50 (*California, a Remarkable State's Life History*, 3rd edn, 1970, 183), while John Kemble ('The Gold Rush to Panama, 1848–1851,' in John Caughey, ed., *Rushing for Gold*, 1949) gives 47,663 for the same period. On the figures for overland travel, however, there is much less agreement. Caughey (*ibid.*) suggests between 25,000 and 35,000. George Stewart (*The California Trail*, 1962, 232, 296) says about 22,500 went via the overland route in 1849 and another 45,000 in 1850 — 67,500 in all. But Merrill Mattes, who has made a special study of the Platte river section of the California Road, estimates that 30,000 used the route in 1849 and 55,000 in 1850. Of course not all these were going to California (Mattes's *The Great Platte River Road*, 1969, covers the Oregon emigrants too), but the figures can be set in the context of an average of 2,500 emigrants using the Platte river route per year from 1843 to 1848 (Mattes, 23).

severe cases of cholera. The result is a wide variation in historians' figures* for deaths from the epidemic among the wagon trains, but there is no doubt that the forty-niners themselves were worried about the threat. Hardly an account of the California Trail in 1849 fails to mention a death by cholera, or at least the concern for their health among the party.

Other dangers were more directly related to conditions of travel on the trail. With so many going at once, there was the risk that the grass along the way would run out by mid-summer (in fact 1849 was a wet spring on the prairies, so there was enough for everyone). The heavy wagons were hard to manage up and down steep slopes and while fording rivers, and there was always risk to limb, if not life, from manoeuvres of this kind. It was difficult to judge how much goods and equipment to take along. Too much weight meant the oxen or mules became exhausted just when their greatest effort was needed in crossing the desert between the Humboldt Sink and the Truckee river. Too little (the mistake made by many going in 1850, who had read in the papers accounts of overloading and the subsequent jettisoning of equipment), and they might be unable to repair a broken wagon, or even run out of food.

Then there were the social risks. How would so many strange men behave, thrown together so uncomfortably and so far from civilization? In fact, very well. At least there seems to have been surprisingly little fighting or thieving. There was some bickering, in the trains and especially in the mines. The danger here was that a company or other partnership might break up, with a disastrous effect on the enterprise demanding the cooperation of many. Finally, there was the economic danger that a miner would fail to find gold and be stranded in California up to 3,000 miles from his home.

It is in terms of such superlatives, such heroism, that the history of the Gold Rush has often been told, as though it were the epitome of the great American drive for the West undertaken at other times by mountain men, trappers, explorers and emigrants. Yet the forty-niners were quite different from their precursors in several important respects. Unlike the emigrant parties, most of their number —

* The estimates run from 5,000 dead in 1849 (Hubert Howe Bancroft, *Works,* San Francisco, 1882–90, XXIII, 149) to 400, or less than 2 per cent of the total going by the California Trail in 1849 (Stewart, *The California Trail,* 228).

about 95 per cent — was made up of adult males, many of whom, unlike the pioneers or mountain men, had left wives and families at home. Although many of them were small farmers, a much greater proportion than in any earlier or later emigration came from towns and cities. 1849, writes the historian and novelist George Stewart, might be called 'the year of the greenhorn':

They lacked even the knowledge of camping and woodcraft that is likely to be possessed by the average man of the mid-twentieth century from having been a Boy Scout or having taken a few fishing trips, to say nothing of the many thousands who have slept in foxholes. There were, of course, the veterans of Mexico, and a still large proportion of Western farmers. But the many city-dwellers were definitely men of a soft generation, far removed from the frontier and never having known war. They could learn, and did, but sometimes paid heavily for that tutelage.[5]

The forty-niners also seem to have been peculiarly aware of their role in history or at least of the importance and interest of what they were doing, and they were correspondingly more articulate about their adventures than earlier and later emigrants on the California Trail, who experienced dangers and excitement at least as great as they. The number of extant journals and diaries kept by forty-niners (especially by those who went in 1849) represents a far higher proportion of those going than in any other year except 1841 and for that year the small sample of 100 people is statistically insignificant.* What is more surprising, perhaps, is that the proportion of overland forty-niners keeping journals was at least as high as that of those who went by the sea routes. It may be wrong to assume that the travelers by sea had a better education and were more articulate, simply because they had more money to spend, but what cannot be denied is their greater leisure on the journey. Yet

---

* There are over 150 diaries extant of the California Trail crossing in 1849. Even taking the highest estimate for people crossing in 1849, this gives a ratio of one diary for every 200 who went that year. This is an astonishing figure, considering that there must have been many diaries lost and many still undiscovered. By comparison, Mattes gives a figure of one diary extant for every 500 travelers in 1850 and 1852, 'but in late years the ratio drops off sharply. No ready explanation is at hand, only the surmise that the Californian rush produced more writers in its early climax because of its novelty and excitement. Or it may be that the ratio of diary keepers was just as high in later years, say in the 1860s, but their diaries were apt to be discarded by descendents for some inscrutable reason' (*Platte River Road*, 24). In fact, the sense of the historical importance of the event could be expected to influence both the numbers of diaries written and the interest shown in the diaries by their authors' descendants.

the overland travelers, despite the dust, bad light, and their fatigue, managed to enter daily impressions of the journey in at least as high proportion as the passengers by sea.*

Their motives for going, too, seem to have been various, and certainly could not be generalized within some economic category like the desire to get rich quick. H. M. T. Powell, who went from Greenville, Illinois, to California by the Santa Fe Trail, recorded his feelings on leaving home with his companions:

4th [April, 1849] Started from home with Dr. Burchard about 8 a.m. Parting bitter – bitter. About halfway down the lane Henry came posting after us on Grey Horse to give me a little green and gold paper to give to his brother Walter – it brot tears again to my eyes – but let all that pass – duty sends me away, or I would not go.   (B. C-F 115, vol. 1)†

After the specificity of names and other details, the abstraction 'duty' is almost defensively uninformative; it appears again and

---

* On this subject, too, there appears to be some disagreement. Oscar Lewis, author of the standard work on the 'argonauts', as he calls them, seems to take the common assumption for the fact when he writes: 'those who made the journey by land were no less eager to put on paper a day-by-day chronicle of happenings along the way, but comparatively few were able to carry out that resolve. On the other hand, those who travelled by sea found their journals a welcome relief from the tedium of idle weeks aboard ship. The consequence is that while overland diaries are comparatively rare, there exist today hundreds of diaries, journals, and collections of letters, all setting forth in detail every phase of life at sea on the months-long voyages from the ports of embarcation to San Francisco' (*Sea Routes to the Gold Fields*, New York, 1949, v–vi). My own count of the major holdings of forty-niner diaries and journals suggests a different conclusion. The Coe collection at Yale has 33 overland diaries and four by sea (three by the Horn, the other by the Isthmus); the Huntington Library has about 40 of each; the Bancroft, at Berkeley, has about 95 overland journals and about 75 by sea, of which 45 are via the Horn and 30 the Isthmus (my Bancroft figures include their copies of MSS in other hands, except Coe and Huntington, but excludes short letters or later dictation to Hubert Howe Bancroft). Unless Mr Lewis knows of a cache of sea diaries not represented or noted in the major collections, it would seem that the numbers of extant diary for each main route reflect approximately the numbers going by that route; or, if we take Caughey's estimates of the numbers going by each route (40,000 by sea, and between 25,000 and 35,000 by the California Trail) the proportion of diaries remaining is actually greater for the latter.

† Citations from the forty-niner diaries have been simplified to the following scheme: where published, date of publication followed by page number; where unpublished, library where manuscript is held (in practice this will be either 'B.' for Bancroft or 'H.' for Huntington) followed by call number. No attempt has been made to cite page, or leaf number of unpublished manuscripts, which are often unpaginated in any case, but the date of the entry is given. A fuller description of these sources appears below, pp. 208–11.

again in these accounts, especially in letters home when the men try to explain to their wives and parents why they have gone. But even when they were more articulate about their motives, the forty-niners mentioned the gold, if at all, as only one of their reasons for going. Niles Searls went by the California Trail on the 'Pioneer Line,' an organized wagon train that sold passages almost as on public transport. His entry for 15 May, 1849, puts a wide range of possible motives:

We have launched out upon those broad plains which for months must be our home & what is the object of our present journey? Are we led on by a kind of indefinite wish to roam over creations broad expanse without any particular object in view, or are we led on by the all absorbing mania for getting gold, or by the more laudable one of seeking for knowledge at her primeval source, of surveying and admiring the majestic works of Providence as displayed in their native grandeur? (B. C-F 46)

Clearly the 'mania' for gold did not rank high in Searls's priorities of prestige. This is not to suggest that he was not interested in striking it rich, only that he seems to be imagining himself in the steps of Bonneville and Frémont as much as contemplating a timely speculation. David Staples left Boston for the California Trail on 16 April, 1849, for the nicely balanced reasons of 'bettering our condition on money matters & seeing the country. I left home with regret as it is no easy matter for me to leave *Wife home friends* & attachments' (B. C-F 165).

Others were concerned to make some social space for themselves. Henry Sturdivant, who left late in 1849 to go West by the Isthmus route, expressed his motives in terms of goods and property to be bought with California gold, but his project is set in the frame of humiliation at not having made his mark in his home town:

Unwilling to live any longer in a town, to which I have no earthly [?clame], save that of nativity; having never yet been able to own a foot of land within it, though many an hour of toil has been spent to gain a foothold among the friends of my boyhood; & live amid the scenes I have cherished from childhood, with a fondness not soon to be forgotten; I must to day say good bye to that I love in Maine; & number myself among those who are going to hunt gold in California. It seems as if fate had determined that I should have nothing of this worlds goods, unless I seek it among strangers. (H. HM 261)

And in the middle of 1850, David Dewolf wrote his wife back in Springfield, Ohio, that he had made some money in the mines, and was now making even more driving a team hauling provisions:

You want me to come home this Fall but you need not look for me as soon as you think I can get home by the last of January with I think three thousand dollars & by staying until the first of March I can get home with five thousand now I leave it for you to say shall I come home this Fall or wait until Spring. . . . Oh! Matilda oft is the night when lying alone on the hard ground with a blanket under me & one over me that my thoughts go back to Ohio & think of you & little Sis [their daughter] & wish myself with you but I am willing to stand it all to make Enough to get us a home & so I can be independent of some of the Darned sonabitches that felt themselves above me because I was poor.

(1925, 220–1)

The question of why so many Americans emigrated to the West during the nineteenth century (or, for that matter, why a third of the American population changes address every year even now) has never been easy to answer. Ray Billington, the senior historian of the American West, has shown that large westward migrations have never been directly motivated exclusively by economic need; in fact, that it always took a certain amount of capital to make the venture.[6] For the same reason, and for others as well, American working men and European immigrants newly arrived in the country rarely emigrated further West but were content, exhorted or constrained to remain within their tightly knit communities in large urban centres of the East. But the American middle-class family, freed perhaps for the first time from the most pressing need, but still feeling that their life could be improved, could think of joining that westward drift that had always been such an important part of American progress. And contrary to popular opinion, it was not the enterprise of individuals, but the efforts of the nuclear family that settled the farmsteads of Illinois, Ohio, Indiana, Missouri, and the rest of what is now called the Midwest in the early nineteenth century. The more children you had, the more land you could clear for eventual farming, and the more firmly you established yourself. Conversely, parents, in-laws, and anyone else over the age for manual labor were a liability. Hence the primacy of the nuclear family in the enterprise of the western clearings.

Hence also, perhaps, a certain *ennui* felt by the first and second generations of these families. The very strength of the family unit in the work of clearing the wilderness — the mutual physical and moral support of its members — could seem confining after the most urgent need for such cooperation had passed. Outside the family, the small town might be intolerant of deviant behavior, including poverty. After all, had not the opportunity to own property and accumulate goods been offered equally to everyone when the town was first settled? Surely poverty could be the result only of carelessness, or laziness? (Alternative explanations, such as that in the older towns, like the one in Maine from which Henry Sturdivant was escaping, a fairly inflexible striation of class and wealth had had time to establish itself through inheritance, were not consonant with America's idea of itself in the middle of the nineteenth century, and were therefore inaccessible to the collective mentality of a New England town.)

The best way to understand the forty-niners may be to think of them as men on a kind of vacation from Protestant communities in which holidays were no part of normal life. For a season — and they would not have wanted it any longer — men broke away from their wives and small children; adolescents freed themselves from a dominating father; and (in a few cases) social deviants escaped an accusing community. No other account of their motives will serve as well. Were they after the gold itself? Most of the diaries discount this as a primary motive, whether out of genuine scepticism about the morality of such desires, or as a defense against their eventual disappointment and that of their families. Was it to possess California? No doubt the advocates of western expansion, like Bryant and Polk, would have liked nothing better, but the diaries suggest that few of the miners settled in California, on their first trip West anyway, and fewer still set out in the hope of doing so. Was it, as Niles Searls wrote, for the sake of 'seeking for knowledge at her primeval source,' or 'surveying and admiring the majestic works of Providence'? Certainly many forty-niners wrote as though their journey had a vaguely scientific or exploratory purpose, but after the government surveys from Lewis and Clark to Frémont, and after a decade of emigration to California, could anyone seriously argue that the West, especially as seen from the same old route through the Platte valley, still needed to be mapped, measured and described? No, they were going for fun, for adventure, for relief from an existence that was not so much economically depressed as simply boring, or emotionally cramped. They went, as the common phrase had it, 'to see the elephant.'

But holidays in America, expecially the all-male ones, have always carried a lot of meaning. Even now they can be gestures to the legendary past of American western exploration and a way of cultivating the virtues connected with that exploration. So a modern hunting or fishing trip in the wilderness may both reenact the conditions of life of the old frontiersmen, and celebrate the hardy, undomestic side of life thought to be so important to American success in the world. A vacation of this kind may even serve as a kind of initiation into these values of the younger members of the party, an introduction to American adulthood. All this is well enough known; but now apply it to the holiday (if that is what it was) of 1849–50. Could this too be read as a reenactment of a movement thought to be important to a shared past — perhaps an imitation of the real westward migration undertaken by the parents and grandparents of the forty-niners? It would not be entirely far-fetched to imagine their generation being told endlessly of their forbearers' achievements, and wishing to vindicate themselves by at least a token migration of their own. But like the modern hunters and fishermen, they too, of course, possessed earlier, and more widely shared historical legends — models of American development fashioned by the romances of Cooper (where the family is the beginning and end of western adventure, but never its locale) and by the not-entirely-functional explorations of Frémont and Irving's *Bonneville*. And for them too, the trip could be a gesture against the domestic setting (despite all their denials to their wives at home) and a rite of passage. This idea was both very deep in the American consciousness, originating in the experience of breaking away from the mother country, and celebrated in legend and fiction, like Irving's story of Rip Van Winkle, the henpecked family man who went to sleep for twenty years, and woke to find his wife dead and his country an independent republic; and in Hawthorne's fable, 'My Kinsman, Major Molyneux,' in which a young man tries, but fails, to find his well-connected 'kinsman,' before realizing that he is old enough to fend for himself. It is even in Irving's *Tour on the Prairies*, where he advocates a western journey for any young American wishing to achieve 'that manliness, simplicity, and self-dependence most in union with our political institutions.'

For the phrase 'seeing the elephant' implied more than a pleasant outing; the elephant was not our familiar attraction in the local circus (indeed, the animal was not introduced to American circuses until the 1870s) but a mythical beast at the ends of the earth. Once you had seen the elephant you had seen everything, and could count yourself a man. The trope was common, and it entered quickly into the iconography of the Gold Rush. An enterprising publisher, realizing that the forty-niners wrote a lot of letters home, began to produce printed letter blanks, a kind of picture postcard suitable for pony-express post, and a nice instance of the holiday aspect of the California venture. Most of them showed scenes of the California landcape (then, as now, the giant redwood figured large), life in the mines, maps of San Francisco, and so forth. But among the most popular views was a drawing of a miner aghast at a huge elephant rearing before him. This was the one un-naturalistic view, a late echo of the popular emblem book. The forty-niners needed an image of their powerful feeling that they had grown up during their journey to the mines; the result was an odd translation of their verbal figure into a pictorial 'view.'

The notion that the western adventure was a maturing experience worked so powerfully on the forty-niners that even those most discouraged at their social position on setting out for California began to cheer up, the more they accomplished by their own hand. David Dewolf, so abashed by the 'sonabitches' who looked down on him, wrote his wife before he headed West from West Port, Missouri:

Matilda I never had such feelings in my life as I have had since leaving home. Men have taken sick and died all around me with the colery and even one of my own comrades has died with the disease and one or two others have had it in our mess but I have been generally healthy myself.

But it would be a consolation to me if I were to be sick if I had my loved one to chafe my temple and wipe the cold sweat from my brow.   (1925, 186)

But by the end of the year, after he had completed the journey and begun to make money in the mines, was able to make light even of the dreaded 'colery.' He wrote Matilda on 12 December, 1849, 'My health at this time is very good I was taken with Colery Morbus but am getting better but they are trouble with the Dioreah & Scurvey'

(217). In time even the scurvy got him, but by early the next year it was all one to him. 'My health at this time is very good,' he again reassured Matilda; 'I expect I am more fleshy than you ever saw me I have had the Scurvey a Complaint that is very common here It is caused by eating salt food which are compelled to live on here for vegetables are very scarce & tremendous high' (219). Time, and the experience of the disease he only imagined before, convert his sentimental fears into laconic acceptance. Even the scurvy is the source, not of self-pity, but of quiet boasting; it is the badge of a select brotherhood cut off from the produce of the domestic market garden.

To Henry Sturdivant, apparently less robust both physically and emotionally than Dewolf, the sense that he was growing through his western experience came more slowly and less evenly. Besides, a passenger on a ship could hardly claim he was roughing it. But once landed at the Isthmus, he and a companion 'engaged a log canoe, propelled by three natives,' and started up the Chagres river. Their first night was spent in a tiny native village, where:

we crawled up into the top of a hut, & lay down on some poles in the most filthy place, I have ever thought of lying down to sleep. It was inhabited by one old niger, who lay in the shape of a hoop, too far into sleep to know that he had company. I now became conscious that I was taking my first view of the *Elephant*.

(H. HM 261)

At the mines he learned quickly enough that (as he wrote on 1 April, 1850) 'gold even in California, is not to be got without labor, & that the most laborious.' But illness kept interrupting his work in the mines: first diarrhoea, then a mysterious numbness, then palpitations of the heart, finally a sore throat. He could not keep his thoughts from comparisons between being sick at home and in a mining camp. 'There I slept in a bed, in a room with a fire in it, & two or three to wait upon me — here my bed is an india rubber one, that leaks . . . by the time we get into bed the fire goes out; & it is no warmer in the tent than out side.' By July, his health was still poor ('I have all the ails of a confirmed Dyspeptic, & living base is unfavorable for me'), but he was determined to carry on as long as he could work, 'for I cannot bear the thought of going home poor.' But by the end of the year his mood had eased from grim stoicism to positive hope. And the reason for the improvement was not money. This is part of his entry for New Year's Day, 1851:

What advancement I shall make the coming year in any pecuniary affairs I have but little idea of. A year ago today I supposed by this time I should be rich but I find my worldly possession yet a minus quantity. But I have a mind now that is not easily troubled. I think that I have not been so happy since I was twelve years old, as within the last few months. I have heard it said that people get weaned from home in about two years, I hardly think it will take me so long.

By March he was earning between $50 and $60 a week, but the adventure of the mines was gradually ebbing, leaving only the tedium of regular manual labor. It was on experiencing this that most of the diarists began to think of returning home. Sturdivant discovered that he was not, after all, an exile from his small home town in Maine but would quite like to see his childhood friends again:

would that I could mix in social circles with the friends of my youth, Were I an outcast, one whom the world looks coldly on; Were there no friendly greetings to wellcome me to my early home – did I wish to shun the gaze of men, [California] should be my chosen home; as it is I shall not content myself to live here much longer.

He sold his claim; then, with some friends, bought and sold a schooner, and with the profit bought a passage for San Juan de Nicaragua and New York, where he arrived early in 1852. His story is the very paradigm of the concept, made explicit by Irving but also generally believed, of the West as a field of romance in which a youth could prepare himself for his proper place in the society of the East.

This sense of romance probably explains why the forty-niners referred even to the actual hazards on the trail in an oddly impersonal and abstract way. It is true that David Dewolf admitted to homesickness, but this was in a private letter and probably no bad tactic in a message addressed to his wife. Anyway he later incorporated his weakness within the plot of the wilderness as initiation. On the other hand, the diaries and journals – that is, those accounts written partly to inform posterity of the man's western adventure, even if that posterity was limited to his own descendants – express their feelings in the general terms of an anxiety at being so far beyond the borders of civilization. Overton Johnson's *Route Across the Rocky Mountains,* the widely used trail guide published in 1846, had developed this idea especially fully (like Bryant's book, it was more than just a collection of practical hints and a table of distances). His preface compares the landscape of the East with that of the West, following comparisons made by Willis and others between Europe and America. 'Nature appears to have created [the West] upon a grander scale. The mountains are vast; the rivers are majestic; the vegitation is of a giant kind' (*Route*, XIII). As he crossed the prairies, Johnson's feelings were 'of no common kind,' and his syntax rose to the occasion:

> when the past; all that we had left behind us – nothing less than the whole civilized world, with all of its luxuries, comforts, and most of its real necessities – society, friends, home, – all that is in this world dear to man: – when the future, dark and uncertain, presenting nothing but a vast extent of drear and desert wastes, uninhabited save by the wild beast and savage, filled, perhaps, with thousands of unknown difficulties and dangers, hardships, and privations, – rushed at once, in mingled confusion, upon the mind, and impressed upon our feelings a full sense of the loneliness of our situation and the rapidly increasing space that was separating us from all communion with the civilized world.
>
> (*Route*, 3)

The forty-niners took up the theme. As he approached the South Pass, cold and worn down with fatigue and worry at nursing a companion with a disease of a 'typhoid character,' Solomon Gorgas could not suppress his gloom at what lay around him:

> Surely the great Creator has never designed this dreary country to become the habitation of the white man – of the civilized & the intelligent – for all here is a dreary waste of sandy hill & miry hollow, no timber no fuel but the wild sage – No, No, This is evidently the region designed by Him for the range of the wild beast & the home of the Red Man of the forest who knows nothing of the comforts, refinements & blessings of life, who knows nothing of the arts and sciences – The Lord grant to deliver us speedily from the cold & gloomy region.
>
> (H. HM 651; 16 June, 1849)

A Dr Thomas was struck particularly by the contrast between Fort Laramie and the wilderness surrounding it. As with Johnson and Gorgas, the ambitious meditation seems to require long, complex sentences. In this case, however, the syntax falls apart – significantly at the point where his nostalgia at the sight of the national flag, the symbol of what he has left behind, refuses to be subordinated to the rest of his sentence:

> The rooms are fitted up very neatly, to be transported from any part of the States to this place, without seeing the intervening country, one would involuntarily exclaim, How lovely, How neat, but after travelling through the boundless, wild, and desolate plains and not seeing the least semblance to civilization until all at once you hove in sight of a tasty edifice from whose summit floating upon the delightful breeze which is ever present on the plains, the Star Spangled Ban-

ner, the sight of which sends a thrill of joy deep into the breast of every true American. The contrast is too great when I see the fine workmanship, the conveniences of the Fort I am reminded of home of Civilization, but step outside and cast your eye over the boundless extent of space, not to find a single object upon which to rest its wearied vision save the high tops of Rocky Mountains, and you become almost as wild as the Indian for whom this country appears so particularly adapted.   (B. C-B 383:1; 3 June, 1849)

Even when they did think about specific dangers, the forty-niners usually set their concerns within the more general frame. Thus David Staples, after witnessing a fight in which a man, pushed and kicked by another, threw a hatchet at his assailant, commented, 'men get cross some times on this trip and having all restraint thrown off they act rash' (B. C-F 165; 30 July, 1849). Thoughts of illness and death, especially, put the men in mind of the comforts left behind them. David Dewolf could not contemplate the cholera without wishing for Matilda to chafe his temple and wipe the cold sweat from his brow, and even Henry Sturdivant's thoughts turned to home when he fell ill. George Staples, David's brother, died of cholera after being ill for almost two weeks. David and his uncle did their best to mark his grave and fix its location in their memories:

we found a large sandstone & he engraved his name & where from & age on it in good deep large letters his grave was dug in a conspicuous place on the main road 30 miles west of the Big Blue river on the right of the road near the junction of three tracks & a small stream runing south from it.   (*ibid.* 8 June, 1849)

But it was no substitute for a civilized burial. Besides, even the precious paper record could be lost. On 21 August they came across the letters, papers and sermons of an Episcopal clergyman, 'the writings of many hours scatered to the wind,' the last entries in whose journal 'showed rather a depressed spirit.' 'Poor fellow,' added Staples, he was one of the 'many who started to improve their health on this trip [who] have found a grave on these plains.'

It was the tableau of the unattended graves in the wilderness that most clearly emblemized for the forty-niners their distance from civilization. Some made an almost frantic effort to preserve a record of them. Following his last journal entry for 7 October, 1849, James Mason Hutchings (B. 69/80 C) listed 112 names on graves he saw between Missouri and California, entering details of place of origin and cause of death, where these were available. But, as he noted sadly, his record was bound to be incomplete. 'Many of the graves were nameless, some having been written on paper and nailed to the board; others had neither board nor name on them.' J. Goldsborough Bruff, the draughtsman for various government agencies including the Bureau of Topographical Engineers, copied every epitaph he encountered when he led a party overland in 1849. So faithful was he in this activity that in some places his account of the journey seems to consist of little else but memorial messages. The introduction to one of his many notebooks explains that the record was kept for the benefit of those back home who might otherwise have known nothing of the circumstances in which their loved ones had died, but his act was also a more general gesture against chaos.

The graves of the lamented dead, and the harried way-side inscriptions . . . may have been erased and destroyed by beasts of prey of the sacrilegious savage. Yet not a few of them will be found as faithfully preserved . . . as though . . . memorized in marble, in the grave-yard of their native village.

(Cited in 1949, lx)

Those who were not moved to keep lists could acknowledge the dead through poetry. John Wood, who went overland from Cincinnati in 1850, summarized his experience on the California Trail:

I have sat in the stilness of the night, solitary and alone, and watched the last gasping breath of a dying comrade, and stood around the graves of many more, and saw the sand shoveled over their remains, far from home and friends, where no rose tree or monumental stone will ever tell where they lie, and here

'The storm that wrecks the wintry sky,
    No more disturbs their deep repose,
Than summer evenings latest sigh,
    That shuts the rose.'

(1871, 110)

And for others again, the thoughts of death rooted themselves in the rather thin soil of legend. One of the few popular stories of the Overland Trail attached itself, significantly, to Scott's Bluff in western Nebraska, one of the most striking and least likely topographical features on the trail. It was said to have been named after a fur trader who died there alone after being abandoned by his companions. Dr Edward Tompkins was only one of many who meditated on Scott's death when he passed the Bluff, and his entry for 18 June, 1850 celebrates one Scott in the language of another:

'Scotts Bluffs' are so called from a man by name of Scott who formed one of a company of fur traders who abandoned him at this place when sick and unable to assist himself. Here Scott died far, far away from his home and friends surrounded by fiendish savages and all the wild romance of capricious nature's fanciful freaks – O it was a wild lonely, aye a desolate place in which to die. Here he breathed his last sigh alone with nature's gloom, and with nature's God.

(H. FAC 222)

All these responses to the understandable fear of death on the trail or in the mines show an almost superstitious faith in the power of formal verbal construction, whether alluded to or composed afresh, as a wall against barbarism. Even more symptomatic, perhaps, were the elaborate constitutions drawn up by many of the wagon companies before starting out. These were not always entirely functional – being overformal and unenforceable in many particulars – but they were a nostalgic piece of home and a shield of American republicanism against the outer wastes. Silas Newcomb tipped into the bound ledger book in which he kept his meticulous diary the constitution of the Beloit Company, with whom he went overland in 1850. It is *set in letterpress* and consists of a formal preamble and many resolutions, of which the following is only a brief selection:

Whereas we are about to leave the frontier, and travel over Indian Territory, exposed to their treachery, and knowing their long and abiding hatred to the Whites; also many other privations to meet with. We consider it necessary to form ourselves into a company for the purpose of protecting each other and our property, during our journey to California. . . .

Resolved, That there shall be one selected from the suitable and capable to act as Captain or Leader, and to hold his office until removed by a two-thirds vote of the company. . . .

Resolved, That the Christian Sabbath shall be observed, except when absolutely necessary to travel.

Resolved, That each and every member shall pay strict and proper respect to the feelings of each and all the Company. . . .

Resolved, That in the case of a member's dying, the Company shall give him a decent burial.

(H. FAC 4)

Yet not all these formal responses to the wilderness were so gloomy or obsessional. Another pattern commonly imposed was the familiar exoticism of the pastoral. The same Dr Thomas who was so appalled by the desert spaces around Fort Laramie, wrote this about the landscape of the Black Hills, only three days, or about forty miles, further west:

The hand of Nature has done more to enrich the delightful scenery here by interspersing at irregular intervals, that most beautiful of all trees, the pine than the most expert horticulturalist in the world. This [? sublime] Paradise Garden of Eden cannot be contemplated without exciting all the finer feelings of Man's nature and as I feasted my delighted eyes, I could not but think if man was always surrounded by such pretty [?chaste] and lovely scenery, he would never dare think evil, much less perpetrate sin. (B. C-B, 383:1)

The outdoor meal was an especially popular topic. When two members of an emigrant party rode over to visit Bryant's camp:

We invited them to partake of our humble fare, and if they thought proper, a bed in our spacious chamber. The first consisted of bacon broiled on a stick over a fire of buffalo chips; and the last was the illimitable canopy of the heavens.
(*What I Saw*, 102)

Only a month after his affecting meditations on the cholera, David Dewolf jauntily wrote his wife: 'You would laugh I know to see me going along with a bag on my back gathering Buffalo dung to cook with but we have to do it. The darn stuff burns fine in a stove for I'd have you to know we have a cooking stove along with us in our Company & we live fine we have Pork & Beans' (1925, 191). By 14 July they were 'still getting a better view of the elephant,' camping on a small creek and letting 'our stock brouse on plumb brushes' (198). And on 16 December, 1849, Allen Varner wrote his parents in Indiana to reassure them that he was well and making money:

This portion of the country is remarkably healthy   I am told the scurvy is quite prevalent in some parts of the mines; but one of my messmates being quite a hunter we have had plenty of fresh venison and are as healthy as need be   I sleep on a bedstead the cords of which are boards the bedding a buffalo robe & blankets we have good flour Pork venison beans rice sugar coffee tea & dried fruit
(H. HM 39983)

Passages like these imply, almost allude to, similar accounts of meals in Irving and Frémont, where the effect of the open air, on human fellowship no less than on the appetite, promotes 'humble fare' above the 'perfumed feast' of the 'Roman epicure.' Common to all these accounts of eating and sleeping in the wilderness is the old pastoral comparison between civilized and rustic manners. The substitutions are listed item by item: bacon on a stick instead of a three-course meal; the 'canopy of the heavens' instead of a ceiling;

buffalo chips for a stove (this adjustment to the wilds especially caught the forty-niner's fancies); boards for bed cords, and a buffalo robe for blankets and sheets. The juxtaposition works partly as the traditional satire on the over-civil (even though their homes were not universally luxurious — witness Varner's bed cords), and partly as an expression of nostalgia for home comforts. As for the comic confusion of the products of culture and nature (tents and stoves as against buffalo skins and chips), this is also a serious celebration of a sort of reformed domesticity; as though they had recapitulated the best of civilization — its fellowship, its organized effort against chaos — without the worst.

The diaries and letters of the forty-niners were not taken up solely with their adventures and feelings, however. A good proportion of many of them was devoted to what Niles Searls called the 'more laudable' task of 'seeking for knowledge at her primeval source, of surveying and admiring the majestic works of Providence as displayed in their native grandeur.' And as in Flint, Hall and Frémont, they often described the same thing twice over, once admiring and once surveying. Here is Bryant's response to a mirage on the salt desert west of the Great Salt Lake:

as we advanced, beautiful villas, adorned with edifices, decorated with all the ornaments of suburban architecture, and surrounded by gardens, shaded walks, parks, and stately avenues . . . renew[ed] the alluring invitation to repose, by enticing the vision with more than Calypsan enjoyments or Elysian pleasures. These melting from our view . . . in another place a vast city, with countless columned edifices of marble whiteness, and studded with domes, spires, and turreted towers, would rise upon the horizon of the plain. . . . But it is vain to attempt a description of these singular and extraordinary phenomena. Neither prose nor poetry, nor the pencil of the artist, can adequately portray their beauties. *(What I Saw,* 174–5)

The last sentence is not entirely rhetorical, apparently, because he goes on to give an entirely different view, not of the desert's illusory beauty but of its material basis:

For fifteen miles the surface of this plain is so compact, that the feet of our animals, as we hurried them along over it, left but little if any impression for the guidance of the future traveller. It is covered with a hard crust of saline and alkaline substances combined, from one-fourth to one-half of an inch in thickness, beneath which is a stratum of damp whitish sand and clay intermingled. Small fragments of white shelly rock, of an inch and a half in thickness, which appear as if they once composed a crust, but had been broken by the atmosphere or the pressure of water rising from beneath, are strewn over the entire plain and imbedded in the salt and sand. *(ibid.* 175)

However bound they may have felt to admire the works of nature, the forty-niners were unhappy in the mode of picturesque description – more so even than Hall. Their descriptions of landscape are either stiffly clichéd or curtailed in embarrassment. Silas Newcomb isolated his descriptive passages with self-conscious marginalia, labeling them as 'descriptive' or even 'merely descriptive.' Clearly they were not part of the serious work he was about. In other diaries words like 'sublime,' 'magnificent' and 'romantic' are applied routinely to prairies and especially mountains, and often have the effect of freezing an otherwise fluent narrative. These terms were nothing more than the vestiges of an earlier mode, probably only partly understood in any case. Hiram Pierce, who came via the Isthmus in 1849, began his diary in California 'for future reference by my self and Family,' and developed a good vernacular style attentive to the concrete facts of his daily existence. But when it turns to scenery, his narrative nervously tries on finer garments:

The scenery in some places is grand & Sublime in the extreme. At one place as we were assending the side of the Mountain, on our left lay a vale or bason far below us, shut in on all sides by lofty ranges. This contained pines interspersed through it with a great variety of wild flowers & shrubery all clothed with the freshness of Spring, while far above us on our right toward the black & rugged Peacks of the Mersais Mountains. That beautiful language of the Poet was forcibly brought to mind:

> Was the rich vail that proudly Shone
> beneath the morning beam &c

(1930, 54–5)

Often the description itself is elided, leaving only the object selected for description and its effect on the observer. A common instance of this is the brief statement that this or that mountain, or whatever, was such as to elicit wonder. Sometimes the account displays a slightly more ambitious version of the same formula, as when Ezra Bourne crossed the Sierras on 1 August, 1850, and wrote: 'After the bare and moldy Rockies, these seemed sublime. The music of the mountain streams tumbling and flowing under snow and down the mountains is something I shall hear in my ears always' (B. C-F 142). The music died with the author. So did the tableau not described by Joseph Warren Wood on 23 June, 1849, the evening after they forded the north fork of the Platte: 'The smoke from our stoves curl up among the branches & presents a scene of rural beauty enchanting to the imagination' (H.HM 318). For John Wood, the sight of the Devil's Gate, where the Sweetwater had cut its way through dramatic, nearly perpendicular walls on its way down from the South Pass, could be expressed in dimensions, but 'The sublimity and grandeur of the place are indescribable and is certainly a great display of God's works, and is well worth any travelers' attention' (1871, 43).

A variant of the elided description is what might be called the figure of the future painter (or writer, or other creative artist), the idea that someone better qualified than themselves, like the poet 'brought forcibly' to Hiram Pierce's mind, would come one day to the job they could not manage. Frémont himself had expressed the hope that one day the 'grandeur and magnificience' of the Rockies would find 'pens and pencils' – that is, writers and artists – to do them justice (*Report*, 255). Bryant had suggested that the prairies, with their 'delicate shading and coloring' 'would charm the enthusiastic landscape artist in his dreaming sketches' (*What I Saw*, 36). On the evening of 27 May, 1849, David Staples and his party made camp 'on a beautiful rise with a creek on our right & the Kansas on the left'; it was, he thought, 'a grand scene for a painter' (B.C-F 165). And Mary Stuart Bailey, seeing Scott's Bluff, thought of 'some Ancient City with high walls, gates, towers. . . . I could not compare it to anything else & would like to have spent days there – what a theme for the novelist' (H. HM 2018; 21 June, 1852).

The wish expressed by Frémont and the forty-niners for writers and artists to celebrate the spectacle of the prairies and the Rockies was not an unmixed compliment to the western terrain. The implication is that for time being practical men needed to get on with the important business of mapping, surveying and retrieving specimens. 'Mere description' was itself a barren exercise on a voyage of discovery. For even the forty-niners, late as they were in the field, thought of themselves as explorers. Bruff's plethora of notebooks, his sketches, diagrams, maps and tables, are only the most elaborate in a large number of pseudo 'reports' of largely mimetic 'expeditions.' Most of the forty-niners' diaries also aspired, to a greater or lesser degree, to the example set by Bonneville and Frémont. But if there had been some doubt as to the scientific value of these earlier expeditions, there could be none in the case of the later. Their route had been amply surveyed and described, and the forty-niners knew it. Had they not, after all, read the earlier reports? For them exploration and topographical description was not functional science but rhetoric, like their picturesque passages and their pastoral moralizing, another formal grid to place over the wilderness.

Except that they lent their energies to the rhetoric of science with greater gusto than to the other descriptive modes. They annotated, sketched and measured to a degree well beyond what their time, energy and skill would seem to have allowed. They kept tables of distances; they noted the weather. Silas Newcomb inscribed the longitude, latitude and altitude of the better-known landmarks, taking most of his figures from Frémont. (Entries for longitude and latitude are also a common feature of 'argonaut' diaries, the figures coming from the daily noon fix, posted for the passengers to see.) Bruff and Elijah Howell (B. C-F 121) entered daily air temperatures on their journeys in 1849, the former more assiduously than the latter. Quoting from Joseph Ware's *The Emigrant's Guide to California,* Howell inserted the following 'promiscuous extracts,' as he called them, into his narrative: 'South Pass is distant from Fort Laramie 300 miles, and 950 from the mouth of Kansas River. It is in Latitude 42 deg. 27' 15"; Longitude 109 deg. 27' 32"; Altitude 7490 feet.' From the 'Mormon Guide Book' he took the altitude of the South Pass, and the bearings of Pacific Creek 4½ miles south of the South Pass, the position of Steam Boat Spring, and even of Salt Lake City (B. C-F 121, 26 June and 5 July).

Newcomb also kept 'specimens' of flowers in a press. Others collected berries and flowers, as well as geological samples. At the back of the first of his six-volume diary, Joseph Warren Wood (H. HM 318) made a list of his specimens:

No 1 Carbonate of Lime from Black Hills, it is an isolated specimen. I saw no more.
   2 A Pebble from Warm Spring, the gravel of the spring was Quartzose
   3 Fragments of chimney rock
   4 Conglomerate from the range of hills North of Laramies Peak − . . . it appears to be Cemented with lime − in some places large Boulders entered into its composition. . .

And so on. In the left hand margin he wrote later, 'Some of these are thrown away.'

Two geographical features especially, both of them already famous by 1849, attracted the attention of the amateur scientists. One was a group of hot springs along the Bear river, on the route between the Green river and Fort Hall. The other was the assortment of buttes and pinnacles along the North Platte; Courthouse Rock, Chimney Rock and Scott's Bluff. These were the first glimpse, for most of the forty-niners, of the strange, angular landscape that has since become familiar through western films. The springs had been mentioned in Irving's *Bonneville* and described in detail in Frémont's account of his expedition to Oregon and California, the second part of his *Report* of 1845. The chief attractions were Beer (or Soda) and Steamboat Springs, named, very roughly, after the taste of one and the noise of the other. Frémont took samples of their water and the surrounding deposits, analyzed their mineral content, and published the results in tables in the *Report*. He also fixed their appearance and general character with great verbal precision, of which the following description of Steamboat Spring is a fair instance:

In an opening on the rock, a white column of scattered water is thrown up, in form like a *jet-d'eau,* to a variable height of about three feet, and, though it is maintained in a constant supply, its greatest height is attained only at regular intervals, according to the action of the force below. It is accompanied by a subterranean noise, which, together with the motion of the water, makes very much the impression of a steamboat in motion. . . . The rock through which it is forced is slightly raised in a convex manner, and gathered at the opening into an urn-mouthed form, and is evidently formed by continued deposition from the water, colored bright red by oxide of iron. (*Report,* 477)

The forty-niners could not leave it at that, though. William Swain, who went overland from Michigan in 1849, described Soda and Steamboat Springs exhaustively in his diary entry for the night of 14 August, arriving at dimensions much the same as Frémont's. He also found time to take samples of the minerals deposited by the springs, and of some petrified wood that lay nearby. Elijah Howell, copying out his notes more than twenty years after he had made the voyage, nevertheless found his memory settling on measurements made by Frémont:

The Steamboat Spring is in one or two rods of the bank of the river, I think. The water in it comes gurgling and sputtering up through an irregular opening in the flat rock, some six to twelve inches in size, and froths and spouts up (according to my recollections) some 2 ½ or 3 feet high, and then sinks gurgling still, back into the ground to rise and spout up again (I think, now, in 1872) in about 40 or 50 seconds.　　　(B. C-F 121, following original entry for 23 July, 1849)

But nothing encouraged the scientific mode more than Chimney Rock. This is a natural spire rising from a cone, one of those erosional remnants that give the 'Wild West' its characteristic look. The whole structure, which looks like an inverted funnel, stands about 325 feet high, or 470 feet above the river.[7] So remarkable seemed the phenomenon that even Irving, when he came to that part of Bonneville's journals describing the feature, thought it best to retire from the narrative, as though to impress upon his readers that the description was not a figment of the ghost-writer's fancy. The result is one of the few paragraphs of 'scientific' prose in Irving's work:

Opposite to the camp at this place, was a singular phenomenon, which is among the curiosities of the country. It is called the chimney. The lower part is a conical mound, rising out of the naked plain; from the summit shoots up a shaft or column, about one hundred and twenty feet in height, from which it derives its name. The height of the whole, according to Captain Bonneville, is a hundred and seventy-five yards. It is composed of indurated clay with alternate layers of red and white sandstone, and may be seen at a distance of upwards of thirty miles.　　　(Bonneville, 21–2)

Frémont, did not, himself, describe the Chimney, because while his main party traveled up the North Platte, he and a few men made a detour up the south branch of the river to take some astronomical positions and to scout possible sites for military forts. But he cut in excerpts from Preuss's journal describing the rock, so that the account appears in the appropriate place in the Report. He also continued to describe geological formations on his route that were like the more famous phenomenon: 'our road soon approached the hills in which strata of a marl like that of the Chimney rock, hereafter described, make their appearance' (Report, 191). 'It is composed of a soft earthy limestone, and marls resembling that hereafter described, in the neighborhood of the Chimney rock, of the North fork of the Platte, easily worked by the winds and rains, and sometimes moulded into very fantastic shapes' (Report, 207). Preuss's description of the Chimney is not much longer than these, because he also drew a picture of his subject:

76

To several of these localities where the wind and rain have worked the bluffs into curious shapes, the voyageurs have given names according to some fancied resemblance. One of these, called the *Courthouse,* we passed about six miles from our encampment of last night, and toward noon came in sight of the celebrated *Chimney Rock.* It looks, at this distance of about thirty miles, like what it is called, the long chimney of a steam-factory establishment, or a shot-tower in Baltimore. . . . *July* 10 . . . after a day's journey of twenty-four miles, [we] encamped about sunset at the Chimney Rock, of which the annexed drawing will render any description unnecessary. It consists of marl and earthy limestone, and the weather is rapidly diminishing its height, which is now not more than two hundred feet above the river. Travellers who visited it some years since placed its height at upwards of five hundred feet.   (*Report,* 215–17)

Irving's *Bonneville* and Frémont's Preuss established the descriptive mode and the salient details of Chimney Rock, though they got the details wrong. Bonneville overestimated its height, and Preuss underestimated it by over a half. Both exaggerated the degree to which it was wearing away. U.S. Geological Surveys have since shown the spire to have lost only 17 feet between 1895 and 1965.[8] There seemed very little more to say about what, after all, was only a column of rock (or column of something), however striking. But Bryant would not be the last to feel he had his own contribution to make, though his account contains nothing that could not have come from Preuss. And the forty-niners, almost without exception from those that passed that way, added their own accounts. Most of these were 'scientific' at least to the extent of expressing the experience largely in figures.

In this respect their descriptions were often at odds with other parts of their discourse. For example, when Dr Edward Tompkins wanted to describe the various cities through which he passed on his way to the frontier in 1850, he found the words flowing from his pen as on to a chamber-of-commerce brochure. 'Eirie contains many very fine buildings which principally surround a very large public square or park, situate on a plain at a considerable elevation above the lake.' Cincinnati was 'a charming city and possesses all, all that refinement of taste and exquisite finish that characterises the most aristocratic of eastern cities. It can boast a great elevation of Literature, science, and art. . . . Its public houses are finished in the best possible style and afford the choicest accomodations.' And so on, down the list of public buildings, through the 'temples of science and learning' to the 'Grand Masonic and Odd Fellows

Halls.' But the sight of Courthouse and Chimney Rocks, for all their resemblance to architectural features, reduced him to numbers, as soon as their barren reality manifested itself:

Court House Rock' This is a very remarkable eminence indeed . . . and appears in the distance like a magnificent Castle. On approaching it is found to be an eminence of hard clay mixed with pebbles. It is about 260 feet high and perhaps 300 feet across its base. A detached spire stands within 40 feet of it which is perhaps 240 feet high and 170, across its base. Some call the main rock 300 feet high. . . . The base of Chimney Rock is about 250, square and runs up in a pyramid form some 125 feet . . . surmounted by a column which is about 10, feet through from north to south and 20, feet from east to west.

(18 June, 1850)

Joseph Warren Wood wanted 'to study the Botany of the plants' he encountered along the route, but could not 'do anything satisfactory on acc't of the plants not being fully described in Mrs Lincoln's work.* I have not time to carry out the various descriptions myself & consequently cannot pursue the study with interest' (H. HM 318; 7 June, 1849). But with the aid of Bryant, whom he mentions having read, and Frémont, whom he almost certainly read as well, Wood could at least describe Chimney Rock:

The Chimney is of the same material as the [Court House] but a little more sandy, it stands upon a high mound of clay & is about 100 ft high the elevation of the whole mass is 250 or 300 ft high. I judge of its height by comparing it with men standing on its side & viewing it from a distance.

The Chimney is about 30 ft in Diameter at the base & 20 at the top, it is regular in its proportions & cannot be ascended it will not endure many years.

(9 June, 1849)

Others, though, found the existence of prior texts on the subject something of a strain, and were anxious to add their own contributions to the descriptive tradition. When he caught sight of the 'famous landmark & curiosity' in 1849, Charles Glass Gray thought it 'resembled the chimney of a *sugar refinery'* (1976, 30, my italics), and as if that burst of ingenuity were not enough, later compared a still unnamed butte to 'the capitol at Washington . . . which the men all thought it very much resembled' (32). Silas Newcomb had no sooner reached the area of the Courthouse and Chimney than he broke off his narrative to give a complete bibliographical account of

* Presumably, Almira H. Lincoln, *Familiar Lectures on Botany for the Use of Higher Schools and Academies*, Hartford, 1829.

78

the guidebook used by his party (William Clayton's *The Latter-Day Saints' Emigrant's Guide*), then quoted Bryant verbatim on how Scott's Bluff got its name. At last, his eye fell on the unnamed bluff seen by Gray almost a year earlier: 'Opposite to our camp, on the south side, and between "Chimney Rock" and "Scotts Bluff", is a remarkable – unnamed – elevation, resembling the Capitol at Washington so much that I took the liberty to call it "Capitol Rock" (H. FAC 4; 4 June, 1850).

Poor Newcomb; like many another researcher in an overworked field, he was just a year too late. Who knows how many hundreds of forty-niners also saw and named that nameless rock, thinking that they had, at last, made their own contribution to the descriptive geography of the American West? Even Frémont once got entangled in this network of claiming and naming, when he and his party called Steamboat Spring after its sound, 'without knowing that it had been already previously so called' (*Report*, 477).

What can possibly account for this great concentration of interest on the hot springs and especially the rock formation along the North Platte? Why were these places described with the anxious attention, and in some cases the meticulous reference system, of a scientific dissertation? The simple answer, the efficient cause as it were, is that these sights were famous because they were famous, to borrow another phrase from Daniel Boorstin; that is, the sights had been noted repeatedly by early explorers, who described them scientifically, so the forty-niners followed suit, uneasily aware that they were not first in the field. We are back at the model of the family parked by the Grand Canyon, looking at the scene in their View Master. Modern holiday makers (Boorstin would say *especially* modern ones[9]) commonly visit places made famous by the perceptions and descriptions of other people, and do not look at the places when they get there. Insofar as their journals were the forty-niners' holiday snaps, this explanation fits them as well as it would the subjects of Boorstin's critique.

But what made these places especially noteworthy in the first place, more than (say) the Humboldt Sink and the passes over the Sierras? The answer, I think, is that the springs and bluffs were not simply strange, but both strange and beguilingly familiar. They were a paradox, a perfect figure for the uneasy tension between culture and nature sensed by so many travelers in the West. The

79

springs bubbled diabolically, like outposts of Hell, yet they were almost perfectly round, and might have been made of marble or porphyry, like fountains in a municipal garden. The buttes and pinnacles on the Platte were uncultivatable, oddly out of scale and not softened by erosion like the hills of home, yet they suggested any number of architectural forms – domestic and public, ancient and modern. Edward Tomkins, so good at describing cities, was particularly eloquent about the possible shapes to be read in this mysterious landscape, but other accounts, from Irving's *Bonneville* and Bryant's *What I Saw,* down to most of the forty-niners' journals, found similar analogies coming to mind:

The whole country seems overspread by the ruins of some of the loftiest and most magnificent pallaces that imagination of man can reach in its most extravagant conceptions. Here lays the ruins of a lofty Pyramid, there a splendid Castle. On one hand is a tremendous Citadel, on the other the grand Hall of legislation. Yonder is the facsimile of our nations Capitol at Washington – and there again is the City Hall at N.Y. only enlarged perhaps a dozen times or more.

On all sides lay the ruins of more grandeur than man has ever had a conception of. Even the ruins of Rome, Athens, Bagdad and Petria fall into perfect insignificance by the side of these apparent ruins of a city that must have been inhabitated by giants. (H. FAC 222; 18 June, 1850)

When he discusses the hot springs, Frémont takes a moment to explain that Beer Spring was named for its 'effervescing gas and acid taste' by 'voyageurs and trappers of the country, who, in the midst of their rude and hard lives, are fond of finding some fancied resemblance to the luxuries they rarely have the fortune to enjoy' (*Report,* 477). He might have applied the same acute comment to himself, for whom similes like *'jet d'eau'* were no doubt a consolation for civic splendors denied him, at least for the time being. Whether in the simple, Adamic project of naming the wilderness, or in the more sophisticated process of 'fancying resemblances' to the shapes they discerned, the travelers in the wilderness were attempting to cultivate the awesome sight of Chimney Rock, Courthouse Rock and Scott's Bluff by reference to what best represented the civilization they had left behind: centers of the law and government, like the courthouse and the Capitol; or foci of an even older 'tradition' like castles, cathedrals and the ruins of antiquity.

In this more fundamental respect the only difference between the *voyageurs* and the forty-niners who came after them was the latter's knowledge that the scenes had been described so often already. But this awareness only added to the paradox presented by the features. They were strange; they looked familiar; by 1849 they were known to be loaded with the textuality of geographical description. The most plotless of American landscapes had been overplotted before the forty-niners arrived to see it for themselves.

But why the language of science? Here again, the answer must go beyond the forty-niners' inclination to imitate their sources; after all, when he got to Chimney Rock, even the æsthete Washington Irving allowed Bonneville's scientific description to surface through his own narrative. Again the most likely answer lies in the anxiety produced by the paradox of culture and nature. The problem was that the similarities between bluffs and buildings, or springs and fountains, were, as Preuss and Frémont said, only fancied. Like Hall's comparison of the prairie to the parks and 'massy architecture' of Europe (and unlike Frémont's '*jet d'eau*,' which at least bears the weight of description, illustrating the shape and motion of the geyser in Steamboat Spring), the architectural shapes discerned in the valley of the North Platte were mirages of cultural artifacts; not similes at all. Dr Tompkins knew, even as he wrote at such length about what these strange formations suggested, that they were really 'hard clay mixed with pebbles.' That is why he had to resort to numbers when he came to describe the thing itself, close up. And he seemed to sense the insubstantiality of his daydreams when he continued from the passage cited above, as follows:

It is vain to attempt a description of these enchanting wonders. Even the strange creations of fancy which give Alladin's lamp such wonder-working powers could never display to the dreamy mind a tenth of such astonishing grandeur as is displayed on these places where nature has made such a *mockery* of the works of art. (*ibid.*)

Nature's 'mockery' is not only of the works of art, but of the force which gives those works their form – the imagination. As Joseph Warren Wood wrote on 11 June, 1849, after listing the architectural analogies suggested by the 'various fantastic shapes' (castles, domes, chimneys and towers), 'you can conceive them to be just what you please.'

What seems to have happened is that a number of ordinary people suddenly found themselves beyond the borders of what they took to be their culture. Faced for the first time with an absence of plots, they began to plot for themselves, beginning with the process of figuring resemblances to what they saw — similarities themselves drawn from what they had left behind. But the project was too desperate, too obviously unsubstantiated; and besides the authors were unsure of their talents as creative writers. Unaware of a possible distinction between fancy and imagination, yet only too painfully conscious that what they were fancying had no basis in reality, they came to suspect the imagination too, and all its works. The effect was so powerful that it was felt by the relatively sophisticated Washington Irving, if only at Chimney Rock. In this dilemma, furthermore, there was no 'tradition' to help them. Though Irving and Frémont had managed to adapt certain European descriptive traditions to the American landscape (the picturesque for the oak openings on the prairies and the sublime for mountains, to take two examples), there was no ready formula for describing geometrically shaped bluffs and hot springs.

The result, again and again in these narratives, was a process of advance and retreat; a foray into the speculative figures of admiration, followed by a withdrawal into the quantitative science of surveying, exactly as patterned in Bryant's two treatments of the desert south of the Great Salt Lake. The insubstantial figures in the mirage had to be countered by, ballasted by, the language of incontrovertible fact. Science offered Irving, Bryant and the forty-niners exactly what it offered Frémont at the top of the Rocky Mountains: authentication. The rhetoric of science bestowed the comfort of a universal language known to be true.

The forty-niners, then, experienced certain anxieties beyond those one might have expected from the dangers they faced. Perhaps they felt guilty at leaving wives and families to cope with farms and small businesses; certainly they were homesick; they were alarmed at the scalelessness of the western wilderness. These feelings they met with certain verbal formulae: abstract talk of 'duty,' rhetorical structures borrowed from the pastoral or the picturesque. As in the case of James Hall, however, their acutest problem may well have been about how to write. In one way or another they came to suspect figurative language. If it was applied to the barren beauty of the Rockies, it seemed to call for special powers of description of which they felt themselves incapable. If it was employed in the process of projecting domestic or urban patterns on the wilderness, then it would collapse when the reality of the wilderness exposed the process for the cruel delusion it was. The safest retreat — indeed the strategy that embraced all the other tactics — was the 'expedition' or 'voyage of exploration,' a posture offering not only a duty but a universal rhetoric of fact.

There is no need to posit a great sensitivity or literary sophistication in the forty-niners to argue that they were worried about how to write about the West. They must have had a canny suspicion that the primeval wilderness was fast disappearing. Almost within their own lifetimes Ohio, Illinois and Missouri had been transformed from wilderness into cultivated farmland — some of them were escaping from this very fact — and they could have seen no reason why the trans-Mississippi West should be any less vulnerable to the advance of the plow.

Their sense of history was so acute, so precocious. Even California became part of the United States, under their feet as it were, in the midst of their holiday away from home. In this respect, as in others, Chimney Rock (so often and wrongly described as about to crumble away to nothing) was a perfect emblem for their feelings.

Little dreaming of the Civil War, the forty-niners thought of the Gold Rush as the unique adventure of their lifetime. Because most of them planned to return from California by sea, after they had made a little money and the fares had come down, they supposed their overland journey would be their one sight of the remaining American wilderness. For many of them their narrative of this journey would be their only gold, the only tangible evidence of the elephant seen, the rite of passage achieved; the only thing to leave their offspring. No wonder so many forty-niners wrote journals, and no wonder their narratives were so self-conscious.

4

THE UNOFFICIAL GOLD RUSH

It is not that the forty-niners were unable to think, read and write in realistic detail about the material conditions of daily life on the Overland Trail, rather that they were reluctant to enter this on the official record (as it were) left to their posterity. Their guidebooks, too, reflect these two strata of ceremonial and informal prose. They seem literally to have used two sorts — one for citing and emulating in their own texts, the other for actually getting them to California. Silas Newcomb quotes Bryant verbatim on Scott's Bluff (H.FAC 4; 4 June, 1850), but mentions having used the extremely functional Mormon guidebook by William Clayton, *The Latter-Day Saints' Emigrant's Guide* (1848). Sarah Royce, who went by ox-drawn covered wagon with her husband from Rochester, New York in 1849, and finally settled in California (their son Josiah, born in Grass Valley in 1855, became the celebrated professor of philosophy at Harvard), recalls beginning their journey 'guided only by Frémont's *Travels*' (1932,3), but later on in the journey refers to 'guide-books' advising them on the supply of timber stage by stage on the trek across the plains (1932,20). West of Salt Lake City they used a hand-written pamphlet on two small sheets of notepaper sewn together, grandly titled 'Best Guide to the Gold Mines, 816 miles, by Ira J. Will[i]s, [Great Salt Lake] City' (1932,34).

An idea of the solid prose in which these practical guidebooks offered their advice can be gathered from a brief look at J. M. Shively's *Route and Distances to Oregon and California* (1846). From the beginning, the book is bracingly unromantic:

When the emigrants start to the sun-down diggings of Oregon, they should not fancy that they are doing some great thing, and that they need military array, officers, non-commissioned officers, &c; all this is folly. They will quarrel, and try to enforce non-essential duties, till the company will divide and subdivide, the whole way to Oregon.   (Shively, 3)

Other advice is similarly deflationary. The single man should 'have nothing to do with the wagons nor stock,' but instead buy two horses or mules in his home town, later trading them for Indian horses: 'and be not too particular; for the shabbiest Shawnee pony you can pick up will answer your purpose better than the finest horse you can take from the stable' (*ibid.*). Culinary arrangements should be simple too:

You should take with you an iron pan, the handle so jointed as to fold up; a kind of knife, fork, and spoon, that all shut in one handle — such knives are common in all hardware stores. In addition to this, you will need a fire-proof iron kettle, to make tea, coffee, boil rice, make soup, &c.; a tin pan, quart cup and a butcher knife, will about complete your kitchen; delay no time to kill game, unless it comes in your way. (Shively, 4)

The route itself is described with only the slightest deviation into editorial opinion, and with no practical detail overlooked:

You are now 640 miles from Independence, and it is discouraging to tell you that you have not yet travelled one-third of the long road to Oregon. Be off from Larima [Fort Laramie] 12 miles to a spring at the foot of the Black Hills; about 4 days will take you through these dreary hills, and you again come to North Platte. Keep up the stream to the red butes, cross and fill your kegs, – for it is 20 miles to any water fit to drink, – fill your kegs again at the Willow Springs. 20 miles will bring you to the Independence rock on Sweet Water – 830; here, a little to your right, is a great basin of Saleratus [sodium bicarbonate], white as snow; fill your bags with it – it is very good for use, and quite scarce in Oregon. (Shively, 8)

So utilitarian is Shively's text that his rare passages of reflection come as a surprise. But his account of the route between the Oregon Trail and California, through what is now western Nevada, shows how capably his spare, hard prose could rise to the more complex business of analytical description:

This is the most sterile desert on the Continent of America, for a distance of 350 miles; not a tree nor shrub, except the hated sage and gresewood [sic]; can be seen. The water is all strongly tainted with mixed minerals, and hundreds of lakes in winter are now dry, and form a crest at bottom as white as snow. The water, before evaporated, is like lye – the white pearlash [potassium carbonate] at bottom is of the same nature, and is used in California for making soap. Here you will see hundreds of Indians destitute of a particle of clothing, living on snails, crickets, worms, and grass, (where there are any.) They are the last link in the chain of human beings. They occupy the country from Mary's [now the Humboldt] river to Snake river. They dig holes in the ground to shelter them from the storms of winter, and must lie in a partial torpid state 'till spring, when they leave their burrow, and wander over the wide plains of desolation, without the means of killing the few antelope that are thinly dispersed over their unparalleled barren country. (Shively, 13)

In all, Shively's guide comprises only fifteen pages, including a table of distances at the end, yet in that short space it gives a more complete sense of the actual requirements and conditions of the overland journey than the whole of Bonneville, Frémont and Bryant. In fact, some of the forty-niners finally achieved something of the plain style of these practical guidebooks, either by learning how to write through the long apprenticeship of making daily entries under trying circumstances, or simply by growing weary of their own rhetoric. After all, even nervousness can be sustained for a season only, and the forty-niners would not have gone West in the first place if they had not tired of plots, including their own. The rhetoric of the journals was concentrated, particularly on the commonplaces of description along the trail, those *topoi* of the 'western experience' like prairies, mountains, the hot springs and the formations around Chimney Rock. Beyond these points (in effect, this means beyond the hot springs), the journals either settled down to a more plain style or petered out altogether. As a general rule, the longer the journals continued, the more they came to justify their name as a record of daily events put down with a minimum of plotting, rhetorical pointing or personal comment. By the time he was climbing the Sierras through the Carson river valley, David Dewolf, for example, was entering his experiences dispassionately, letting the events speak for themselves. Even the sight of a grisly burial, which might earlier have prompted a long meditation on his distance from home, gets put down as it occurs, without comment:

Oct 7th [1849] left camp not very early traveled 5 miles up the river when we forded it 40 feet wide & 2 deep, we continued up the river 6 miles further & halted for noon, we had rough road after crossing the river the valley being narrow & the mountains put close in to the river we had in many places to drive on the side of them. The mountains here are very high & rocky   near where we nooned was the grave of a man that had been buried about 2 weeks he had been partially dug up by the wolves & the flesh all torn off his head, his scull lay some distance from the grave he had been buried not more than 18 inches deep   we halted 2½ hours then hitched up & continued up the river 6 miles & encampt with tolerable good grass the road has been good this afternoon. distance 17 miles.   (1925, 215)

David Staples, for whom tragedy came early on the trail, gives a good sense of the monotony and frustration of the leg between Goose Creek and the head of the Humboldt:

Monday 20[th August, 1849]

To   day we were off in good season   Three miles from camp we crossed a small stream of poor water called Malad Creek . . . a west course after leaving the creek six miles brought us to a warm spring on the side hill   here we filled our tanks expecting to have a long drive to good water   we were not disappointed   the sun was hot in the extreme the roads dusty a kind of powder which would rise in clouds enough to suffocate a person   after twenty miles such roads over some high hills we came to a spring gushing out of a dozen places clear water   men & animals rushed to it as if beside themselves & what a disappointment   just warm enough to be sickish & *salt* ! OH! horrors. we had traveled far as the animals could bear & camp we must & make the best of it   we boiled some for coffee which only made it the *salter*   we have suffered as much today for want of water as any day since we started our men are all well so we can stand it. Distance traveled to day 29 miles.   (B.C-F 165)

And Solomon Gorgas, for whom the plains east of the Rockies were such an unrelieved wilderness, felt more cheerful after his party had crossed the South Pass. His entry for 20 June, 1850, is almost psalmic in its rhythms and its recourse to the materials of physical contentment:

Left camp at 5½ O.C. Drove 12 miles and halted – crossed a deep stream. Not rapid but deep. Wet our breadstuffs, left our pleasant resting valley & rose upon the hills – our noon halt is on a beautiful valley – plenty of grass & water – afternoon crossed some hard hills & steep descents & descended again in the valley of the Fork – drove 30 mi   Plenty grass & wood & the finest of spring water.

If some of the forty-niners finally learned to write plainly (or unlearned how to write pretentiously), the few women who went West with husbands and fathers around the time of the Gold Rush seem to have possessed this skill almost from the beginning of their narratives. They were, after all, different from the men, in at least three ways. First of all, their social role made them supportive and passive rather than active and aggressive; they were expected to confine their concern to the practical details of the family economy, not trouble their minds with abstract speculations and cosmic doubts. Secondly, they traveled with their families, so had the security of a family group, except when the group itself was threatened with some extraordinary danger from outside. They were, in other words, emigrants rather than adventurers; certainly they were on no sort of vacation.

Finally, the women had read different books from the men. The forty-niners were born too early for universal free schooling,* so

* According to Lawrence Cremin's *American Education, the National Experience, 1783–1876* (New York, 1980), 178, the aggregate national school enrollment was only 35 per cent of whites between the ages of five and nineteen in 1830, and that figure includes private, fee-paying schools of all sorts. Emma Willard founded the first women's high school in 1821, but even New York City did not establish public elementary schools until 1832.

unless their parents had paid for their education, and done without their labor on the farm or in the shop, their reading would have been confined to what they could forage for themselves. A young man might go about and find himself a copy of Frémont, but a young woman, socially and spatially more confined, would be restricted to books in the house thought by her parents to be suitable. In practice this meant the Bible, *Pilgrim's Progress,* perhaps a pious 'captivity narrative' of a woman kidnapped by the Indians, almost certainly an almanac. Even Sarah Royce, who 'had a careful, old-style academy education, supplemented . . . by much reading and study' (according to her daughter in law) would have had little acquaintance with say, sentimental novels, much less with the progressive curriculum (including science) of The Mount Holyoke Female Seminary, where the young Emily Dickinson, though born in 1812 and very much a homebody, received the best formal education available to an American woman at the time.

Those differences from the men would explain, perhaps, why the women are given to few flights of rhetoric, and then only of an unambitious kind in response to particularly severe pressures. At the outset of the journey, when the anxiety of leaving home and friends was sufficient to outweigh the security of the family unit, the writing could be more formal than usual. This was especially true when the author felt emotional stress additional to the worries of leaving home. Mary Stuart Bailey went overland with her husband in 1852, after the death of their only child, Harriet. Their journey seems to have been as much an escape from this tragedy as a search for new fortune, and her feelings on leaving must have been even more powerfully ambiguous than those of others at the same stage of their journey. If only here, and if only to the level of a rather sentimental piety, her style rose along with her heart:

April Wed 13 1852

> Left our hitherto happy home in Sylvania [Ohio] amid the tears & parting kisses of dear friends many of whom were endeared to me by their kindness shown to me when I was a stranger in strange land, when sicness & death visit our small family & removed our darling our only child, in a moment as it were such kindness I can never forget. The sympathy I received from all was truly consoling & while life lasts will never be forgotten.   (H. HM 2018)

Or to put it another way, the allusion to the strange land is applied not to the wilderness — concretely experienced or abstractly anticipated — but to her emotional condition at home.

Something similarly extraneous, and additional, to the normal anxieties felt on the trail seems to have prompted Sarah Royce's few modest excursions into formal expression. Once on the Great Plains, when their party had experienced violent thunderstorms, when one of their company had died of cholera and two more were ill with it, she wrote in her contemporary diary, from which she quotes in her later narrative:

Now indeed a heavy gloom hung round us. The destroyer seemed let loose upon our camp. Who would go next? What if my husband should be taken and leave us alone in the wilderness? What if I should be taken and leave my little Mary motherless? Or, still more distracting thought – what if we both should be laid low, and she be left a destitute orphan, among strangers, in a land of savages? . . . I poured out my heart to God in prayer, and He gave me comfort and rest. . . . I said from my heart, 'Thy will be done.' Then peace took possession of my soul, and spite of threatening ills, I felt strong for duty and endurance.

(1932, 17)

On another occasion they had lost their way in the Utah desert and were almost out of water, when they came across a dreary scene. A fire left by campers of Indians had spread, blackening what little vegetation the desert afforded. Suddenly one smoldering bush burst into flames:

It was a small incident, easily accounted for, but to my then over-wrought fancy it made more vivid the illusion of being a wanderer in a far off, old time desert, and myself witnessing a wonderful phenomenon. For a few moments I stood with bowed head worshiping the God of Horeb, and I was strengthened thereby.

(49–50)

These two tiny plots in which desolation is recapitulated in the Word of God are reminiscent of the minor typologies of Puritan history and spiritual autobiography, such as William Bradford's history *Of Plymouth Plantation,* and of the enormously popular captivity narratives, like that of Mary Rowlandson, first published in 1682 and into its fifteenth edition by 1800. The dangers that provoked such narrative strategies may be thought sufficient to explain them, but it seems that Sarah Royce may have been under the additional pressure, when she edited and composed her final account of the journey, of concern over the faith of her philosopher son. Josiah Royce spent much of his profession trying to compose a kind of Christianity that could embrace the modern complexities of the *Origin of Species* and the German Higher Criticism, but her faith was the old Puritan one in the literal truth of the Bible and the possibility of remarkable providences. She wrote her narrative for her son, over thirty years after she had kept her 'Pilgrimage Diary' on the trail, when he was writing his *California . . . a Study of American Character* (1886), and in it she embedded this subtle message for him.

These exceptions apart (among the cases I have seen), the women noted the trans-Mississippi West without formulae. They did not miss the idea of home or civilization so much as actual people and places. The wilderness impressed itself upon them in terms of specific comforts lacking. If they felt themselves growing or maturing through the experience, they expressed this feeling in the context of the possibility that they might actually settle in California. With them almost everything noted had the solidarity of a possible use.

The scientific mode is notably absent. For Sarah Royce Chimney Rock was nothing more than 'an immense natural tower visible for many miles' (22). Mary Bailey, still feeling homesick perhaps, described one of the buttes along the Platte as 'like the bust of an old lady sitting alone looked as though she felt lonely' (16 June). The illusion projected by Courthouse Rock was briskly dismissed; it looked 'like a large public building of stone but the fact is it is mostly composed of earth' (19 June). Phenomena that might have moved the men to long technical descriptions prompted from her a brief, homely metaphor. 'Have noticed a substance on the surface of the earth resembling salt the cattle lick it up' (10 June); 'Passed over some very dry alkeline country the mountains look very much like snow drifts in shape' (4 September).

Unfamiliar plants caught the attention of Algeline Ashley, who set out for California with her husband, shortly after they were married in 1852:

Clear, windy and cool. Rough road. It is a new route, said to be shorter and fords the river but once. The old road fords seven times. We have been gradually rising, for three of four hundred miles, to the summit of the dividing ridge between the waters of the Atlantic and the Pacific. Greasewood grows along the road in great abundance. The first that we saw was a little below Fort Laramie. It is two or three feet high and looks some like cedar only brighter green; the new shoots are white. It is thorny. When rubbed between the fingers it is slippery or greasy. It burns rapidly. It grows in patches about a foot square, the flowers are snowy with an orange center, and about the size and shape of the bunch pink, they are very fragrant. Also a plant spreading on the ground about an inch high.

Leaves like the mullen-pink – flowers like a pea – very small and bright purple, covering the leaves entirely – it is handsome. Rain and hailstorm severe, two hours, clear now. Camp near Sweet Water, poor grass. Passed four graves.

(H.HM 16773, 9 June)

It would be easy to underrate the precision and energy of this passage, with its homely comparisons to plants with which her readers might be familiar. Unlike Joseph Warren Wood, Algeline Ashley was not abashed by the lack of Mrs Almira H. Lincoln's *Familiar Lectures on Botany;* she could see, touch and smell for herself. She was no less fascinated than the men in the strange growths of the wilderness, but for clarity, her account of the flora surpasses all but the best of their more ambitious attempts at technical description. And for all its apparent simplicity, the passage is amazingly varied in its rhythms; alternating between note form and connected prose, between short and long sentences, subtly accenting her particular interests.

Not being on a disguised holiday from their families, the women could admit to holiday spirits and even the occasional tourists' excursion. Almost everyone who passed Independence Rock, east of the South Pass of the Rockies, climbed it to carve or paint his name on its top, but often the men make the ascent sound like a minor feat of exploration. It comes as something of an anticlimax, then, to read that Sarah Royce managed the effort *carrying her infant daughter.* * 'Of course I had to lift her from one projection to another most of the way; but we went leisurely, and her delight on reaching the top, our short rest there and the view we enjoyed, fully paid for the labor' (25). 'Leisurely,' 'delight' and 'enjoyed' seem more appropriate words than the 'duty' of 'surveying' which the men so often took from Frémont. Others climbed the rocks of Devil's Gate, the natural chasm cut by the Sweetwater river just west of Independence Rock. A twelve-year-old girl named Sallie Hester did this in the company of several other youngsters 'not over fourteen' on their way West with their families in 1849. They were gone so long that men from the train were sent out to look for them (1925, no. 2528,3). Fifteen-year-old Mary Warner climbed the Devil's Temple in the

---

* Not that Independence Rock is a formidable climb. It is a small volcanic plug whose bare surface affords sufficient grip for at least one four-year-old boy to have made it safely to the top in a little over five minutes – wearing plastic sandals. Devil's Gate is a larger feature.

Platte valley, accompanied by 'Mrs Lord, Mrs Hayward, Fannie, [and] Aunt Celia', to see the view and pick up 'some relics' (B.C-F 66A; May 11, 1864).

Relics,* not specimens. The women were not afraid to name things as they were. Nothing was beneath the dignity of their notice: the tedium of unloading wagons to free the wheels from boggy 'sloughs' (Royce, 5); the dosage of calomel given for 'mountain fever' (Ashley, 12 June); the sound of the wind flapping the makeshift shroud covering a man dead of cholera, lying overnight outside their wagon (Royce, 15). Mary Bailey recorded the condition of the grass, the state of the road, even the high cost of supplies at Fort Laramie, now in Wyoming: '50 cts a pound for sugar, raisins, 75 cts for saleratus, 80 for a paper of tacks &c,' (23 June). Algeline Ashley even noted the more domestic details of Indian life: the prices the Sioux charged for animals ('from $100 to $125 for horses and mules, and from $65 to $75 for ponies' (29 May)); and what the Paiutes ate:

Camped near a beautiful spring and creek with cool, green willow growing around them. Excellent mountain grass. Saw the Utah Indians gathering locusts in old basins and bags to eat. They gather them very fast, pulling one wing off so they cannot fly. They are very low Indians and very ugly looking.

(HM 16773; 20 June, 1852)

Along with their attention to the ordinary, material details of vernacular life, the women diarists were careful to preserve a record of character and motivation on the trail. Mary Bailey's anthropomorphism for the butte along the valley of the Platte is the sort of figure that came naturally to mind, and even Sarah Royce's formal expression of anxiety at the thought of their death in the wilderness attaches itself to specific victims and a particular cause. Her youth and intelligence gave the twelve-year-old Sallie Hester a remarkable degree of dispassionate insight into the feelings of the grown-ups. 'My mother is heartbroken over this separation of relatives and friends,' she wrote when the family left their home in Bloomington, Indiana, on 20 March, 1849. 'Giving up old associations for what? Good health, perhaps. My father is going in search of [Mother's] health, not gold' (1925, no. 2528,3). They seem to have found it.

---

* The deconsecrated use of 'relic' as 'souvenir' the Oxford English Dictionary records from as early as 1601.

When the party left St Joseph, her mother 'had to be lifted in and out of our wagons,' but by 21 May, 'she walks a mile or two without stopping, and gets in and out of the wagons as spry as a young girl. She is perfectly well' (*ibid.*). In California they built a small house, of two rooms, out of clapboard with a puncheon floor. 'On this mother has a carpet which she brought with us and we feel quite fine as our neighbors have the ground for a floor' (1925, no. 2529, 3). But come Christmas and mother was homesick again. 'It's hard for old folks,' wrote Sallie, with her preternatural understanding:

to give up old ties and go so far away to live in a strange land among strange people. Young people can easily form new ties and make new friends and soon conform to circumstances, but it's hard for the old ones to forget. Was invited to a candy pull and had a nice time. Rather a number of young folks camped here. This is a funny looking town anyway. Most of the houses are built of brush. Now that the rains have set in, people are beginning to think of something more substantial. Some have log cabins, others have clapboards like ours.   (*ibid.*)

It is from the diary of Mary Warner that we get one of the few accounts of the personal quarrels that occasionally divided a wagon train and to which the masculine journals allude only obliquely. She went to California in 1864 with her Uncle Chester and his bride Lizzie, her mother Mary, her brothers John and Elon, her sisters Mary and Cora and her Aunt Celia. Others in the train included a Mr and Mrs Lord, who were to prove incompatible with the Warner family. Chester had already been twice to California, and Mary's father, who joined the party at Salt Lake City, had already established a cattle ranch in the Sierras. So their journey was not speculative or even especially adventurous; they were moving, finally, to a home already set up in California.

The trouble with the Lords is first noted when an injured horse kept them from traveling, and to kill time, Mary and her Aunt Celia played chess, 'which Mrs. Lord thought was the first step toward gambling' (B.C-F 66A; 10 June). After Mary's father joined them, an argument broke out in the train:

One of the boys refused to do something which he was asked to do, which caused some trouble, and Mr. Lord was referred to and he rather upheld the boy, which made the matter worse. Pa (who was taking charge of the train) refused to do so any longer, and Uncle Chester would not. Mr. Lord was not going to at first, but as they would not settle it, he consented to during the day. After going about

eight miles we stopped to bait, and as Mrs. Lord ordered dinner cooked it was
done.   (13 June)

They decided to split the train. 'Pa and Uncle Chester were to have
two shares of the property and Mr. Lord the other third.' 'First the
horses were divided, then the wagons, harnesses, and then the provisions, stores, and other things, which we had considerable sport
over' (14 June). Then the rival trains seem to have challenged each
other to a race. On 18 June:

We did not leave camp until one o'clock this morning, and Mr. Lord's train was
not far behind us. About daylight we came to Grubs wells after going twelve
miles. While we were there some of the other trains visited us, but we did not
pay much attention to them, *especially* Mrs Lord.

Does Mary Warner's account of this little squabble represent a
truth about the forty-niners' parties suppressed in their accounts?
Possibly not, but one would never know from the reticence with
which they record, without delineating character or imputing
motive, occasions on which single people or whole groups of wagons
left the train. As for the quarrels, the men sometimes mention melodramatic encounters with dangerous weapons producing horrible
wounds, but seldom the petty verbal exchange. They had left home,
if only temporarily, and wanted to forget any reminder of domestic
tedium. The women would have been happy to bring their homes
with them; so they carried on gossiping and noting the price of
things.

It is this sense of an unofficial view, a peep behind the scenery,
that one gets again and again from reading the diaries and letters of
the few women who emigrated alongside the men having their Gold
Rush adventure. The forty-niners thought of themselves as engaged
in a heroic moment, historical in its public resonance, and in the
sphere of private morality, purifying the human character of its
meanest instincts. The women, as good observers of the minutiae
of human behavior, could not help noticing another reality; the
comic misadventures, the tiresome quarrels.

And this is why the women's one repeated address to the romance
of the West comes over as so convincing. They were no less sensitive
than the men to the idea of the journey West as a rite of passage to
independence and maturity. It was partly a matter of health, and of
course it was based on fact as much as myth. Sallie Hester's mother

really did get well, or so Sallie says. Algeline Ashley was surprised to find that she did not 'get tired of the journey'; 'on the contrary,' she wrote on 18 June, 'I like it better every day.'

Along with the awareness of improved health came something else, a confidence that one could adapt to new circumstances, perhaps even the glimmer of an expanded social role. On 17 May the homesick Mary Bailey 'Went into the woods & slept out the ground for the first time. it seemed as though it would kill us to sleep out doors without anything but a canvass to protect us from the dews of Heaven it did not make any of us sick.' A month later, just beyond Fort Laramie, she was more positive: 'We enjoy ourselves better as we get used to this *way* of *traveling* & living out of doors. We have good appetites & plenty to eat although we sit down & eat like the Indians.' As she accustomed herself to the rough life, her account begins to show signs of a certain independence of judgement too. For instance she records two difficult river crossings. In the first she was all fear and service, as her domestic role demanded:

Tuesday 15th [June] . . . We went on untill we came to the end of the road –. when we had to cross the Platte River – had to raise the bed of our wagons got over safely but were somewhat frightened when we saw them go into the water – The Dr was thrown from his horse, we were very much frightened – But were very thankfull to get over safely. we got everything ready for supper for the men when they got the goods all over.

But by the second, over a month later, she had begun to question the stereotype into which she had been cast:

Tuesday 20 [July] Forded the Green River had to raise our wagons, did not get into the water although we were somewhat frightened – do not know as there was much danger but the *men say* the women must always be frightened.

Even on this point – their sense of their increased independence – the similarity between the men and the women was limited, however. They were both, no doubt, conforming to an old American triad: the need for space; the tribulations in the wilderness; the achievement of the Promised Land. The difference is that the men were following, or responding to, Washington Irving's packaging of this impulse as a temporary phase in the training of the young; for him the West could become an American substitute for the grand tour, a pastoral interlude ending in the return of the youth to his eastern home. This was the pattern followed by David Dewolf and Henry Sturdivant, who for all their surprise in their increased confidence and improved health seem to have partly expected that result (witness Sturdivant's anticipation of 'the elephant' in the hut near Chagres and Dewolf's quiet pride in his undomestic life in California).

But the women, many of them, were not going home. The pattern they followed was the more ancient path of the Israelites, as the title and organization of Sarah Royce's 'Pilgrimage Diary' make clear. So for them the awareness of an archetypal rite of passage – an improvement in health, an easing of social constraints, or simply going through puberty – had to be set within the context of a real, fundamental change in their social and physical geography. And the way the two polarities of change, the archetypal and the actual, interpenetrate and qualify each other is the most interesting feature of their diaries.

It is this complex dialectic between the idea and fact of emigrating to the West that makes the collected letters of Mary Jane Megquier, written home from San Francisco between 1849 and 1856, one of the minor classics of the Gold Rush. Although she and her husband came to California to make their 'pile' and return home, she eventually decided to remain in San Francisco without him. Her letters record her gradual transition from forty-niner's wife to independent settler. They show the mental process by which she worked out her own version of the rite of passage, now testing events against statements of the archetype, now qualifying the myth with the results of the actual.

Thomas Lewis Megquier (the family pronounced the name 'Megweer') had practiced medicine for twelve years in Winthrop, Maine, when he decided to try his luck in California. Mary Jane was reluctant to leave their children, two sons and a daughter named Angeline Louise to whom most of the letters are addressed, but as she wrote to a friend before they sailed from New York, 'the Dr is very anxious for me to go with him, as it is very difficult to get any thing done in the way of womens help' (1949,3). Besides, women were paid well for 'service,' and for a time after their arrival in San Francisco, after a voyage via the Isthmus and a wait in Panama of over two months, she seems to have worked as a maid. Was this a difficult adjustment for a doctor's wife? Possibly, but then San Francisco was a topsy-turvy society anyway, as she wrote her 'Very Dear Cousin and Daughter,' probably in September, 1849:

As for giving you a description of my situation and those around me, it is impossible, it is a complete farce, a change comes over one, that you can with difficulty recognize your intimate friends, the greatest dandies wear their beard long, their hair uncombed, a very dirty colored shirt. . . . Professor Shepard from one of the first institutions in the states is driving a cart from Sacramento city to the mines, from which he is coining a mint of money.   (1949, 26)

It is not certain whether this records her own observation or something she read in the papers. Both the point about the dandies roughing it and the joke about the professor were standard journalistic tropes about Gold Rush society; nice images of the exoticism and classlessness of early San Francisco life. Other instances of social inversion meant more to her personally. They started to build a drug store, and when she wanted to see how the construction work was progressing, she had only to put on a decent hat to transform herself from a housemaid into a lady of fashion:

I have put my bonnet on last week for the first time since I have been housekeeping and walked down in town to see the store. I have so much to attend to I have no time to gad. The ladies have called on me but I do not care for society as I intend to go home when I get my pile.   (to Angeline, 31 October 1849, 28)

The curious logic of the last sentence is the result not only of pride but of the debate, already beginning within her, about whether she really wanted to leave. In her letters she often affirmed her intention to return home, but seldom without mentioning an overriding reason for staying in California. So furious was the interior dialogue that it sometimes led her away from her subject altogether:

Our motto is to make hay while the sun shines, we intend to sell the first good offer and return forthwith, although there are many good things here that are better than in the states yet I cannot think of staying from my chickens a long time, and it is not just the place for them at present, no schools, churches in abundance but you can do as you please about attending, it is all the same whether you go to church or play monte, that is why I like, you very well know that I am a worshipper at the shrine of liberty. The land is very rich would yield an abundance if it was cultivated, but no one can wait for vegetables to grow to realize a fortune.   (to Very Dear Friend, Milton, 11th November, 1849, 30)

Already she was beginning to formulate her experience in San Francisco in the traditional opposition between the domestic East and the liberated West. When she wrote her mother in April of the next year, again about churchgoing, she evoked, full-blown, the myth of the West as the site of a further reformation:

I suppose you will think it very strange when I tell you I have not attended church for one year not even heard a prayer but I cannot see but everything goes on as well as when I was home. The churches are very well attended without any of my help. . . . Among the many that have died in this country not one that I have heard of has expressed the least anxiety about the future which plainly shows to me that it is the circumstances that surround them that causes so much anxiety as to what will become of them after death, as it respects proffessors [*sic*] they lay by all outward forms of religion and have none but the vital part left, there is no such thing as slander known in the country no back biting, every ones neighbor is as good as himself. (40-1)

But as they grew more settled, she came to value San Francisco more for their attachments there than for its social freedom. 'There is so many of my friends coming I fear I shall have some ties to sever,' she wrote a 'Dear Friend' in February, 1850. 'A few weeks ago I could have left without regret, but we are beginning to live like civilized beings, we have two theatres one of which we attended last week' (36). They were also prospering and increasing their own real estate. At first they lived above the drug store; then they started to build their own house, in which they planned to take boarders. She wrote her daughter in April, 1850:

We are having our building raised . . . it gives us a fine view of the bay . . . and makes the cook room delightful as you have a fine view. I can stand by the stove and watch the porridge and take a look at the big ships, as they are rolling lazily on the water.

We had a nice little dance the other [night] at the store of one of our borders. I was engaged four dances ahead, isn't that smart? I suppose you will have a good laugh to see your mother tripping the light fantastic toe. (39)

And as their prospects improved, she came to ally herself with a 'spirit of aristocracy' in San Francisco that she had not mentioned before. She wrote Angeline, probably in the summer of 1850:

There is to be a soiree given by the ladies of the St. Francis which is said to be very select, there is quite a spirit of aristocracy prevailing here which in my opinion is composed of those that have been cramped in the states and they are the ones to set themselves up as being somebody but it is uncertain how they will succeed, at the last party they sent one home, she was taken there by an unsophisticated youth from Oregon. I think some one introduced him, to impose upon him, but he was so green he did not suspect any thing, although she kept a cigar and liquor store, but she was told the carriage was ready very soon after her arrival, I expect the ladies are trying to prevent any thing of the kind happening again. (48)

99

She does not say whether she was yet included within this new exclusivity, and certainly her tone keeps its distance, here, from 'the ladies,' but she is, at least, beginning to share their values. Clearly a cigar and liquor store was a few notches down from a drug store and boarding house, even if its owner was, like her, one that had 'been cramped in the states.'

She was also experiencing the property owner's trouble with servants. As early as the end of November, 1849, she had 'a black man . . . who pretends to be a cook but he don't know as much as a jackass' (33), and at the end of June, 1850, she complained to Angeline, 'I have got another woman but I do not know how she will do, but there is not much doubt but I shall have to work hard while I am in Cal' (45). Three years later she was still having trouble with the help, this time encountering an ingenious form of freelance industrial action:

My China boy was so ugly that I could do nothing with him . . . he drove a nail into the tea kettle, he would knock the noses off the pitcher against the fasset of the water barrel, put grease on the stove to make a smoke and laugh when I scolded him: he would come up behind me and stick burning matches under my nose . . . if I chanced to have a clean cloth on the table, he would put all the slops in a cup and tip it over, the Dr asked him why he did it, he said, more money, We thought it best to let him go and we now have a small French boy but he knows nothing of the kitchen and it makes my work very hard.

(to Angeline, 22 April, 1853, 76–7)

Even the alarming China boy was no match for Mary Jane Megquier. In fact, she does seem to have worked hard for herself and 'the Dr.' When they built a new boarding house in 1852 it was she who got it ready; sewing, washing dishes, buying furniture. She also had to do the daily shopping, as she complained to Angeline on 15 August, 1852: 'I get up every morning by five and go to market where I meet all the negroes and spanish in town. I do not like it but your Father cannot tell what is wanted therefore I must do it' (66).

She remained apparently undecided about whether to remain in California. By the middle of 1850 she had made up her mind to return. 'We are getting ready for home as fast as possible,' she wrote Angeline on 14 August, 1850, 'perhaps [via] the mines as I do not like to go home without seeing more of Cal' (48). But they did not leave until early the next year, and they were back in San Francisco in May, 1852. Friends welcomed them on their return and urged them to stay for good this time, 'but never shall I give up the idea of making that nice little farm [in Maine] my home at some future time, but if we have our health it will not be until we can carry out our plans in some measure,' she wrote her 'Dear Loved Ones at Home' on 30 May, 1852. Also, they were kept in California by prolonged litigation following the death of a man called Richmond, who seems to have been in business with the Doctor and laid plans to cheat him. 'In this country, a person must attend to his own business, or it is not done,' wrote the Doctor to the children in July, 1852 (64). Besides, compared to San Francisco, with its increasingly sophisticated entertainments, Winthrop, Maine, had come to look decidedly dull in retrospect:

I am right glad to hear [the family at home] are enjoying themselves so much but I have seen so much of things a little more exciting I fear I shall never feel perfectly satisfied with their quiet ways again. Here you can step out of your house and see the whole world spread out before you in every shape and form. Your ears are filled with the most delightful music, your eyes are dazzled with everything that is beautiful, the streets are crowded the whole city are in the street. We have near us a splendid ice cream saloon which surpasses any thing I have seen in the states, very large windows with magnificent buff silk damask curtains with lace like those that Newhall Sturtevant boasts so much of, two large rooms are connected by an arch hung with the same material marble tables, floors and counters and as light as day at all hours of the night.

(to 'My Dear Children', 8 April, 1853, 75–6)

Yet she made one final trip back to New England. That summer, when the California grass began to turn its seasonal yellow, she wrote Angeline and Charles, 'with you everything is beautiful, I do want to see it and if I live shall another spring, whether your father comes or no' (82). It is the first sign in the letters of a growing split between her and the Doctor. In the spring of the next year, she went home again, leaving him to follow. His health was failing. Finally they separated, and she returned to San Francisco alone. 'My Dear Angie,' she wrote on 4 November, 1855, 'After the usual amount of hardships which seem my fortune to encounter, I am at last in the good city of San Francisco' (82). And at the end of that month:

The very air I breathe seems so very free that I have not the least desire to return. I do long for the time when I can sell the property and send some money home. . . . I assure you I have never for a moment regretted that I left Winthrop, that beautiful house has no charms for me at present (84–5).

Back home, meanwhile, the Doctor was encountering the hardship of actually dying. Mary Jane was sorry to hear of his illness, but:

> if he should be taken away it will only be what I have wished that might come upon myself, rather than live with one who was ever wishing me to sacrifice my health to his gratification. I endured it I thought as long as I could, I know what the world will think of me, but my regrets are that I have no money to send.
>
> (to Angeline, 3 December, 1855, 87)

But she had escaped that world, the one that would censure her behavior and with which she had, by now, cut off all correspondence, except through her daughter. In her new world, 'there is not a day I do not receive kind words and wishes of friends which are so very unlike what I will meet at home, excepting my children,' she wrote to Angeline on 4 March, 1856 (90). By now the Doctor had been dead three months, and she had a new beau. 'Mr Johnson of whom you often hear me speak is my gallant,' she wrote Angeline on 4 February (87); and later she described a party at his house:

> We had strawberries put up in France, champagne in abundance, one little unique bottle stood in the centre of the table neatly encased in straw, with a little glass which would take a table spoonful to fill, which I found was for me, it was a kind of cordial as smooth as oil, with no intoxicating quality. I felt I was kindly cared for, as it no doubt took a smart five to buy it, if not ten, We had bon bons in abundance which in pulling apart suddenly explode like torpedoes, no doubt arises from the vast amount of sentiment they contain. . . . Night before last we went to a little quadrille party at Mrs Martins, Yesterday I spent the day with Mrs Davis. . . . We had two tables of euchre [a card game], between eleven and twelve we had tea made from the flower of tea, which I assure you was fit for the Gods; served in little cups the size of a hens egg, fancy cakes, nuts and raisans.
>
> (19 March, 1856, 91–2)

What a hard woman she must have been; quite unlike the protagonist of an English novel, let alone a Cooper heroine. No liberal sensibilities, no chaste patience. Self-centered, self-pitying, hard working; responding as a powerful, simple organism to stimuli of light, space and comfort; she was determined to free herself even if it meant betraying her oldest attachments. Her dénouement too was unlike that of the novel plots; she was not punished for casting off the Doctor in his illness to take up with Mr Johnson. Indeed her transgressions seem to have been rewarded by her long delayed entrée to the glittering society of the San Francisco 'ladies.' Even the muse of vernacular narrative withheld judgement. Though Mary Jane's prose freezes into a defensive rictus, false even by the standards of sentimentality, when she delivers her chilling dismissal of the Doctor's illness, it blossoms as never before as she dwells on the delectable tokens of her emancipation.

How unlike, too, the usual view of the forty-niner and his wife – the adventurous Josiah Royce (Senior) and the pious Sarah, say. It is surprising that her letters should have survived at all; the long-suffering Angeline must have been very tolerant or very loyal not to have destroyed them as shaming the family honor.

Was this, then, the reality of the western adventure? Does Mary Jane Megquier represent the true voice of the vernacular West? Was this Howell's western realism at last? It should be. Her story is both actual and paradigmatic. She really left the cramped circumstances of her old life, traversed a kind of wilderness of disrupted family ties and confused social setting, and settled in a magical city on a hill, which she both conceptualized and experienced as a reformed community. Yet when Howells met a version of that story, in the form of Dreiser's *Sister Carrie* (for Mary Jane Megquier was, of course, the real-life Carrie of the West), he could not accept it, and shut Dreiser out of his normally warm hospitality to new talent.* Even now Dreiser's novel is one of few in English in which a heroine of quite ordinary sensibilities gains social freedom and material wealth without experiencing either qualms or retribution for her infidelities. And even fifty years after the Gold Rush a substantial eastern publishing house did not consider its sophisticated readers ready for *that* story. The book appeared, surreptitiously, only after a publisher's reader at a rival house, a young man called Frank Norris, read it and loved it. Was it only a coincidence that Norris was brought up in San Francisco, or had his acquaintance with that city made him peculiarly responsive to plots of social liberation, however unsuitable to the genteel sensibility of the American East?

* Larzer Ziff, in *The American 1890's* (New York, 1966, 341) suggests that Howells, for all his respect for social realism in the novel, 'found unspeakable the suggestion [in *Sister Carrie*] that the social shift, which had resulted in an immense labor pool, had also resulted in the destruction of a sense of community for thousands upon thousands of Americans.'

THE JOURNALISTS' CALIFORNIA

The glamor of the Gold Rush attracted professional writers too. Some were commissioned to report on the phenomenon; others wrote on speculation, though with a good idea of where to place their material and who would read it. In either case, these were the writers for whom there was little doubt but that their impressions of the West would find a recognizable audience sooner or later. They were writing neither just for themselves nor for their faceless posterity, but for a readership whose tastes and range of experience they knew well. Four of them seem particularly representative of the professional journalists of the Gold Rush: Leonard Kip, J. D. Borthwick, Bayard Taylor, and Louise Amelia Knappe Smith Clappe, better known, for obvious reasons, by her pseudonym, 'Dame Shirley.' The last two will be familiar to anyone who has begun to read around the subject, and are still enjoyed by a small lay readership, especially in California. The others are now known mainly to historians and students of the period.

Leonard Kip, the brother of the first Episcopal Bishop of California, came from a well-off New York family, was educated at Trinity College Hartford, and Yale. He studied law in Albany before he went to California in 1849, prospecting for gold and a likely law practice. He was disappointed in both, and was soon back in Albany, where he opened a law office and published his book on the Gold Rush, *California Sketches With Recollections of the Gold Mines,* both by the end of 1850. The book was made up of sketches he had intended for the daily papers, as well as a brief account of his own experience in California. Later he became a prolific romancer.

John David Borthwick was a Scottish traveler, artist and journalist. Born in 1825 and graduated from Edinburgh Academy, he corresponded for *Blackwood's Edinburgh Magazine,* published drawings in *The Illustrated London News,* and even exhibited at the Royal Academy in London. He seems to have been in the United States from sometime after 1840 until he went to Australia in 1854. His *Three Years in California* was published by Blackwood's in 1857, and later reprinted in various American editions.

Bayard Taylor had always had literary aspirations. With a good high-school education behind him, he started out as a professional journalist, working first as a typesetter and copy boy on a local paper in Pennsylvania. After publishing a volume of romantic verse, he traveled in Europe from which he sent letters to Horace

Greeley's *New York Tribune*. A version of his European travels, *Views A-Foot* (1846) landed him a permanent job with the *Tribune,* and when the gold fever broke out at the end of 1848, it was Taylor whom the paper sent to report on the occasion. The result was *Eldorado: or, Adventures in the Path of Empire.* It appeared first in London in 1850, where it was instantly pirated by two other houses, then in New York that same year. Within the following decade it went through eighteen editions in the United States alone, and it was joined by six further volumes of the author's travels in Africa, the Near East and Russia. Taylor also wrote short stories and poetry, and four novels set in New York and his native Pennsylvania.

Louise Clappe came West in 1849 with her husband, yet another doctor, called Fayette Clapp (she added the terminal 'e'). Brought up in Massachusetts, she had been educated at the Charlestown (Mass.) Female Seminary and Amherst Academy, and formed a friendship with Alexander Hill Everett, the diplomat and author, and brother of Edward Everett, the editor of the *North American Review.* Everett encouraged her to read widely and write often, and seems to have arranged for her first publication, a poem, in 1844. She first used the pseudonym 'Dame Shirley' for some sketches and poems published in the *Marysville* (California) *Herald* in the spring and summer of 1851. That same year Dr Clapp decided to try practicing in one of the mining communities, partly because he thought the climate of the foothills would suit him better than in San Francisco; so the Clapps moved, first to Rich Bar, then to Indian Bar, both thriving mining towns on the Feather river. From here, startled by the new scenery and fascinated by the vigorous masculine society, 'Dame Shirley' wrote what purports to be a series of letters, signed by her pseudonym, to her sister at home in Massachusetts. At least, that is how they appeared when they were published in *The Pioneer,* San Francisco's fledgling literary monthly, in every number of its short life between the beginning of 1854 and the end of 1855. By that time she had been back in San Francisco for two years, working as a school teacher, and separated from the Doctor (they were finally divorced in 1857), and there she remained until 1878, when she returned East to live with her actress friend, Genevieve Stebbins, in New York.

The West, as it appeared to these professional journalists, was as unruly and out of scale as that perceived by the forty-niners crossing the country, and the journalists were as articulate as were the forty-niners about their situation 'on the borders of civilisation,' as Dame Shirley put it (*Letters*, 184). But their verbal responses to this feeling were far more resourceful and self-assured. They were secure in their sense that they were professional writers communicating with an eastern audience, with whom they shared certain indices of decorum. By training and inclination they were disposed to notice the social, rather than the physical, signs of western unruliness (or, as in their observations on the size of San Francisco, the physical as an index of the social). Furthermore, they had come to California by sea; so their first encounter with the West, as they got off the boat in San Francisco, was not with craggy buttes and untenanted prairies, but with a society that, however unlike the towns and cities with which they were familiar in the East, was at least a body of human beings living together in a recognizable commercial and political order. The same was true even of the rough mining camps.

San Francisco was the social equivalent of Chimney Rock and Scott's Bluff— both like and unlike the cities at home. It was apparently solid, yet insubstantial, having grown prodigiously between 1848 and 1855 from a small Mexican outpost of about a thousand people living in adobe huts, wooden shacks and the cabins of beached sailing ships, to an American city of 50,000 more-or-less permanent inhabitants rejoicing in opera houses, banks, restaurants and hotels, as well as business houses and residences built after the latest eastern and European patterns. But whole tracts of it could burn down in a single night, and one of the most popular 'views' on the letter blanks showed a map of the huge area of the city destroyed in the fire at the beginning of May, 1850. Others showed earthquakes, another reminder of the city's fragility. The famous earthquake and fire of 1906 was only the largest in a series of natural disasters made good in breathtaking time. Then there is the upsetting climate of San Francisco: colder in summer than in winter because of persistent sea fogs drawn in off the cold Humboldt Current by the summer heat of the Central Valley. San Franciscans, though they seldom admit it to strangers, have never quite got over the feeling that they live in the house built on the sand (as, in fact, many of them do): that the city, for all its opera, symphony, 'little' theater, universities, good hotels and restaurants, substantial banks and skyscrapers, a renovated city center and surely the best system of public transport outside of Russia — that all this, plus its cosmopolitan toleration of the most varied life styles, is somehow still hollow at the center, too rapid and pat a synthesis of eastern patterns; like their famous Victorian houses, shipped out in pre-cut wooden sections and thrown up on foundations of sand and wood within a few days of their arrival. This anxiety probably lies behind the hearty claims, still made quite frequently in the city's press, to the sophistication, cultural attainments, social complexity and general metropolitan grandeur of San Francisco. It is a city that talks about itself a great deal.

No wonder, then, that the journalists of the Gold Rush dramatized the wild proportions and the sensory paradoxes of San Francisco life at mid-century. To Leonard Kip, the very substance of the place was an illusion, the effect of a clever, commercial *trompe d'oeil*. 'I peeked into many [gambling houses],' he wrote, 'and was surprised to see how easily French paper, fine matting, and a small chandelier, can convert the rough ribs of an old barn into an elegant hall' (*Sketches,* 4). Meanwhile, the solid and (relatively) ancient Franciscan Mission 'was falling rapidly into ruins, as well as the few houses which clustered around it. The once beautiful gardens were almost broken up and destroyed, and, of the natives who had once congregated for instruction, but a few remained' (*ibid.* 7).

However illusory its décor, the city was unmistakably growing. Returning to San Francisco after a brief attempt at mining, Kip:

found that less than two months had worked a mighty change in that city. The spirit of speculation having walked abroad uncontrolled during the interval, new streets had been laid out and new houses built in every direction, until the place had grown far up the hill behind it and far down the side ravines. . . . And still the tide rolled on, and still night and day, week-day and Sunday, the noise of hammers could be heard; and while new houses rise by magic, it seemed as though each month, the city would be doubled in its straggling proportions.

(*ibid.* 54)

To Kip, clearly, no city could grow so rapidly without breaching decorum, whether conventions like resting on the Sabbath, or the 'proportions' ideally appropriate to a city in that geographical setting. Or, as Bayard Taylor put it, 'Every newcomer in San Francisco is overtaken with a sense of complete bewilderment. The mind, however it may be prepared for an astonishing condition of affairs, cannot immediately push aside its old instincts of value and ideas of business' (*Eldorado*, 44). He, too noticed a growth in San Francisco, which, he was sure, would 'tax the belief of the future':

I speak only of what I saw with my own eyes. When I landed there, a little more than four months before, I found a scattering town of tents and canvas houses, with a show of frame buildings on one or two streets, and a population of about six thousand. Now, on my last visit, I saw around me an actual metropolis, displaying street after street of well-built edifices, filled with an active and enterprising people, and exhibiting every mark of permanent commercial prosperity. Then the town was limited to the curve of the bay fronting the anchorage and bottoms of the hills. Now it stretched to the topmost heights. . . . Then the gold-seeking sojourner lodged in muslin rooms and canvas garrets. . . . Now lofty hotels, gaudy with verandas and balconies, were met with in all quarters, furnished with home luxury, and aristocratic restaurants presented daily their long bills of fare, rich with the choicest technicalities of the Parisian cuisine.

(*ibid.* 226)

And so on. The Old World, which is to say, everything that was 'lofty,' 'aristocratic' and 'Parisian,' was rushing to engulf the new almost before Taylor's balanced prose periods could orchestrate the confusion.

Borthwick, too, commented on the rapid development of San Francisco, and also on another remarkable civic growth. One night the whole of Sonora, the mining town in the foothills of the Sierras, burned down; by the middle of the next day it was being rebuilt:

In the afternoon the Phoenix began to rise . . . posts began here and there to spring up; presently cross pieces connected them; and before one could look round, the framework was filled in with brushwood. As the ground became sufficiently cool, people began to move down their goods and furniture to where their houses had been.

(*Three Years*, 350)

As for the state of society in towns and cities so beyond the customary scales of time and size, how could it be anything but chaotic? Everyone noted the disruption of the social bandings of class and profession. 'Dress was no gauge of respectability,' wrote Taylor in a chapter devoted to 'Society in California.' 'Lawyers, physicians, and ex-professors dug cellars, drove ox-teams, sawed wood, and carried luggage; while men who had been Army privates, sailors, cooks, or day laborers were at the head of profitable establishments and not infrequently assisted in some of the minor details of Government' (*Eldorado*, 236).

Taylor had learned an early, personal, lesson in the classlessness of California. On landing in San Francisco, he had asked his new landlord to send a porter for his trunks. ' "There is none belonging to the house", said he; "every man is his own porter here." I returned to the Parker House, shouldered a heavy trunk, took a valise in my hand, and carried them to my quarters, in the teeth of the wind' (*Eldorado,* 43). Borthwick too realized quickly that:

Every man was his own servant, and his own porter besides. It was nothing unusual to see a respectable old gentleman, perhaps some old paterfamilias, who at home would have been horrified at the idea of doing such a thing, open his store in the morning himself, take a broom and sweep it out, and then proceed to blacken his boots. (*Three Years,* 46)

For Borthwick, the outrageous proportions of California life extended even to the vegetable products of the region. These, apart from potatoes and onions, were scarce but 'upon a gigantic scale. A beetroot weighing a hundred pounds, and that looked like the trunk of a tree, was not thought to be a *very* remarkable specimen' (*ibid.* 48).

As professional writers, the journalists of the Gold Rush were naturally interested in how the forty-niners spoke, and inverted commas appear frequently in these accounts, as assertions of the difference in linguistic register between observer (and reader), and observed. Borthwick was amused when an acquaintance did not appear at the table of his boarding house, and the landlord suggested 'that perhaps he was "strapped", "dead-broke" – *Anglicé,* without a cent in his pocket.' Later, when the man admitted that this was, in fact, the case, 'I told him, in the language of Mr. Toots, that it was of no consequence' (*ibid.* 254–5). Borthwick cites a notice in a barroom as a sign, also, of the ultra-democratic principles upheld in public places frequented by the forty-niners. A sign in the 'bar-room of the most fashionable hotel' in Panama 'requested' the 'Gentlemen' awaiting ships to California 'to wear their coats at table, if they have them handy' (*ibid.* 26). A similar figure caught Dame Shirley's attention:

If [the miners] wish to borrow anything of you, they will mildly inquire if you have it 'about your clothes.' As an illustration; a man asked F.[ayette] the other day, 'If he had a spare pick-axe about his clothes.' And F. himself gravely inquired of me this evening at the dinner table, if I had 'a *pickle* about my clothes.' (*Letters,* 52)

She had no praise for the miners' 'swearing propensities.' 'Those of course would shock you,' she wrote her sister; 'but though you hate slang, I know that you could not help smiling at some of their *bizarre* cant phrases' (*ibid.*). Less amusing was the blacksmith ('not the "learned" one') who called on her husband one day when he was out, and decided to wait for him:

'Who writ this 'ere?' is his first remark, taking up one of my most precious books, and leaving the marks of his irreverent fingers upon the clean pages. 'Shakespeare,' I answer, as politely as possible. 'Did Spokshave write it? He was an almighty smart fellow, that Spokshave, I've hear'n tell,' replies my visitor. 'I must write hum, and tell our folks that this 'ere is the first carpet I've seen sin I came to Californy, four years come next month,' is his next remark. For the last half-hour, he has been entertaining me with a wearisome account of the murder of his brother by an Irishman, in Boston, and the chief feeling which he exhibits, is a fear that the jury should only bring a verdict of manslaughter. But I hear F.'s step and his entrance relieves me from the bore.   (*Letters*, 182–3)

The professional journalists were also sensitive to the forty-niners' rhetoric in their non-verbal style. Borthwick was critical of the forty-niners' equipment, which he saw (no doubt, rightly) only as so much romantic paraphernalia. On landing at Chagres, he wrote, some of the men:

seemed to shrink within themselves, and to wish to avoid being included in any of the small parties which were being formed to make the passage up the river. They were those who had provided themselves with innumerable contrivances for the protection of their precious persons against sun, wind and rain . . . and who were completely equipped with pistols, knives and other warlike implements. They were like so many Robinson Crusoes, ready to be put ashore on a desert island; and they seemed to imagine themselves to be in just such a predicament, fearful, at the same time, that companionship with anyone not provided with the same amount of rubbish as themselves, might involve their losing the exclusive benefit of what they supposed to be so absolutely necessary. I actually heard one of them refuse another a chew of tobacco, saying he guessed he had no more than what he could use himself.   (*Three Years*, 9–10)

Leonard Kip noticed that the style of dress in Stockton divided itself into the flamboyant and the ostentatiously humdrum. Members of the local establishment opted for the latter. 'The Alcade himself rode about on his mule, in all the republican simplicity of uncovered shirt sleeves,' while the ordinary citizens affected 'hats . . . looped up at the side with a silver tasselled cord . . . and many a man, whose legs never crossed a mule, stalked along with most terrific spurs clattering at his heels' (*Sketches*, 16).

At one point, and in the most literal sense, Borthwick collaborated in producing the image of *farouche* romance when he met a

German doctor in a more tattered condition than anyone he had seen before, even in California. 'He was a complete caricature of an old miner, and quite a picture of himself, seen from any point of view':

There is as much vanity sometimes in rags as in gorgeous apparel; and what he wanted of me was to make a sketch of him, rags and all, just as he was . . . I begged him . . . not to think of combing his hair, which, indeed, to judge from its appearance, he had not done for some time.   (*Three Years*, 240)

He did sketch him, as he did many other characters from the mines and San Francisco life, and he formulated his own version of Kip's rule: 'men of a lower class wanted to be shown in the ordinary costume of the nineteenth century — that is to say, in a coat, waistcoat, white shirt and neckcloth; while gentlemen miners were anxious to appear in character, in the most ragged style of California dress' (*ibid.* 203).

It is this confident, distanced neutrality with which they annotate the paradoxical styles of California that makes the professional journalists so convincing in their accounts of everyday life in the Gold Rush. Coming from outside that society, 'reporting' on it rather than becoming involved in any of its poses or factions, not even (for the most part) risking their luck in the mines, the journalists could afford to be tolerantly amused at the peculiarities of California life. Or just tolerant. Borthwick, at least, was determined to be fair to San Francisco society. He found there:

more eating and drinking, more smoking, swearing, gambling, and tobacco-chewing, more crime and profligacy, and at the same time, more solid advancement made by the people, as a body, in wealth, prosperity, and the refinements of civilisation, than could be shown in an equal space of time by any community of the same size on the face of the earth.   (*ibid.* 49)

Every social evil was balanced by a corresponding good. 'If there was a lavish expenditure in ministering to vice, there was also munificence in the bestowing of charity. Though there were gorgeous temples for the worship of mammon, there was a sufficiency of schools and churches for every denomination' (*ibid.* 67).

They were sufficiently confident even to admit incongruities discomforting to their own self-image. Dame Shirley relates an instance in which her meditation on the forty-niners' favorite theme of death in the wilderness was rudely interrupted by an inappropriate touch of comedy. A young man had his leg so badly crushed by a fall of rock that Fayette had to amputate it. She nursed him through his precarious recovery, feeding him, teaspoon by teaspoon, on milk fetched from a 'Spanish Rancho.' The situation prompted sentimental reflections: 'My heart aches as I look upon his young face, and think of "his gentle, dark-eyed mother, weeping lonely at the North," for her far away and suffering son' (*Letters,* 38). Just then the funeral procession of another young man, killed by a fall into an open mining pit, passed by the window. Her invalid mistook the cortège for the procession celebrating the Independence of Chile, the anniversary of which was being observed that day:

I did not tell him

> 'That the weary sound, and the heavy breath,
> And the silent motions of passing death,
> And the smell, cold, oppressive and dank
> Sent through the pores of the coffin plank,'

had already informed me that a far other band than that of the noisy South Americans, was solemnly marching by. . . . About a dozen persons were carrying an unpainted coffin, without pall or bier (the place of the latter being supplied by ropes) up the steep hill which rises behind the Empire [Hotel] – on the top of which is situated the burial ground of Rich Bar. (ibid.)

She then goes on to describe what the mourners were wearing; expresses her 'strange horror of that lonely mountain grave-yard'; reflects on her preference for 'cheerful' burial places, quoting Lamb, Shakespeare and Dickens in the process. Then her mood was interrupted:

My eyes were yet moist from the egotistical *pitié de moimeme* in which I had been indulging, at the thought of sleeping forever amid these lonely hills, which in a few years must return to their primeval solitude, perchance never again to be awakened by the voice of humanity – when the Chileno procession, every member of it most intensely drunk, really *did* appear. I never saw anything more diverting than the whole affair. Of course, *selon régle,* I ought to have been shocked and horrified – to have shed salt tears, and have uttered melancholy Jeremiads over their miserable degradation. But the world is so full of platitudes, my dear, that I think you will easily forgive me for not boring you with a temperance lecture, and will good-naturedly let me have my laugh, and not think me *very* wicked after all. (ibid. 39–40)

She conveys the sense here, though perhaps insisting on it too coyly at the end, of events happening, not as 'good taste' would dictate, or as she would have expected them to happen, but as they actually occurred. The Chileno procession interrupts her discourse, as it does her sentimental reverie, forcing them off the track determined by her eastern notions of decorum. And there is no doubt that she has something of this opposition in mind when, again using herself as a foil, she relates an encounter with some emigrants who have just come across the country by wagon train:

I always had a strange fancy for that Nomadic way of coming to California. To lie down under starry skies, hundreds of miles from any human habitation, and to rise up on dewy mornings, to pursue our way through a strange country, so wildly beautiful, seeing each day something new and wonderful, seemed to me truly enchanting. But cruel reality strips *everything* of its rose tints. The poor women arrive, looking as haggard as so many Endorean witches; burnt to the color of a hazel-nut, with their hair cut short, and its gloss entirely destroyed by the alkali, whole plains of which they are compelled to cross on the way. . . .

One day a party of immigrant women came into my room. . . . Some observation was made, which led me to enquire of one of them if her husband was with her.

'She hain't got no husband,' fairly *chuckled* one of her companions; 'She came with *me,* and her feller died of cholera on the plains!'

At this startling and brutal announcement, the poor girl herself gave a hysteric giggle, which I at first thought proceeded from heartlessness; but I was told afterwards, by the person under whose immediate protection she came out, and who was a sister of her betrothed, that the tender woman's heart received such a fearful shock at the sudden death of her lover, that for several weeks her life was despaired of. *(ibid.* 198–9)

To say that this account had the 'ring of truth' about it would be as much an understatement as a cliché. Read after the transcontinental diaries (even those by the women) it comes as one of those massive, delayed revelations in a play, in which the proceeding action is suddenly shown from a wholly new point of view; as when, in the last act of Shakespeare's *Henry the Fifth,* the Duke of Burgundy reveals the horrible devastation visited upon French husbandry and society by the heroic war with England, or Brecht's Mother Courage goes into the town of Halle to buy cheap supplies abandoned by fleeing shopkeepers, leaving her crippled daughter to be shot by the invading soldiers. It is in passages like these that the professional journalists come closest to the western realism prophesied by Emerson, and later by Howells and Garland — passages, that is, in which the intense factuality of the West banishes the stylistic prototypes of 'eastern' behavior and writing.

And yet their realism is not quite what it seems, however attractive and however it invites the reader's conviction that at last he is learning the truth about life in the Gold Rush. The professional journalists were not simply neutral observers (there is no such thing) making an objective record as things as they were in California. In the first place, the genres in which they wrote infiltrated their subject matter, and affected their tone as much as did their expertise, their sense of audience and their idea of themselves as professional reporters. Taylor wrote in the tradition of Irving (that other European traveler gone West), Flint, Hall, Frémont and Bryant. *Eldorado* is an exotic narrative of western 'exploration,' ballasted by the occasional passage of scientific detail, as when he goes into the zoology of the shoreline near Monterey, in chapter 17. Dame Shirley's book, as her first editor put it, no doubt inelegantly, but accurately enough, was 'penned in that light, graceful, epistolary style, which only a lady can fall into.'[1] That is to say, not simply that it was presented in the form of letters (as, after all, Flint's *Recollections* had been), but followed in the wake of the lady's epistolary novel. J. D. Borthwick's book is after the fashion of other British travelers to America, like Thomas Moore, Dickens and Frances Trollope; noting, for example, the rapidity and savagery of American mass feeding ('some still masticating a mouthful of food, others picking their teeth with their fingers, or with sharp-pointed bowie-knives, and the rest . . . making horrible motions with their jaws.') (*Three Years*, 172); and forever wondering at the democratic formlessness of the place. Finally, Leonard Kip saw California in the shape of local-color sketches that would fill a column or two of newspaper back home in Albany, New York. Indeed, his book is called *California Sketches,* and is prefaced by a late example of the eighteenth-century author's disclaimer, a protestation that the studies 'were intended for one of the daily papers, but the friend to whom they were sent (in the absence of the author), has assumed the responsibility of publishing them in this form for the benefit of those who are meditating a voyage to the El Dorado of the West' (*Sketches,* 'Notice,' n.p.). His book includes the narrative of his own brief experiences in the mines, but his 'sketch' chapters, with titles like 'Gold Digging,' 'Life in the Mines' and 'Tent Scene,' are typical, rather than personal, in their reference — like the letter blanks showing characteristic views of California life — and quite set off from his own story.

So popular had this mode become, presumably through the

newspapers, that some of the ordinary forty-niners also wrote sketches of California life, separate from their record of daily events. Ezra Bourne, whose diary is elsewhere clear, concrete and content to let commonplace stand unembellished, gears himself up for something special when he comes to write his piece on California gambling houses:

The gambling saloons with their piles of silver and gold dust or nuggets broke down all barriers. It was a strong temptation. The Americans liked 'Faro,' the Spanish preferred 'Monte,' and the French 'Roulette.' . . . To a country boy brought up in a home of refinement it was a scene from a play. Everybody was moving, watching, and finally seized by the whirlwind, would sit down by the table to try his luck. 'Make your bets, gentlemen,' was heard all over the room. 'Jack and deuce,' 'Bet on the Jack,' 'Seven and Ace,' 'The game is made,' such a clatter; one's head swam. (B. C-F 142)

His elegant variation ('liked . . . preferred' and 'moving, watching . . . seized') is signal enough that Bourne is taking more trouble here with his writing than is usual for him, more's the pity. He is careful, too, to void the scene of any trace of personal observation: 'one's' head swam, not 'mine.' The balanced phrases and the passive voice also contribute to this effect. The same changes come over the journal of Henry Sturdivant (H. HM 261), when he devoted seven of his fifty-five pages of manuscript to another study of gambling in San Francisco. So it seems that the objectivity and neutrality of the professionals may have come from the genre in which they worked as well as from their status as reporters and their detachment from the anxieties of California life.

Another problematic feature of the journalism is its use of formal diction, or other ostentatiously 'high-falutin' devices like allusions to literature and to modes of civilized life unavailable to the people being observed. This could be a way of projecting, and maintaining, the pose of the detached reporter; at its best it was a means of dramatizing the easterner's experience in the West, by exploring the divergence in stylistic levels appropriate to each place. In other places it seems less functional, as when Leonard Kip takes such pains to explain that the coyote does not, on the whole, eat people, but that 'this forbearance . . . is not owing to any scruples concerning the expediency of feasting upon live food, for in such consists his especial delight. It is rather owing to his indisposition to court unnecessary danger' (*Sketches*, 22). What seems almost about to take off as a piece of western humor, like Mark Twain's treatment of the same animal in chapter 5 of *Roughing It,* collapses into a plain statement of fact, for which the fancy diction seems pedantically excessive. Bayard Taylor, too, seems to work against himself, when he recalls his nights in Sacramento City: 'Some of the establishments have small companies of Ethiopian melodists, who nightly call upon "Susanna!" and entreat to be carried back to Old Virginny.' But then, as though surprised by his unintended facetiousness, he hastens to add: 'I confess to a strong liking for the Ethiopian airs, and used to spend half an hour every night in listening to them . . . the Ethiopian melodies well deserve to be called, as they are in fact, the traditional airs of America' (*Eldorado,* 206).

Then too, even in the journalists' accounts, one cannot always be certain that what looks like a freshly observed fact of California life has been affected by traditional ways of looking at the West. Dame Shirley, for example, comments in her first letter on the beauty of an Indian woman they met on the way to the diggings, a 'wildwood Cleopatra' with 'those large, magnificently lustrous, yet at the same time, soft eyes, so common in novels, so rare in real life.' Her husband ridicules her interest in Indians, and she has to admit:

that those who bear that name here, have little resemblance to the glorious forest heroes that live in the Leather Stocking Tales; and in spite of my desire to find in them something poetical and interesting, a stern regard for truth, compels me to acknowledge, that the dusky beauty above described, is the only even moderately *pretty* squaw that I have ever seen.   (*Letters,* 15).

This is constructed on the same principle as her accounts of the Chileno procession and the appearance of the women emigrants: the dialogue between eastern conventions and western fact. But here the 'reality' half of the opposition is itself a contemporary convention. According to the great authority on American folklore and humor, Constance Rourke, the false romanticism of Cooper's sentiment for the Indian was already being burlesqued on the New York stage by the 1840s, in sketches by John Brougham and William Burton[2] — so by the time Mark Twain got around to the topic, in his letters home from Nevada in the early 1860s, and in 'Fenimore Cooper's Literary Offenses' (1895), it must have been positively stale.

Indeed, a second look even at the episodes about the Chileno procession and the overland women shows them to be more complex than a simple opposition between eastern tropes and western reality. It is true that Shirley's romantic or sentimental visions are interrupted by the discordant actuality, not only of what she sees, but hears. The rudest vernacular shatters the pallid stained glass of her diction: ' "She hain't got no husband," fairly *chuckled* one of her companions; "she came with *me,* and her feller died . . .".' Yet when Shirley learns the awful truth behind this *galgenhumor*, she restructures it in language calculated to soften the impression made on her and her sister back home. The 'feller' becomes her 'betrothed'; the woman a 'tender woman,' and the terrible event, 'the sudden death of her lover.' Thus the strange encounter is naturalized in the language (once again) of sentimental romance, and the *haut ton* is maintained. Not that the episode becomes, by this observation, any less convincing, but that its major interest in the narrative is concentrated in its impact on Dame Shirley and her efforts to accommodate it.

So the language of eastern convention is not banished, once and for all, by the unassailable concrete facts of the West, but discarded and reassumed as the dramatic role requires. And Dame Shirley is not the neutral observer she seems to be. In fact, 'Dame Shirley' is a literary character befitting her name, quite distinct (especially at moments like this) from Louise etc. Clapp(e). She is a masque, a foil, a preposterous *papier mache* of the eternal easterner: spouting allusions to Shakespeare and Dickens, lurching into French tags like 'pitié de moimeme' and 'selon régle,' and generally lording it over the natives, while occasionally deigning to notice their quaint mannerisms. No wonder she was so often discomfited by the rude facts of western life. For what Louise Clappe is doing, of course, is dramatizing the old American encounter between the greenhorn and the westerner.

The traditional outcome of the encounter is the maturation of the greenhorn, because this is another field in which the old American rite of passage is played. Dame Shirley's meetings with the Indian, the Chilenos and the overland women are all scenarios through which Louise Clappe explored her feeling, shared with so many other travelers to California (forty-niners, emigrants; men and women alike), that the rough, western wilderness was a moral force; that there were tongues in its trees, books in its running brooks, sermons in its stones, and good in every part of it. Elsewhere in the letters this feeling is made explicit. 'How would you like to winter in such an abode?' she wrote her sister as a preface to her own version of James's famous negative catalogue of American life:

in a place where there were no newspapers, no churches, lectures, concerts or theatres; no fresh books, no shopping, calling nor gossiping little tea-drinkings; no parties, no balls, no picnics, no *Tableaux*, no charades, no latest fashions, no daily mail, (we have an express once a month,) no promenades, no rides nor drives; no vegetables but potatoes and onions, no milk, no eggs, no *nothing?* Now I expect to be very happy here. This strange, odd life, fascinates me. As for churches, 'the groves were God's first temples,' 'and for the strength of the hills, the Swiss mountains bless him.' (*Letters*, 61–2)

Only a year later, however, the prospect of spending another winter in the mountains appeared 'fearful.' Besides, they had 'not laid in a pound of provisions' ('not so indifferent a matter as it may at first appear to you', she added, as though anticipating an objection) (*ibid.* 209). In any case, Rich Bar was played out, and 'the whole world (*our* world,) was, to use a phrase much in vogue here, "dead broke" ' (208). So they prepared to leave. Wildernesses are for a season, not forever. But 'My heart is heavy,' she wrote in her last letter, 'at the thought of departing forever from this place. I *like* this wild and barbarous life' (*ibid.* 215). Then follows an apostrophe to 'divine Nature'; her 'solomn fir trees,' her 'watching hills' and 'calmly beautiful river,' her 'moon-lighted midnight.' And finally, Shirley's conclusion (of the letter as of her entire discourse) draws the lesson of her sojourn in the wilderness:

Here, at least, I have been contented. The 'thistle-seed,' as you call me, sent abroad its roots right lovingly into this barren soil, and gained an unwonted strength in what seemed to you such unfavorable surroundings. You would hardly recognise the feeble and half-dying invalid, who drooped languidly out of sight, as night shut down between your straining gaze and the good ship Manilla, as she wafted her far away from her Atlantic home, in the person of your *now* perfectly healthy sister. (*ibid.* 215)

It makes a good story, beautifully told. And the same plot, or fragments of it large enough to indicate an outline of the whole, was repeated by the other journalists of the Gold Rush. Bayard Taylor's account of an outdoor dinner 'in a sheltered glen' between Monterey and San Francisco enacts the pastoral meal in the tradition of Irving, Frémont and the forty-niners themselves. They found a providential 'stock of wood' left by 'some benevolent predecessor' and lit a fire. Taylor tried his hand at making coffee, 'while the others spitted pieces of meat on long twigs and thrust them into the blaze.' Afterwards they smoked the 'pipe of peace – never omitted by the genuine trapper or mountaineer' (though, of course, they were neither). Then 'we spread our blankets on the ground and looked at the stars through the chinks of the boughs, till we dropped asleep. There is no rest so sweet as that taken on the hard bosom of Mother Earth' (*Eldorado*, 146). Perhaps this almost paradisal view of California is what conditioned his judgement of California society as almost preternaturally reformed. 'Nothing in California,' he wrote, 'seemed more miraculous to me than [the] spontaneous evolution of social order from the worst elements of anarchy' (*ibid*. 197). Borthwick too, discerned the pastoral paradox of civility discovered in the wilderness:

> It may seem strange, but it is undoubtedly true, that the majority of men in whom such a change was most desirable became in California more humanised, and acquired a certain amount of urbanity; in fact, they came from civilised countries in the rough state, and in California got licked into shape, and polished. (*Three Years*, 122)

And if the journalists were not wholly immune to the traditional associations of travel in the West, they were also bothered (professionals though they were) by the customary problems of writing about the experience. How best to annotate, in 'scaled invention or true artistry' (as Ezra Pound would say) the outrageous dimensions and rootless styles of California? For the sophisticated professionals, the readiest device was humor. The chaos could be indicated lightly at a distance, kept at arms' length by the joke shared with the readers back home. Yet in places, this remedy seems to have occurred only just in time. Leonard Kip, riding through the San Joaquin valley, had the same illusion of culture experienced by others before him on the great prairies of the Middle West:

> Moreover, being thickly studded with large oaks . . . it seemed as though we were travelling through some old English park, rather than a wild tract of the western wilderness. So naturally was the idea forced upon us all, that if we had suddenly seen the turrets of an old castle rising between the trees before us, I hardly believe that it would at first have caused any astonishment.

Trapped in the old confusion between the imagination and the fancy, perhaps embarrassed by it, he extricates himself, not (as the forty-niners would have done) through a flurry of statistics, but by a joke: 'But of course no such building deigned to make its appearance; perhaps because on that road [which led to the mines] air castles enough had been built to compensate for the absence of any earthly one' (*Sketches,* 20).

But Bayard Taylor, for whom amused detachment was not a natural mode, faced the problem more squarely than did the other three writers. 'One knows not whether he is awake or in some wonderful dream,' he wrote of his first days in San Francisco. 'Never have I had so much difficulty in establishing satisfactorily to my own senses, the reality of what I saw and heard' (*Eldorado,* 44). He too met some of the overland travelers, and he, like Dame Shirley, sensed that the reality of their experiences banished all the dusty old tales of adventure they had brought with them from the East:

Standing as I was, at the closing stage of that grand pilgrimage, the sight of these adventurers as they came in day by day, and the hearing of their stories, each of which had its own peculiar and separate character, had a more fascinating, because more real, interest than the tales of the glorious old travelers which so impress us in childhood. (*ibid.* 211)

Here the plot drawn is that of similar juxtapositions in the *Shirley Letters* (the reality of the West educates the easterner out of his childish fictions), but Taylor goes on to articulate a problem only implied in Dame Shirley:

The experience of any single man, which a few years ago would have made him a hero for life, becomes mere commonplace when it is but one of many thousands; yet the spectacle of a great continent, through a region of one thousand miles from north to south, being overrun with these adventurous bands cannot be pictured without the relation of many episodes of individual bravery and suffering. (*ibid.*)

Nothing in these accounts so illuminates the ambiguity of 'reality' in the Gold Rush. Reality (as factuality) authenticates the apparently impossible stories told by the overland emigrants. But reality (as the opposite of fiction) drains those same stories of interest; because instead of forming a unified action mediated through the artistic consciousness, being 'real,' they fall into the repetitious babble of a thousand vernacular voices. Here is the problem of western scalelessness applied, if only tentatively, to the problem of narrative. The efforts of the forty-niners in crossing the plains were heroic, because requiring such reserves of individual bravery; true, because their adventures really happened and were not part of a story; commonplace, because repeated so many times over. Could the problem be resolved? Not by Taylor, who goes on to write, not wholly rhetorically, that he 'will not attempt a full account of the emigration' (*Eldorado*, 211–12).* He may have sensed that the 'full account' would emerge only in the hundreds of imperfect, sometimes barely articulate, diaries and journals kept by the participants themselves.

For Whitman, who had the courage to throw over the entire cargo of 'eastern' aesthetics, the problem could be attacked by reversing the traditional associations, when applied to the West, of words like 'common,' 'average,' and even 'monotonous.'† For Taylor, on the other hand, the best course seemed to be to plot the indescribable West, ultimately, within a traditional, indeed an ancient, pattern. For instance, he too projected onto the vague screen of the undeveloped San Joaquin valley whatever associations came to his mind of the literature and culture of the Old World. His days there, he wrote:

were the realization of a desire sometimes felt, sometimes expressed in poetry, but rarely enjoyed in complete fulfilment. In the repose of nature, unbroken day or night; the subtle haze pervading the air, softening all sights and subduing all sounds; the still, breathless heat of the day and the starry hush of the night – the oak tree was for me a perfect Castle of Indolence. Lying at full length on the ground, in listless ease, whichever way I looked my eye met the same enchanting groupage of the oaks, the same glorious outlines and massed shadows of foliage; while frequent openings, through the farthest clumps, gave boundless glimpses of the plain beyond. . . . It was an abandonment to rest, like that of the 'Lotos-Eaters,' and the feeling of these lines, not the words, was with me constantly.

(*Eldorado*, 60)

He then goes on to cite lines 60–8 of Tennyson's 'The Lotos-Eaters' ('Why should we toil alone . . . "There is no joy but calm!" ').

There is a certain bravado in this. Instead of regretting the ambiguity of the landscape as Kip does, Taylor works openly to soften its outlines even further so that he may superimpose on it the images of the older culture he has brought with him. But he is not

---

* In fact he allocated only this chapter of less than ten pages to the subject, which he treats by describing the general conditions of the route from East to West.
† See, for example, in *Specimen Days*, 'Two Hours on the Minnesota': 'the sample promises of its good average capacities'; and 'The Prairies': 'the grandeur and superb monotony of the skies of heaven'; the word 'common' was already half-way to redemption via the phrase, beloved of Whitman, 'the common man.'

just showing off; nor is he retreating, ultimately, from the perplexities of the West into what was most familiar to him. The allusions are not an evasion but a form of typology. The Castle of Indolence is here perfected; made true. From the 'Lotos-Eaters' it was the 'feeling,' not the words, that was with him constantly. The literal and the literary alike are shed, leaving the reality of the experience, the kernel of truth, hitherto buried in the conventions of expression.

Coming back to San Francisco from Sacramento City, on an unusually clear winter's day, Taylor was enthralled by the colors of the sky and hills surrounding the Bay. The sight was almost unreal, more strange than art: 'Could the pencil faithfully represent this magnificent transfiguration of Nature, it would appear utterly unreal and impossible to eyes which never beheld the reality.' Yet it was no illusion, no projection of the artistic imagination, 'no transient spectacle'. But how to describe it except in terms of painters' colors?

The cloudless sky became gradually suffused with a soft rose tint, which covered its whole surface, painting alike the glassy sheet of the bay, and glowing most vividly on the mountains to the eastward. The color deepened every moment, and the peaks of the Coast Range burned with a rich vermillion light, like that of a live coal. This faded gradually into as glowing a purple, and at last into a blue as intense as that of the sea at noonday. (*Eldorado*, 221)

To resolve the paradox of the painting that could never be a painting, Taylor reinvents the conventions of the picturesque in a new typology. Sunset on San Francisco Bay both was, and was not a painting, because it was the final perfection of the Old World itself. It was what the old paintings would be if they could:

I have seen the dazzling sunsets of the Mediterranean flush the beauty of its shores, and the mellow skies which Claude used to contemplate from the Pincian Hill; but, lovely as they are in my memory, they seem cold and pale when I think of the splendor of such a scene on the Bay of San Francisco. (*ibid.* 222)

This appears in a chapter called 'The Italy of the West,' but apart from this oblique reference, via mention of the Mediterranean, Italy is not even alluded to in the chapter, though Taylor draws extensive climatic and topological analogies between Italy and California elsewhere in the book. Here the chapter heading works as the title on one of George Herbert's poems both taking on and bestowing meaning as the body of the work is read. For what the chapter adds to the title is the sense, not that California was merely a pale copy of Italy, a sort of decadent branch of the original tree; but its antitype, its final perfection, in the sense in which Christ is said to be the antitype of the Old Testament prophets, priests and kings who prefigure Him. Other people had made the comparison between the two areas, notably Frémont in his *Geographical Memoir upon Upper California* (1848), but it was Taylor who, as Kevin Starr has written, 'gave aesthetic amplitude to Frémont's topographical model.'[3] The comparison with Italy became a potent image in the development of California, affecting not only its idea of itself, but hence also material facts like the rate of its growth, the pattern of its immigration, its architecture, its landscape. And it was Taylor who first propagated the image widely. It was his gift, not only to the emerging state but to the self-esteem of his country, because in it he found at last a text for the American picturesque.

For the other journalists of the Gold Rush, allusions to the culture of Europe and the American East were a way of backing off from the West; of begging allegiance to the readership, and at best, of establishing a secure cultural platform from which to regard the California scene with detachment. But Taylor used allusions of this kind to embrace California. His vision of it as paradisal is underpinned, as all convincing apocalypses must be, by a typological system drawing on facts verified by his own experience – facts, that is, of his European travel and reading. For him California was not to be measured by the distance by which it fell short of a European or eastern model; instead the 'model' is seen only as a pale convention shrouding an idea, or feeling, or perception, waiting to be perfected in its new incarnation in California.

If California developed almost too quickly, so did its sense of its own history. No sooner had the emigrants arrived than they were forming themselves in exclusive 'pioneer societies' (Mark Twain was to find the one in San Francisco especially pretentious), preserving their journals and other memorabilia, and collecting stories from the 'old timers.' The San Francisco bookseller and historian, Hubert Howe Bancroft, began to assemble his great library of West-Coast source materials in 1859, only ten years after the Gold Rush began and nine after California became a State.*

* The pattern was repeated in other parts of the West developing at the same time. Only six years after it entered the Union in 1848, Wisconsin appointed the frontier historian

The legends and jokes of the Gold Rush accumulated as preco-
ciously as its historiography. Barely three years after the publication
of Taylor's *Eldorado* and Kip's *California Sketches,* their observations
on California society had permeated the American consciousness
enough to allow a humorist to write his own burlesque account of
life during the Gold Rush, counting on his readers (including those
who, like himself, had never been there) to get the joke. In other
words, in less than three years the fresh observations of the journalists had become stale commonplaces, either because of *Eldorado* and
California Sketches or, more probably, because what Taylor and Kip
reported was true to the perceptions of hundreds of other journalists
of the Gold Rush too.

The author in question is one Joseph Glover Baldwin, a minor
Southern humorist who made his name with a series of sketches in
the *Southern Literary Messenger* from January, 1853, on 'The Flush
Times of Alabama and Mississippi.' So his sketch on California,
published in November of the same year and entitled 'California
Flush Times . . . Letter from an Emigrant,' is as much a takeoff of
his own style as of the tropes of Gold Rush journalism. Baldwin
selects a few of the more often repeated observations of California
life: the rapid growth of San Francisco; the phoenix-like revival of
San Francisco and Sonora after their fires; the reversal of class and
professional roles in society; the climate. His technique is simply to
take each of these observations in turn, and build on it. Here are
some samples:

You have heard of our fires. They throw light on our character: we burn down a
city in a night and build it in a day. The ashes are not cold, before we are
building again: contracts for new buildings are signed by the light of the fire that
is consuming the old.   ('Flush Times,' 13–14)

You see that barren hill sloping towards the sea? Well – look good – for you will
never see it again. In a week hence, it will be in the heart of the city, built all
over with fine houses; and stranger yet, within two weeks, there will be no sea

---

Lyman Copeland Draper as director of its state historical society. Draper had already
roamed the Appalachians through Tennessee and Virginia collecting material from old
court records and taking dictation from pioneers of the region. In Wisconsin he collected manuscripts on the early Wisconsin fur trade, made files of early newspapers,
and put together the foundation of one of the great American historical libraries. Reuben Thwaites, the editor of *Early Western Travels,* trained there and eventually succeeded
Draper as the society's director; and Frederick Jackson Turner used the collection exten-
sively.

there! Some enterprising Yankee will scoop all the water out of it for a quarter of a mile as you would bail out a canoe. *(ibid.* 15)

My greatest complaint is about the washing and ironing. My present washerwoman is Goderich Johnson, Esq., late Professor of Chemistry and Belles Lettres in the University of ——, and author of a 'Review of Vestiges of Creation,'* and a treatise on 'The Unity of the Races,' and a prize essay on 'The Dignity of Labor.' He is not a good laundress; he has a great deal to do; his former reputation operating very much in his favor in his new calling. . . . My chambermaid pleases me better; he makes up the bed and cleans up the room very neatly. He is also of use by giving me some instruction, as he dusts the things, in the Spanish Language . . . which his liberal education at Cambridge, where he graduated with much *eclat* some years ago, enables him to do. . . . I have noticed that the literary and educated men here are just as useful and handy . . . as if they had never seen a college or a book. *(ibid.* 20–1)

And yet, for all his attempt to exaggerate, Baldwin scarcely goes beyond what is presented by the original journalists as literal fact. Were they too overstating the case? Or did the facts have a way of catching up with the wildest exaggerations? Baldwin sensed the problem, and answered the question:

Things here are turned upside down, wrong side out. What is the truth elsewhere is a lie here – a lie here is the truth everywhere else. There is no romance here. We are oppressed by a dreadful and boundless reality. Poetry is out of the question, there is no room for it. A poem cannot be read here at all: it is as tame as a guager's [*sic*] table. Fact has displaced Fiction. The world of illusion has been destroyed to give place to a more poetic world of fact . . . the only office of the imagination here is to enable one to believe what he sees. *(ibid.* 14)

Baldwin tells the story of one Thompson Hicks, 'counted a great liar' in Mississippi, who 'has been trying in vain since he has been here to lie up to the truth. . . . He thinks of addicting himself to Fact, *by way of gratifying his love of the marvellous.*' It is a parable about Baldwin himself, of course, and perhaps even of the fate of 'western humor,' with its love of laconic exaggeration, in California:

He started some sneaking lie about the population – said there were twenty thousand people in San Francisco; the statistics, published the next day, showed 30,000. He came running down [*sic*] street to a crowd before a Broker's shop to tell some wonderful tale about a lump of gold, weighing fifty pounds in the clear:

---

* Such a book actually existed. Written by the Scottish publisher, Robert Chambers, and published anonymously in London in 1844, its full title was *Vestiges of the Natural History of Creation.* According to the modern editors of *Flush Times,* the book anticipated Darwin in several respects.

he had hardly got through before the weigher inside sang out that the lump he had, weighed three hundred! He then turned his invention loose upon the vegetable productions, and reported that he had just seen a watermelon weighing one hundred and fifty-two pounds and an ounce; that the only way to cut it was with a cross-cut saw, worked by two negroes; the rind having first to be started by a wedge: judge his astonishment when he was told that several slabs of a melon had just been brought in from Los Angelos [*sic*] – the melon weighing two tons, and the slabs sawed out at the saw mill – the water of the melon being used in turning the wheel! (*ibid.* 14–15)

What Baldwin explores is not only the problem of writing about California, but also of writing about writing about California. Were the details recorded by the journalists of the Gold Rush literally true, or were they the exaggerations of men and women disconcerted by the formlessness of what they were observing? If their observations had become, in three years, so commonplace as to be the ground bass of Baldwin's jokes, did that fact make them any the less true? It is the same question, exactly, as Taylor's about the overland travellers: if their heroism was repeated thousands of times over, did that make their individual courage any the less real? Who can tell whether the commonality of the journalists' observations comes from their all matching diverse facts to the same preconceived system, or all observing the same objective fact?

Perhaps it was all literally true. Perhaps professors did dig cellars, and beetroots grow to weigh a hundred pounds. Perhaps Dame Shirley really wanted to stay another winter in Rich Bar, and California really was a paradise where social order evolved spontaneously from the most unpromising motives and people. Certainly many Italians came to look on it as a perfected Italy. All we can answer is that even the journalists, for all their training and confidence, and for all their dispassionate reporting, apparently of objective fact, sometimes doubted the literal truth of what they were reporting. California was all so insubstantial, really: founded on the illusory hopes (for the majority who went, anyway) of finding a fortune in the mines; growing too fast for its roots; shallowly civilized, like the gambling houses noticed by Kip, made of barns lined with French wallpaper. This is why 'realism' is such a problematical term, even applied to the dispassionate journalism of the professional reporters. For, after all, the difference between the professional and amateur annotators of the Gold Rush was more of tone than of substance. The reporters were detached, not only from their subject but from themselves; they could watch themselves watching; they were capable of irony. But they too were disconcerted by the lack of scale, whether of landscape or in society. They too experienced doubts about how to write about it. For both professionals and amateurs the facts of the West were perceived in dialogue with stylistic and reference systems brought from home; and more often than not, if the facts discomfited the systems, they were soon enough naturalized by them; parcelled up, as it were, for home consumption.

The documentary style, the objective, neutral stance of the reporter was not enough. Or else it was too much. Either the reality was too removed from the fevered expectation for the literal and the figurative to be brought into any sort of approximation to each other, or the endless replication, the scaleless enlargement of the vernacular reality approached and overtook the wildest romance, whether epic or pastoral – not to mention the cooler exaggerations of the tall tale and the metaphors of conventional poetry. So tenor and vehicle were either too close or too far apart. The only answer (unless the author stayed away altogether, as Baldwin did), was, as Taylor discovered, a full-blooded, unblushing (and partly that because it was a traditional American recourse) mythology of fact; for this, of course, is what typology is: a figurative system in which the most unlikely prophecy is made actual, in which the numinous is also the expected, and in which the fact becomes more exciting than the most feverish fiction.

A final word about Joseph Baldwin. Shortly after the appearance of 'California Flush Times,' he decided to travel to the legendary land about which he had written without visiting it. He set up a law practice in San Francisco, where his wife and children joined him a year later. So successful was his career that it took him finally to a seat on the State Supreme Court. Sometime after he settled in California he started to write a serious version of 'Flush Times'; a documentary account, based on what he actually found there, of San Francisco life during the Gold Rush. He never completed it.

6

MARK TWAIN'S WEST: THE STILLBIRTH OF SATIRE

For William Dean Howells, Mark Twain was the very epitome of a westerner, whose writing spurned the tired literary conventions of Europe and the American East. But just how 'western' was Mark Twain? In what sense can either he or his work be said to embody 'western' qualities? To what extent did his experience in the West contribute to the formation of his famous vernacular style? The simple and surprising answer is that Samuel Clemens was a come-lately forty-niner; he was both a participant in and a journalist of the Nevada silver boom as the Comstock Lode was developed during the 1860s, and he made his name by writing 'western-humor' newspaper sketches in Nevada and California. Indeed, there is something in his early writing of all five journalists examined in the previous chapter, whose work he may well have known: the visionary Taylor, the misanthropic Kip, Shirley the artful greenhorn, Borthwick the detached observer from another culture, and (perhaps most of all) Baldwin the hoaxer.

Clemens came, not from the far West, but from a settled town on the Mississippi over 150 miles to the east of the jumping-off point for the Overland Trail. His first trip West was just such an adventure, and just such a holiday as the forty-niners' excursions to California, except that he was avoiding a war, not the diurnal tedium of work and the domestic routine. Like the forty-niners, he responded excitedly to the outlandish topography and climate of the western landscape; to the romance of the all-male fellowship living to a reformed pattern of existence, and to the idea of the western journey as a rite of passage. Like the forty-niners, too, Clemens was to encounter problems in writing about the West, and crisis of style was to occur as much in his prose as in his life. The dialectic between 'east' and 'west' — not only in his passage both ways between the two areas, but also in the unexpected conflict between genteel and savage values in Nevada itself — would be the making of the writer we now know as Mark Twain, but only after he returned to what he saw as the cultural security of the American East. He was certainly a 'western' writer, but not in the sense meant by Howells.

In 1839, when Samuel Clemens was four, his family moved from what he was later to call the 'almost invisible village'[1] in which he was born, to Hannibal, Missouri. The town is described variously in his fiction and autobiographical sketches. In 'Old Times on the

Mississippi' it is barely civilized, with pigs scoffing garbage in the unpaved streets and the town loafers waking only to the call of a ' "S-t-e-a-m-boat a-comin!".' In *Tom Sawyer* and *Huckleberry Finn* it is cramped and petty bourgeois, with the boys' natural inclinations curbed by fences, small rooms, fundamentalist religion and fussy old maids ('Then Miss Watson she took me in the closet and prayed, but nothing come of it'). In *Pudd'nhead Wilson* it is almost southern-aristocratic, smothered in slaves, climbing roses and First Families of Virginia.

In fact Hannibal was a settled port and market town, where they bought and sold pigs, made whisky and cigars and forwarded freight from the river steamers. When Samuel Clemens was growing up there, it had a population of over 1,000, and it no longer stood on the frontier. For a young man of Clemens's imagination and energy, it might well have seemed cramped and provincial, though scarcely wild. The Mississippi flowed past it, and with the river traffic came rumors of a bigger world to the South; of St Louis and the cosmopolitan New Orleans. And though it was east of the frontier, Hannibal was a port for the transshipment of emigrants, animals and equipment headed west for St Joseph, where the wagon trains assembled before leaving on the Overland Trail. The young Clemens would have seen the forty-niners on their way through, and perhaps set up in type stories in the local paper of their adventures on the plains and the West Coast. No doubt some Hannibal residents themselves began to drift westwards in the 1850s.

In other words, Hannibal was Middle America. For its time, it was an average sized town, situated at the hub of two axes representing the two stylistic parameters of the country: the twin dichotomies of class and urbanization. Very roughly, the South connoted established wealth – the big land and slave owners – and the North, the world of the small freeholder working his land by himself or with his family's help; while, at opposite ends of the 'X' axis, the big cities were in the East and the uncultivated wilderness in the West. Whatever its geographical position, however, Hannibal would have seemed culturally and stylistically neutral to the young Sam Clemens, if for the only reason that people at home never speak with an accent.

When he first left home at seventeen, Clemens headed naturally for the larger towns and cities, where he could most readily find

work as a journeyman printer. In 1853 he worked briefly in St
Louis, then turned east to New York and Philadelphia. His letters
home, written, as was usual, in that semi-public style that admitted
them to the columns of the local paper, reflect the cultural implications of the East as seen from the Midwest. Like the diary entries
made by the forty-niner, Dr Edward Tompkins as he passed
through Eirie and Cincinnati, they convey the sort of guidebook
superlatives that might impress any young man at large for the first
time in a big city (population, size of buildings and bridges, number of ships in the harbor),* but they also show his imagination
stimulated by thoughts of the cultural layers underlying the place.
Philadelphia, he wrote his brother Orion in October, 1853, was
'rich in historical associations.' He saw the grave of Benjamin
Franklin, the Liberty Bell, a pine bench on which Washington and
Franklin had sat ('I would have whittled off a chip, if I had got half
a chance'), portraits of the Founding Fathers, battle flags, and a
piece of the granite step on which the secretary's foot had rested
when he read the Declaration of Independence. He meditated on
architectural details too:

We passed a large house, which looked like a public building. It was built
entirely of great blocks of red granite. The pillars in front were all finished but
one. These pillars were beautiful, ornamented fluted columns, considerably larger
than a hogshead at the base and 25 or 30 feet high. No marble pillar is as pretty
as these sombre red granite ones; and to see some of them finished and standing,
with huge blocks lying about of which others are to be built, it looks so massy,
and carries one in imagination to the ruined piles of ancient Babylon.

Near the city water works he came across a small park:

I entered and found it one of the nicest little places about. Fat marble Cupids, in
big marble vases, squirted upward incessantly. Here stands, in a kind of mauso-
leum, a well executed piece of sculpture, with the inscription — 'Erected by the
City Council of Philadelphia, to the memory of Peter Graff, the founder and
inventor of the Fairmount Water Works.' The bust looks towards the dam. It is
all of the purest white marble . . . at the foot of [the] hill a pretty white marble
Naiad stands on a projecting rock; and this, I must say, is the prettiest fountain
I have seen lately. A half-inch jet of water is thrown straight up ten or twelve
feet, and descends in a shower, all over the fair water spirit. Fountains also gush
out of the rock at her feet, in every direction.[3]

* Two later letters from Philadelphia, written for publication in the paper of which Orion
  was for a while coeditor in Keokuk, Iowa, were actually based on a contemporary
  guidebook to the city, though Clemens recast the descriptions in his own words.[2]

132

It comes as a surprise to anyone knowing Clemens's later writing to find him describing such décor entirely without irony. Even the inscription to the founder of the water works is transmitted reverently. Why? His tone has much to do with youth and lack of sophistication, of course, but it is not unconnected with the feeling that here was a place to respect, not only for its size and multiplicity of experience, but because it was rooted in history. In the life of the American republic, it was the oldest place in a young country. Though Philadelphia stood for certain remarkable discontinuities with tradition, being the place where the Declaration was signed, it remained connected with the past through its own communal memory; a sense of tradition that stretched from the city's water works backwards in time even to the capitals of antiquity. Clemens's imagination, stimulated by this most 'eastern' of American settings, conjured up Babylon. Philadelphia seemed the latest in a line of great world cities.

If a cultural tradition seemed to provide continuity with the past, it also appeared to resolve apparently discordant elements in the present. Later, when he was a pilot on the Mississippi, he wrote home a first impression of the New Orleans Mardi Gras:

At the corner of Good-Children and Tchoupitoulas streets, I beheld an apparition! – and my first impulse was to dodge behind a lamp-post. It was a woman – a hay-stack of curtain calico, ten feet high – sweeping majestically down the middle of the street. . . . Next I saw a girl of eighteen, mounted on a fine horse, and dressed as a Spanish Cavalier, with long rapier, flowing curls, blue satin doublet and half-breeches, trimmed with broad white lace. . . . She removed [her] cap and bowed low to me, and nothing loath, I bowed in return – but I couldn't help murmuring, 'By the beard of the Prophet, Miss, but you've mistaken your man this time – for I never saw your silk mask before, nor the balance of your costume, either, for that matter.' And then I saw a hundred men; women and children in fine, fancy, splendid, ugly, coarse, ridiculous, grotesque, laughable costumes, and the truth flashed upon me – 'This is Mardi-Gras!' It was Mardi-Gras – and that young lady had a perfect right to bow to, shake hands with, or speak to, me, or any body else she pleased.[4]

The ridiculous, the coarse, the grotesque, the apparently unpredictable behavior of a girl in the street – this last scenario was to give Clemens acute embarrassment when it recurred in a less traditional setting – all could be reconciled by the traditional concept, repeated for emphasis, of Mardi Gras. The recollection that there was such a thing as Mardi Gras, and that it customarily licenced flamboyant behavior, was enough to make the unorthodox orthodox. The sense of tradition provided a consistent tone in which to register and transmit the experience.

The Civil War put an end to Clemens's career as a river pilot. In 1861, after two weeks of disorganized soldiering in a Confederate militia unit, he went West to Nevada Territory in the nominal role of private secretary to his brother. While Orion busied himself with the real job of Secretary to the Governor of the Territory, Sam explored the country round about and tried a little prospecting. He visited Lake Bigler (now Tahoe) in the Sierras and staked a timber claim there. He toured the mining districts north and south of Carson City and for over a year after his arrival entertained hopes of finding a rich silver claim. His first written formulations of his experience in the West were letters sent during this period; some of them to Orion and other men about mining matters, and others (a more interesting group) to his mother and sister Pamela Moffett, now in St Louis. These letters home are quite unlike those from New York, Philadelphia and New Orleans. They are full of strong emphases; they convey an excited sense of contrasts; the tone is anything but consistent.

In one of his first letters home, written to Pamela in October, 1861, he says he has just read letters from Pamela and his mother sent on September 8 ('How in the world could they have been so long coming?'), then reassures her that he has indeed laid a timber claim for Pamela's husband on Lake Bigler:

It is situated on 'Sam Clemens' Bay' – so named by Capt. Nye – and it goes by that name among the inhabitants of that region. I had better stop about 'the Lake,' though, – for whenever I think of it I want to go there and *die,* the place is so beautiful. I'll build a country seat there one of these days that will make the Devil's mouth water if ever he visits the earth. . . . Orion and I have confidence enough in this country to think that if the war will let us alone we can make Mr. Moffett rich enough without its ever costing him a cent of money or particle of trouble. We shall lay plenty of claims for him, but if they never *pay* him anything, they will never *cost* him anything, Orion and I are not financiers. Therefore, you *must* persuade Uncle Jim to come out here and help us in that line. I have written to him twice to come. I wrote him today. In both letters I told him not to let you or Ma know that we dealt in such romantic nonsense as 'brilliant prospects', because I always did hate for anyone to know what my plans or hopes or prospects were. . . . I would not say anything about our prospects now, if we were nearer home. But I suppose at this distance you are more anxious than you would be if you saw us every month – and therefore it is hardly fair to keep you in the dark. However, keep these matters to yourselves, and then if we fail, we'll keep the laugh in the family. . . . This is just the country for Cousin Jim to live in. I don't believe it would take him six months to make $100,000 here, if he had $3,000 to commence with. I suppose he can't leave his family though.

Tell Mrs Benson I never intend to be a lawyer. I have been a slave several times in my life, but I'll never be one again. I always intend to be so situated (*unless* I marry,) that I can 'pull up stakes' and clear out whenever I feel like it.

We are very thankful to you, Pamela, for the papers you send. We have received half a dozen or more, and, next to letters, they are the most welcome visitors we have.[5]

The contradictions here are what might be expected in the letters of a young man away from home: assertions of independence and gratitude for papers and letters from home, the confidence and doubt which always attend a new adventure. But there is a new sense of excitement that sets off this letter from others written on earlier trips. For one thing, the stakes must have seemed higher. The possibility of striking it rich in timber or silver was much more delectable in anticipation than that of succeeding as a printer in Philadelphia. The emphatic 'romantic nonsense' shows how anxious he was to defend himself, and the family, from disappointment. Then there is the exhilaration of the wilderness, oddly juxtaposed with the civilizing prospect – not entirely facetious – of a country seat. The prose style, too, is jumbled. The bankerly 'intend to be so situated' sits oddly with the idea of pulling up stakes.

Something of the pressure lying behind these contradictions can be gathered from a violent outburst in a letter to Pamela written about eight months later when he was prospecting with Dan Twing in Esmeralda, California. He had found nothing in the way of gold or silver, and apparently Orion had written home to say that if Sam's luck did not improve, he might consider returning to piloting on the Mississippi at the end of the war:

What in thunder are pilot's wages to me? which question, I beg humbly to observe, is of a *general* nature, and not discharged particularly at you. But it is singular, isn't it, that such a matter should interest Orion, when it is of no earthly consequence to me? I never have *once* thought of returning home to go on the river again, and I never expect to do any more piloting at any price. My livelihood must be made in this country – and if I have to wait longer than I expected, let it be so – I have no fear of failure.[6]

Clemens's established success as a pilot was the achievement of a lifelong dream; in more objective terms, it was a prestigious, well-paid job. Why, then, this vehement rejection of the suggestion that he might, one day, return to the river? The only explanation is that he had come to sense a return from Nevada as deeply unnatural, the reversing of a process as powerful and inevitable as growth itself. There was no going back because there was no reverting to childhood. Nothing shows more plainly how powerfully he had come to associate his western experience, as the forty-niners had done theirs, with a rite of passage. For the facts were surely that when he left for the West, Clemens was already an adult, and had already been initiated (as he was later to tell the story) into the genuine mystery of navigating the Mississippi. Yet his first letters home from Nevada speak of his experience there as though it comprised a wholly unprecedented test of his manhood.

It was certainly a man's world in which he now moved as an initiate. In February of 1862 he wrote his mother and sister:

But I have decided on two things, viz. Any of you, or all of you, may live in California, for that is the Garden of Eden reproduced – but you shall never live in Nevada; and secondly, none of you, save Mr Moffett, shall ever cross the plains. If you were only going to Pike's Peak, a little matter of 700 miles from St. Joe, you might take the coach, and I wouldn't say a word. But I consider it over 2,000 miles from St. Joe to Carson, and the first 6 or 800 miles is mere fourth of July, compared to the balance of the route. But Lord bless you, a *man* enjoys every foot of it.[7]

And like the forty-niners, who so enjoyed cooking out with the heavens for their ceiling and a fire of buffalo chips for their stove, Clemens revelled in the romance of the undomestic. Of his and Dan Twing's miners' cabin in Esmeralda he wrote his mother and sister:

The mansion is 10 × 12, with a 'domestic' roof. Yesterday it rained – the first shower for five months. 'Domestic,' it appears to me, is not water-proof. We went outside to keep from getting wet. Dan makes his bed when it is his turn to do it – and when it is my turn, I don't, you know. The dog is not a good hunter, and he isn't worth shucks to watch – but he scratches up the dirt floor of the cabin, and catches flies, and makes himself generally useful in the way of washing dishes. . . .

You would not like to live in a country where flour was $40 a barrel? Very well, then, I suppose you would not like to live here, where flour was $100 a barrel when I first came here. And shortly afterwards, it couldn't be had at any price – and for one month the people lived on barley, beans and beef – and nothing beside. Oh, no – we didn't luxuriate then? Perhaps not. But we said wise and severe things about the vanity and wickedness of high living. We preached our doctrine and practiced it. Which course I respectfully recommend to the clergymen of St. Louis.[8]

The tone of 'we said wise and severe things' is light enough, but Clemens has become deadly serious by the end of the paragraph. Perhaps Pamela had been quoting him a St Louis preacher against his style of life in the West. This excerpt comes from the same letter in which he explodes at Orion's idea that he might return to the river. In a short space he moves through a vehement assertion that he can make it in the mines, through a description of the manly, undomestic world of the miners' cabin, to an almost millennial view of a reformed society in which the 'religion,' the economy and the fellowship are the perfection of, and a lesson to, the home he has left for good.

But the hopes and disappointments of prospecting, and the sense of the reformed community of masculine enterprise, do not, alone, account for the excitability of these early letters from Nevada. The western animals, the inhabitants, the society, the landscape itself all bristle with unresolved contrasts:

'Tell everything as it is – no better, and no worse.' Well, 'Gold Hill' sells at $5,000 per foot, cash down; 'Wild Cat' isn't worth ten cents. The country is fabulously rich in gold, silver, copper, lead, coal, iron, quicksilver, marble, granite, chalk, plaster of Paris (gypsum), thieves, murderers, desperadoes, ladies, children, lawyers, Christians, Indians, Chinamen, Spaniards, gamblers, sharpers, cuyotes (pronounced Ki-yo-ties), poets, preachers, and jackass rabbits. I overheard a gentleman say, the other day, that it was 'the d---dest country under the sun.' – and that comprehensive conception I fully subscribe to. It never rains here, and the dew never falls. No flowers grow here, and no green thing gladdens the eye. The birds that fly over the land carry their provisions with them. . . . On the plains, sage brush and grease wood grow about twice as large as the common geranium . . . Grease wood is a *perfect* – *most* perfect imitation in miniature of a live oak tree – 'barring' the color of it. As to the *other* fruits and flowers of the country, there ain't any, except 'Pulu' or 'Triler,' or whatever they call it, – a species of unpoetical willow that grows on the banks of the Carson – a *river*, 20 yards wide, knee-deep, and so villainously rapid and crooked, that it looks like it had wandered into the country without intending it, and had run about in a bewildering way and got lost, in its hurry to get out again before some thirsty man came along and drank it up. I said we are situated in a flat, sandy desert – true. And surrounded on all sides by such prodigious mountains, that when you gaze at them awhile, – and begin to conceive of their grandeur – and next to *feel* their vastness expanding your soul like a bladder – and ultimately find yourself growing and swelling and spreading into a giant – I say when this point is reached, you look disdainfully down upon the insignificant village of Carson, and in that instant you are seized with a burning desire to stretch forth your hand, put the city in your pocket, and walk off with it.[9]

Here, in Clemens's own version of the argument from profusion, there are various tensions, between the sense of exhilaration and the laconic jumbling of categories which only partially suppresses it; between the pedantic explanation and the refusal to gloss unfamiliar terms of mining jargon. The difference between this and the letters about Lake Bigler and his mining adventures is that this one is less private, certainly less personal, as though he expected it to be sent on to a newspaper. It has the feel of contemporary 'western' journalism, like Kip's *California Sketches* or Baldwin's *Flush Times* pieces. Indeed, his mother did send this and another letter now lost to the *Gate City* of Keokuk, Iowa, where Orion had run a print shop and been an editor for a time, and Sam had published a few humorous sketches in the mid 1850s. There the two letters were edited into a single piece which appeared in November, 1861.

So though the letter looks much more like something by Mark Twain than anything written by the young Clemens from New York, Philadelphia or New Orleans, it also belongs to a widely shared contemporary tradition in American writing. Far from breaking free from tradition when he went West, Clemens merely adhered to another set of conventions. Just as he tried to emulate the success of earlier miners in garnering the wealth, the adventure and experience with situations of danger that make for maturity, so also, perhaps, he tried to live up to their prose style. He would not have had to look far afield for models. The self-proclaimed adventures of the forty-niners were already widely published by the time Clemens reached his adolescence in Hannibal — indeed, were so well known that Joseph Baldwin was able to parody some of their more infamous exaggerations by as early as 1853 — and Nevada had already begun to develop its own version of the tradition, known as 'sagebrush humor,' or 'Washoe wit.'

The best known, longest running, of the Washoe wits was a friend and colleague of Clemens's on the *Virginia City Territorial Enterprise* who called himself 'Dan De Quille.' His real name was William Wright, and he had come West in 1857, leaving a wife and daughter behind in Iowa. After a period of mining and prospecting he began to write for the San Francisco *Golden Era* and finally joined the *Enterprise* in 1862, remaining with the paper until it folded in 1893. Early in 1860 he wrote his brother in law in Iowa about a long prospecting trip he had made the previous autumn, in

Nevada, Utah and California. It is just such a letter as Clemens wrote home about Carson City and the landscape around it; so for this reason (and also because it is good in itself) it is worth citing at some length.

part of the time the mud was knee deep and the rain would pour down for a week straight ahead. . . . Then '*how* romantic' to camp out on such nights and bake bread and get supper – Then after getting to bed and just when the rain was coming down by pail-fulls and the wind blowing a hurricane over goes the tent, and out we rush to set it up – get it nearly up and a puff takes it from us, some of the pegs pull up and some of the ropes break and away the ——d thing goes, fluttering & pitching down the hill with five half naked and distracted 'hombres' in full chase. I know it sounds 'very romantic' to hear men tell how they done their own washing and mending, baked their own bread and slapjack, and all that kind of thing. but, the fun of it is all in your eye after the first week.

On going down [the western slope of the California Sierras] we had good weather and enjoyed our life as man could under the circumstances. We started early or late in the morning just as we felt like doing went as far as we pleased and stopped where we pleased – went into all the peach orchards we found, and stuffed ourselves at the vineyards to that degree that we were unable to travel more than eight to ten miles per day, and sometimes when the peaches were *very* good, only two miles of an afternoon. . . . We . . . crossed the sumit of the Sierra Nevada Mountains, and slept on it in a snow-storm without a tent or other covering than a blanket, and our softest lullaby was the growl of a grizzly or the rush of an avalanche. . . . You have, no doubt, heard of the '*Big Trees*' – but you can form no idea of their size without seeing them – Why, Ben, if one of the smallest of them were standing in the Street in front of Bishop's drug store, and it should be cut down the butt of it would be lying on the ground so long as to be perfectly rotten before the top got to the ground . . . there is a hollow one – called the Horseback Ride, from the fact that people are in the habit of riding through it on horseback. I saw a man start to ride through it on a horse thirty seven hands high, on the keen lope, and he would have gone through slick enough if his horse had not scared at some men who were about the middle of the log, raising a liberty pole with an American flag on the top, and jumped out at a knot hole. These stories may look large to folks back there but I can't help it – they were not near so big when I first wrote them but this infernal climate is so moist I see they have swelled a good deal since.[10]

Dan De Quille's letter shows all the main features of what has come to be called western humor (and also shows just how completely Clemens had absorbed the convention): the tall tale, explicitly related to the outlandish extremities of the climate; the attention to the vernacular; the laconic disclaimer to 'romance'; and above all, the ambiguity of western 'realism' in general. The narrative voice both tells, and does not tell 'everything as it is.' It quotes the jargon without explaining it. What can Clemens's mother and sister have made of the proposition that ' "Gold Hill" sells at $5,000 per foot' while ' "Wild Cat" isn't worth ten cents'? How would anyone at home understand the use of 'feet' as applied to mining shares? Or 'hombres' for men? Again, the voice seeks to disabuse the reader of expectations of romance, or 'romantic nonsense,' as Clemens would say, yet a good deal of romance remains, surely. Clemens's uncomfortable cabin becomes a moral lesson to the more settled community of St Louis. De Quille's 'hombres' are lusty; they do survive in these exceedingly undomestic conditions; they go to sleep to the lullaby of a grizzly; they get up when, and go where, they want; they raid the more settled, agricultural community, turning it (just as the Jews did Canaan) into a paradise for their delectation.

Western humor is, in other words, a mode built on contrasts. But the contrasts are of style as much as of content. Granted the environment, the content of the western sketch was topsy-turvy. The trees and mountains were so vast that beside them human artifacts, like the pretentiously named Carson *City,* seemed wholly insubstantial. Familiar birds and flowers were missing. Nothing was to scale. But all this was so odd only by contrast to 'eastern' norms. What made it noteworthy, and what gave the narrator's voice such ambivalence of tone, is that the author was himself an easterner gone West. In relating the improbabilities of the western landscape so coolly (the characteristic pose of the western tall tale) the narrative voice is mediating between East and West. It has news that will surprise the East but, as an initiate to western mysteries, it must not betray excitement about that news. The voice is eastern when it puts jargon or other vernacular terms in quotation marks, but western in not glossing the terms it quotes. It may deprecate romance, but manages to convey a sense of romance nonetheless. To be more precise, it may make a point of renouncing the pastoral mode (a favorite target was the Cooperesque Indian, and Clemens wrote a funny letter to his mother on this subject too), yet imply the heroic. The undomestic aspect of the West is frequently stressed, even (quite inaccurately) with respect to such towns and 'cities' as were there. Later in his 'Tell-everything-as-it-is' letter, Clemens claims that there are no churches in Carson – or rather that there is a Catholic church, 'but like that one the New York fireman spoke of, I believe "they don't *run* her now".'

The 'real' Nevada was somewhat less exciting than Clemens's stereotype. For one thing, transportation across the plains had improved since the days when the forty-niners had made the trek westwards. A regular stagecoach now covered the distance relatively safely and much more quickly. In fact, that is how Sam and Orion had traveled. Plenty of women, many of them respectable, had made the trip to join their husbands in Carson City. Both Carson and Virginia City were raw towns in the early 1860s, but not in any sense predictable from the dime novel. Virginia, a rough mining town inhabited by all sorts of people from all over the States and from further afield than that, may have had no definable culture in the anthropological sense, but it was not without *kunst*. By 1864 there were four theaters there, playing Shakespeare as well as farce, minstrel shows and variety entertainment. Lecturers and raconteurs such as J. Ross Browne and Artemus Ward drew capacity audiences. And the *Territorial Enterprise,* on which Clemens was to get his first regular reporting job, was considered for a time to be the brightest paper west of the Mississippi.

Nor was Clemens's life in Virginia City wholly that of a desperado. Though he and Dan De Quille, as reporters on the local desk of the *Enterprise,* were forever writing up stories of shootings, fires and mining accidents, they shared rooms in a respectable boarding house inhabited also by 'Tom Fitch . . . his wife, sister-in-law and mother-in-law,' with whom, according to De Quille, they were the best of neighbors. 'Often when Mark and I got home at night we found laid out for us in our rooms a fine spread of pie, cake, milk and the like,' he added.[11] There were plenty of youthful practical jokes; reporters on a rival paper put it about that Mark Twain and Dan De Quille had hanged a pet cat belonging to Fitch's mother in law, and for a time the supply of pie dried up; occasionally friends would sneak into their rooms to plant buckets of water over the door or rig bells with strings to ring them after the two had gone to sleep. On the whole the atmosphere seems to have been more that of a college fraternity house than of Dodge City in the western movies.

As the seat of the territorial, and later the state government of Nevada, Carson City developed quickly into a married, genteel society, comprised of speculators, lawyers and politicians busy framing the new constitution of the emerging state. The inhabitants of Carson guarded their social pieties carefully, the more so because of where they found themselves. The social tone was probably not far removed from that of Chandrapore in A *Passage to India*. In fact, if one looks as the Keokuk *Gate City* version of Clemens's letter to his mother written on October 25, 1861 – one gets a slightly different impression of Carson from that suggested in the letter cited above:

And now, for your other question, which shall be answered tersely, promptly, and to the point: First – 'Do I go to church every Sunday?' Answer – 'Scasely.' Second – 'Have you a church in Carson?' We have – a Catholic one – but, to use a fireman's expression, I believe 'they don't run her now.' We have also a Protestant service nearly every Sabbath in the Schoolhouse. Third – 'Are there many ladies in Carson?' Multitudes – probably the handsomest in the world. Fourth – 'Are the citizens generally moral and religious?' Prodigiously so.

The tone is light, but it does not prevent the reading that there are real churches and respectability in Carson, especially when this version of the letter is compared to the one cited earlier, in which only the defunct Catholic church, and no ladies or 'prodigious' morality, are mentioned. In this version, too, is the quite serious – indeed emphatic – assertion, rather like an uncertain satirist's 'Seriously, though, folks,' that 'Notwithstanding the extraordinary mixture of folks which I mentioned in the beginning of my letter, one can find as good society, here, of both sexes, as any Christian need desire. Please do not forget that.'[12]

Genteel Nevada, set in that unlikely landscape, was a godsend for the Washoe wits. As the contrast between civilization and barbarism moved within the same field, the tension between the two polarities rose, and with it, the hilarity. Dan De Quille, typically, took as his subject for burlesque the law, politics, grand opera, women's gatherings and weddings: instances of formality which seemed to form grotesque contrasts with the savage environment in which they were discovered. Domestic things, such as children and especially babies, also proved humorous in such an apparently undomestic setting. When Clemens joined the *Enterprise,* he warmed to the theme. Schools, weddings, formal parties, women's fashions – all of which sought (vainly it seemed) to impose a kind of order on powerful passions – appeared funny, and were the staple subjects of the sketches. So were children, apparently so innocent but 'really' unregenerate.

Of course, Samuel Clemens had tried his hand at humorous journalism before he went West. He had written some rather callow sketches for Orion's Hannibal *Journal,* among which were: two supercilious 'news' stories about an Irish family living on Holliday's Hill in Hannibal; a controversy with a reporter on a rival newspaper, a newcomer to Hannibal whom Clemens labeled 'Local,' in which Clemens ridiculed the reporter's half-hearted attempt at suicide after he had been jilted; a mock-serious love poem and a number of imaginary letters debating the stylistic proprieties of the poem. For these sketches Clemens put on a 'high-falutin' style, as though to distance himself as far as possible from his distasteful material. The first of the pieces on the Irish family describes the husband getting drunk:

When he thought his limbs sufficiently recruited, he laid in another 'brick', and about supper time, returned to the scene of his labors. This time he commenced on his wife, and after administering to her a sound beating, he took his stick and leveled a fellow lodger, and while waiting for the fallen gentleman to regain his perpendicular, he was amusing himself by tapping over the women and children, when Marshall Hawkins 'grabbed' the unlucky offender, and marched him off to the Calaboose   (*Early Tales,* 70).

The piece is signed 'W. Epaminondas Adrastus Perkins', the first, and most elevated-sounding, of a number of pseudonyms Clemens was to adopt. Later, when Orion was working in Keokuk, Clemens wrote three long sketches purporting to be travel letters written from St Louis and Cincinnati by one Thomas Jefferson Snodgrass, a local bumpkin at large in the metropolis. Now the style was low, full of dialect, and the outlook was naive. Snodgrass goes to a production of *Julius Caesar* and gets thrown out for asking too many questions and causing a commotion. He is astonished by a railroad journey. He is duped by a woman who leaves him holding her unwanted baby.[13]

At first sight these early sketches look quite like what Clemens was to write in Nevada, and like western humor generally. Like almost all his humorous sketches written in Nevada, the early work betrays a fascination with different styles of speaking, living and writing — his own writing. The important difference is that they depended on a society more settled than that in Nevada. In order to get the joke, or to make it, for that matter, one had to have the sense of a community in which a stranger, an Irishman and a country bumpkin would be branded by their speech and behavior as outsiders. Reacting to his material, the narrator could enrich the humor — though, in this case, the final mixture was still rather thin — by assuming a contrasting stylistic mode, becoming aggressively 'low' in the big city and ostentatiously 'high' when confronting an ignorant laborer. The method exploits understood differences of class and region within a relatively settled social structure.

In Virginia City, however, everyone was an immigrant, and the immigrants came from everywhere. There was no single code of behavior, accent or dress against which subtle variants could be typed as coming from outside the community, unless one was writing exclusively for an 'eastern' readership, in which case certain generally 'western' slang words, or technical jargon used by everyone in the western setting, could be employed. It needs to be stressed that Washoe wit was unlike the rest of western humor (and what later developed into 'local-color' writing) in largely ignoring gradations of custom and speech within the one community, and in eschewing a narrative voice with either a mock fastidious or an uneducated style.

The stylistic variations to be found in Nevada were so extreme as to speak for themselves; so the narrative voice became cool and unaligned. Before and after his Nevada period Clemens told his stories in the comic high or low style and paid close attention to the vernacular (most famously in *Huckleberry Finn*), but the narrative style in his western sketches tried to remain neutral, allowing the behavior observed to declare its own absurdity. At least that was the idea. He only managed to keep the balance for a while, leaving the modern reader with the paradox that his earliest sketches for the *Enterprise* seem the most mature in their control. One of his first humorous pieces for the paper was a report of the 'Sanitary Ball' held in Virginia City in January, 1863 (*Early Tales,* 185–7). The United States Sanitary Commission was an early approximation of the Red Cross, established to help the sick and wounded on the Union side during the Civil War; fairs, auctions and dances were organized around the country to raise money for it. The affair seems to have been a fairly formal occasion, with tickets selling at $6 a person. Clemens's report takes on a narrative voice that is stylistically neutral, though the role in which he casts himself is that of the awkward male intruder into the mysteries of high society. At one point two ladies 'moved off . . . but suddenly broached to under full headway, and there was a sound of parting canvas. Their dresses were anchored under our boots, you know.' About the quality of the supper he is non-committal, until the punch line:

However, as we remarked before, everybody spoke highly of the supper, and we believe they meant what they said. We are unable to say anything in the matter from personal knowledge, except that the tables were arranged with excellent taste, and more than abundantly supplied, and everything looked very beautiful, and very inviting, also; but then we had absorbed so much cold weather in those parlors, and had had so much trouble with those girls, that we had no appetite left. We only eat a boiled ham, and some pies, and went back to the ball room.

He did not apologize for the torn dresses, 'because our presence of mind happened to be absent at the very moment that we had the greatest need of it'; but he 'beg[s] permission to do so now' that he is writing the report. As for the success of the catering, 'All those who were happy that evening, agree that the supper was superb.' All in all, it was 'a remarkably pleasant party, and we are glad that such is the case — for it is a very uncomfortable task to be obliged to say harsh things about entertainments of this kind.'

It is a superb short sketch, one of the best things Clemens wrote in Nevada, because of its subtle suggestion of powerful aggressions reined in. Behind the polite reportage, an anarch is struggling to rip off the women's finery, desecrate the food and heap abuse on the whole pretentious affair. Clemens's technique depends on suggestively circular statements. The failure to apologize 'because our presence of mind happened to be absent' actually explains nothing, and thus implies another, stronger reason; the supper was admired by 'all those that were happy,' but this, again, communicates very little, given that happy people would be less critical than unhappy ones — and anyway, how many were happy?

But the tonal balance between the augustan, reportorial voice that hesitates dislike, and the buffoon who steps on ladies' dresses and bolts whole hams at a gulp, was a great strain. Clemens soon found a formula in which the narrative voice could remain neutral and the clown be split off as another character altogether. He invented 'the Unreliable,' a comic foil based (with mutually acknowledged inaccuracy) on a much respected reporter for a rival paper. In these sketches the Unreliable typically crashes a fashionable dance or wedding, wolfs all the food, drinks a bowl of punch, tries to borrow money from the invited guests, steals the cutlery and disappears into the outer wilderness. At a smart wedding in Carson City, he arrives, unasked, in borrowed clothing, and goes from room to room pestering the guests. Finally, when told he can have no more to eat in the dining room, he returns to the dancing-hall with 'a codfish under one arm and Mr. Curry's plug hat full of sauer-kraut under the other' (*Early Tales,* 208). At a party given by J. Neely Johnson, former Governor of California, then practicing law in Carson City and later to be a justice on the Nevada State Supreme Court, the Unreliable stands on the porch looking in, with his nose pressed against the parlor window. Finally he follows some guests in, asks to borrow a quarter, and then goes after the food. The objective reporter documents his progress:

I have the various items of his supper here in my note-book. First, he ate a plate of sandwiches; then he ate a handsomely iced poundcake; then he gobbled a dish of chicken salad; after which he ate a roast pig; after that a quantity of blanc-mange. . .   (*Early Tales,* 196)

Later the guests settle down to some polite amusement:

Horace Smith, Esq., sang 'I'm sitting on the stile, Mary,' with a sweetness and tenderness of expression which I have never heard surpassed; Col. Musser sang 'From Greenland's Icy Mountains' so fervently that every heart in that assemblage was purified and made better by it; Mrs. T. and Miss C., and Mrs. T. and Mrs. G. sang 'O, Charming May' with great vivacity and artistic effect;

Of course, the Unreliable also wants to sing. He opens 'his cavernous mouth' and displays his 'slanting and scattered teeth' so that 'the effect upon that convivial audience was as if the gates of a graveyard, with its crumbling tombstones, had been thrown open in their midst' (*Early Tales,* 197).

It can be no coincidence that Clemens first began to sign his famous pen name to the 'Unreliable' sketches in the *Enterprise.* It is as though he knew that at last he had found another proper profession, one to rank at least equal with the one he had left behind on the river, to which the new name referred. 'Mark Twain' asserts, though subtly, a body of experience that can measure up to the more traditional western occupations in what it demands of manly courage and responsibility. Above all, the name was stylistically neutral, to suit his new-found narrative stance. Now he was no longer the Pecksniffian W. Epaminondas Adrastus Perkins or the socially awkward Thomas Jefferson Snodgrass (whose surname could be, and was, corrupted to 'Snotgrass'), but Mark Twain. Composed of monosyllables, the name avoids the preposterous and suggests plain speaking. In the navigation of the Mississippi it meant safe waters, though only if the soundings were deepening or holding steady at two fathoms.

Even when he abandoned the 'Unreliable' formula, Mark Twain tried to keep the narrator's voice equidistant between the stylistic opposites it was announcing. But without a stooge to act as a shunt for rising aggressions the first-person narrator could quickly run around. For Mark Twain, social trouble almost always had to do with how to behave with women – particularly in how to judge whether or not they were 'respectable' – and the uncertainty in his social style showed in his prose style too. On a visit to San Francisco in the summer of 1863, he wrote his mother a private letter of an embarrassing encounter:

The first Sunday after arriving here, I went, by previous engagement, to take Mrs. J. B. Winters to Church (I have a special friendship for her, because she is the very image of Pamela.) She introduced me to a pretty girl – Miss Jennie Woodruff – & of course, I showed a particular friendship for the girl, also for that day. The next day, at noon, I met the young lady on the street, & bowed to her – sweetly. She simply stared at me & looked a little indignant. I didn't care a cent, & thought no more about it. Two days afterward, I met her again, & kept my eye on her, but never thought of such a thing as bowing to her – and lo! she smiled lovingly, & bowed to *me*. Shortly afterward – two or three days – when I took my usual seat at the dinner table I beheld my fickle darling opposite me. I smiled – bowed – and blast my skin if she didn't scowl at me as sour as thunder, & went on destroying her hash without ever noticing me again. Well, I just thought to myself, this acquaintance is too spotted – it don't pan out to suit me, & I'll move my stakes & drop it.[14]

He had begun the letter by saying how he dreaded the thought of going back to 'the snows & the deserts of Washoe, after living in this paradise,' but he was happy enough to retreat into the manly slang of the mines when wounded in a metropolitan skirmish. This encounter, or something very like it, found its way into a sketch he wrote during another trip to San Francisco later that summer. 'How to Cure A Cold' is a long and rather tedious account of his experiments with various traditional cold cures. He bathes his feet in hot water, takes a cold shower, drinks a quart of warm salt water ('The result was surprising; I must have vomited three-quarters of an hour; I believe I threw up my immortal soul'). And so on, getting nowhere in particular except nearer the bone. Then comes an odd digression:

> Never take a sheet bath – never. Next to meeting a lady acquaintance, who, for reasons best known to herself, don't see you when she looks at you and don't know you when she does see you, it is the most uncomfortable thing in the world.
>
> It is singular that such a simile as that happened to occur to me; I haven't thought of that circumstance a dozen times today. I used to think that she was so pretty, and gentle, and graceful, and considerate, and all that sort of thing.
>
> But I suspect it was all a mistake.
>
> In reality, she is as ugly as a crab; and there is no expression in her countenance either; she reminds me of one of those dummies in the milliner shops. I know she has got false teeth, and I think one of her eyes is glass. She can never fool me with that French she talks, either; that's Cherokee – I have been among that tribe myself. She has already driven two or three Frenchmen to the verge of suicide with that unchristian gibberish. And that complexion of hers is the dingiest that ever a white woman bore – it is pretty nearly Cherokee itself. It shows out strongest when it is contrasted with her monstrous white sugar-shoveled bonnet; when she gets that on, she looks like a sorrel calf under a new shed. I despise that woman, and I'll never speak to her again. Not unless she speaks to me, anyhow.
>
> But as I was saying, when the sheet-bath failed to cure my cold . . .
>
> (*Early Tales,* 302)

The pressure behind this encounter must have been great indeed to force it into such an unlikely context. And the simile is 'singular' indeed – so much so that it prompts a long digression in support of itself. Both social and prose styles perplex. Yet the sketch deals with the woman by attacking her, not by retreating, as it were, to the mines. She is stripped, first of her gentility, then of her humanity, because, unlike the forward girl in New Orleans, she has no 'tradition' behind her to explain her incongruous behavior.

The aggression here is safely contained by the joke against the narrator, but a similar digression in a later sketch is less pleasant. This occurs in a report on a ball given in San Francisco in November, 1865, by the exclusive Society of California Pioneers. The sketch is the last of three Mark Twain wrote burlesquing the style of newspaper fashion writers:

> Mrs C. N. was superbly arrayed in white kid gloves. Her modest and engaging manner accorded well with the unpretending simplicity of her cos-

tume and caused her to be regarded with absorbing interest by every one.

The charming Miss M. M. B. appeared in a thrilling waterfall, whose exceeding grace and volume compelled the homage of pioneers and emigrants alike. How beautiful she was!

The queenly Mrs. L. R. was attractively attired in her new and beautiful false teeth, and the *bon jour* effect they naturally produced was heightened by her enchanting and well-sustained smile.

Then comes an unexpected change of mood:

Being offended with Miss X., and our acquaintance having ceased permanently, I will take this opportunity of observing to her that it is of no use for her to be slopping off to every ball that takes place, and flourishing around with a brass oyster-knife skewered through her waterfall, and smiling her sickly smile through her decayed teeth, with her dismal pug nose in the air. There is no use in it – she don't fool anybody. Everybody knows she is old; everybody knows she is repaired (you might almost say built) with artificial bones and hair and muscles and things, from the ground up – put together scrap by scrap – and everybody knows, also, that all one would have to do would be to pull out her key-pin and she would go to pieces like a Chinese puzzle. There, now, my faded flower, take that paragraph home with you and amuse yourself with it; and if ever you turn your wart of a nose up at me again I will sit down and write something that will just make you rise up and howl.[15]

Here the fantasy is in no way contained. For all the attention to his own style, for all the apparent energy released by his outburst, he simply ceases to be funny or pointed. The expression 'slopping off' is ill focussed, aggressive vernacular, whether applied to social or physical action; he cannot sustain the momentum of the sense unit running from 'Everybody knows' to 'muscles and things'; and the remainder of that sentence dissipates itself in subordinate clauses. Later revisions of 'How to Cure a Cold' and 'The Pioneers' Ball' deleted the digressions on the haughty girls;* so it seems that on reflection Mark Twain was embarrassed by his embarrassment.

If Mark Twain found it difficult to register the complexities of style in San Francisco, he was to find it nearly impossible in Nevada. When he went to work for the *Enterprise*, he ceased writing

---

* The deletions were not made at the same stage, however. The 'How to Cure a Cold' digression was cut at the first opportunity, in preparation of the first edition of *The Celebrated Jumping Frog . . . and Other Sketches* (New York, 1867); Mark Twain allowed the attack on Miss X to survive through the Routledge edition of the sketches (*Mark Twain's . . . Jumping Frog . . . and Other Sketches*, London, 1872), though he changed 'slopping' to 'prancing'; he finally cut it from the Chatto and Windus edition (*Choice Humourous Works . . . .*, London, 1874).

merely for an audience back home and made himself responsible to a local readership as well. If the absurd contrasts between the savage and genteel in Nevada provided a rich source of the burlesque, when viewed dispassionately as material, the same contrasts made for a local readership socially so diverse that one could not entertain all without offending some. If this was true in a general sense, think how much more true it was for Mark Twain, two of whose readers, Orion and his wife Mollie, were at once members of the genteel Carson set and of his own family.

The fact of the local audience even gave Dan De Quille trouble on occasion. In 1874 he wrote his sister, Lou Benjamin, about a 'horrible yarn' he had almost finished writing, about a party of men who are dying of thirst on the Plains. One of their number is ill with the dropsy — 'swollen as big as a hogshead' — and the others decide to 'tap' him, 'getting a whole keg of water.'

The old fellow who was tapped after a time straddles the keg and with cocked revolver keeps the others away, swearing that the water is his own. I am a little afraid that this will prove too disgusting but I can make the thing quite funny — going after the poor devil to tap him, etc . . .[16]

No doubt his friends and neighbors who remembered the rigors of crossing the Utah desert to get to Nevada were greatly amused. In fact, as he wrote his sister later that year:

My story of 'The New Rock of Horeb' has been a great success here — in one respect; it has made everybody sick. The day it was published it spoiled the breakfast and dinner of all who read it. Common writers only aim to influence the mind; but a man of genius goes clear down to the stomach — he at once assails the citadel of man![17]

. . . and so on, for another four sentences of equally defensive joking. But Lou did not find the idea of the story disgusting; 'Your account of "The Rock of Horeb" amused me much to-day,' she wrote him on getting his letter in December.[18]

Mark Twain's first stylistic slip in Nevada, as elsewhere, was a violation in the fullest sense of 'style' — that is, not only do the words on the page strike a reader today as in questionable taste, but they produced a strenuous contemporary reaction too. In October, 1863, he wrote a newspaper hoax about a supposed 'bloody massacre' near Carson City. The story seemed to be a news report of a multiple murder involving several members of a family. A man named Philip Hopkins had taken fright and sold his interests in the best Virginia and Gold Hill mines when he read in the San Francisco papers of the Nevada mining companies' practice of 'cooking' their dividends – that is, paying out unnaturally high returns on capital invested in them– in order to inflate the value of their stock. He transferred his capital to the San Francisco Spring Valley Water Company, only to find that that company really had 'cooked' their stock when the source of their water had dried up. The despair at losing all his savings drove him to kill his wife and seven of his nine children, then to cut his throat. The 'report' is full of ghastly detail; Mark Twain's imagination seems to have responded warmly to the theme:

The scalpless corpse of Mrs. Hopkins lay across the threshold, with her head split open and her right hand almost severed from the wrist. Near her lay the ax with which the monstrous deed had been committed. In one of the bedrooms six of the children were found, one in bed and the others scattered about the floor. They were all dead. Their brains had evidently been dashed out with a club, and every mark about them seemed to have been made with a blunt instrument. The children must have struggled hard for their lives, as articles of clothing and broken furniture were strewn about the room in the utmost confusion.

(Early Tales, 325)

The newspaper hoax was a fairly common feature of western humor, and nothing so clearly illustrates the dialectical nature of this kind of writing, especially as intended for an eastern audience. The hoax was nothing without some 'uptake'; someone, somewhere – preferably an eastern or metropolitan newspaper editor – had to be gulled by it. The best hoaxes teased their readers along with a string of 'documentary' details, manoeuvring them into accepting a preposterous conclusion. Dan De Quille used pseudo-science to achieve plausibility. He wrote an account of a powerful pump that could draw sand out of a mine and another about 'spirit stones' moved mysteriously by the earth's magnetism. One of his cleverest hoaxes concerned an invention called the 'Solar Armor,' a device worn as clothing to protect the wearer from getting overheated in the desert. Employing the principle that evaporation causes cooling, the 'armor' was a suit of sponge kept moist by water ejected from india rubber bladders under the wearer's right arm. The first man to try it was discovered frozen to death in the desert in the blazing midday sun. De Quille was particularly delighted when the story was copied by the London *Daily Telegraph,* even if the reporter was cannily non-committal about the story's credibility.[19]

But if the newspaper hoax, to be complete, had to gull the big-city newspapers, it could not merely deceive them; it had to be a fiction, not a lie. The gulls had to be seen as gullible. The story had to contain an element of self-falsification so that, ultimately, the editors and metropolitan readers could have nothing to blame but their own careless reading. De Quille's hoaxes obeyed this convention, and so did an earlier hoax of Clemens's, a slight but witty piece about a 'petrified man' found in the mountains south of Gravelly Ford:

> The body was in a sitting posture, and leaning against a huge mass of croppings; the attitude was pensive, the right thumb resting against the side of the nose; the left thumb partially supporting the chin, the forefinger pressing the inner corner of the left eye and drawing it partly open; the right eye was closed, and the fingers of the right hand spread apart (*Early Tales,* 159).

The petrified man, in other words, was thumbing his nose. The story caused a certain amount of local merriment, and Clemens was pleased when it 'culminated in sublime and unimpeached legitimacy in the august *London Lancet.*'[20]

But the massacre hoax broke the rules. It was not self-falsifying. True, there is a suspicious confusion of sharp and blunt weapons, and, as Mark Twain later maintained rather piously, the piece mentions a non-existent forest and two towns, Empire City and Dutch Nick's, which were really the same place, but there is absolutely no way an editor unfamiliar with local geography, however carefully he scrutinized the words on the page, could have verified the story. When the deception was uncovered, the papers copying the story were understandably displeased. Perhaps the mildest response came from the Sacramento *Union:* 'It may be considered by the editors of the *Enterprise* very pleasant and harmless amusement to trifle with the sympathies of its readers, but many will not see it.'[21] The local reaction, however, was furious, the more so because of the sense that Nevada had enough real savagery to contend with, without multiplying melodrama in the imagination. The following excerpt from the Virginia *Evening Bulletin* of 23 October, 1863, is typical;

while displaying a certain provincial defensiveness, it makes an acute critical point about satire as well:

In matters of fun, or for the purpose of 'pointing a moral,' we would grant every license to the imagination of a scribe, but in matters that effect [*sic*] the character of a community or an individual, truth is an indispensible necessity. Now in the item referred to, there is not a particle of truth, but unfortunately people at a distance may not be able to detect [this] . . . God knows our Territory has a reputation of being the theater of scenes of blood and violence that really do occur bad enough to satisfy our bitterest enemies. There does not exist any need to paint our characters any blacker than they really are.

But the disturbance over the mock massacre was nothing compared to the response to his editorials in the *Enterprise,* written in the absence of the paper's editor, Joseph Goodman. Much had been written about the uproar following this little editorial excursion: how Mark Twain so angered the local population that he was nearly involved in a duel, and how he was forced to depart suddenly, with his friend Steve Gillis, for San Francisco.[22] Mark Twain himself later provided two accounts of the episode, conflicting and both inaccurate. In *Roughing It* he says that he was asked to take over the paper while Goodman was away, wrote editorials that left the editor, when he returned, with six duels on his hands, then left town rather than become an ordinary reporter again.[23] A later version, which appears in A. B. Paine's edition of Mark Twain's autobiography, names one of the offended parties, James Laird, editor of the Virginia *Daily Union.* Apparently Laird issued a challenge, which was accepted. Steve Gillis, acting as Mark Twain's second, showed him how to shoot by blasting the head off a sparrow at thirty yards. Laird, arriving moments later and thinking the small corpse the result of his opponent's marksmanship, retired in some confusion. Twain and Gillis had to leave the State to avoid being prosecuted under a law forbidding duelling.[24]

In fact, his problem seems not to have been the law, or a fear of demotion, but another miscalculation as to the style of the West. There was only one challenge; it was issued by Mark Twain himself, and it arose over an editorial he had written claiming, with what justice or motive it is not clear, that the staff of the *Union* had not paid their promised contribution to the Sanitary Fund. Their vehement repudiation of the charge, strengthened, perhaps, by a determination not to be found wanting in support of the Union which gave their paper its name, stung Mark Twain to challenge Laird. By the end of the day, May 21, 1864, and after five furious letters had crossed between the offices of the two papers, the affair blew itself out without recourse to shooting.

The second editorial wounded local feelings more deeply still. The ladies of Carson City, Mollie Clemens among them, had organized a ball to support the Sanitary Fund. Twain wrote an anonymous report on the affair insinuating that the funds raised had gone to a miscegenation society in the East instead of to their proper destination. No doubt he considered the old Southern canard that organizations existed in the North to promote marriage between the races as sufficiently farfetched to pass as a joke; or perhaps this was his last shot in a war he had not fought on the Confederate side. In any case, the ladies took the suggestion as a grievous affront to their sense of racial and cultural integrity. Mollie was quick enough to forgive him when he wrote her a plausible account of how the story came to be published, and one of the other ladies also wrote him a private note of forgiveness, though her husband was less easily placated. For the record, however, their wrath was terrible indeed. They sent a letter to the *Enterprise* repudiating the charge and demanding the name of the author of the report. The *Enterprise* published neither their letter nor the name of the offending author.

Just when everything seemed to be dying down, Mark Twain made the incomprehensible tactical error of publishing the letters between him and the *Union* office. It is anyone's guess what effect he intended to produce, but the result was, or ought to have been, predictable. Everyone involved in the duelling affair was made to look ridiculous, and those of the public who had not guessed it already were now given a fairly strong clue to the authorship of the anonymous miscegenation piece. In retaliation, the *Union* published the ladies' rejoinder, of which it had secured a copy, and Mark Twain's humiliation was almost complete.

Almost, but not quite. For when the *Union–Enterprise* letters were published, other western papers reviewed the episode and greeted it with glee. One story was headed 'Coffee and Pistols for Several,' nicely conveying the *mélange* of violence and civility the affair seemed to evoke.[25] Another paper said: 'the easiest and most honorable way they can end the trouble is to go to a cheap grocery, take a little "tarantula juice" and say no more about it. After so much wind they must need some stimulus.'[26] Yet another questioned whether the 'use of language which was resorted to' was justified, and said: 'The sentiment of a civilized community revolts at the appeal to the bloody code on every trifling cause of offense.'[27] As with their reaction to his massacre hoax, the inhabitants of the geographical West, as opposed to the Wild West, felt they had had enough of gunplay, and when it loomed in the inappropriate theatricality of a Southern-style duel, the violence appeared ludicrous as well as reprehensible.

Mark Twain was almost certainly bored with Nevada anyway, but humiliation, possibly fear, and certainly his sense that the conventions of his adopted community were forever being changed without warning — all these prompted his flight to San Francisco at the end of May, 1864. He had failed to find a style appropriate to Nevada, failed, above all, to accommodate himself to its uneven, unpredictable respectability. As part of the West, it should have been a heroic arena in which the gentlemen could prove their manhood, and in which the gentility of everything left at home in the East would be shown up as sham. Yet just as the final conflict seemed about to materialize, all the wrong rules asserted themselves. The family, after all, he had always with him (even if Mollie forgave him, she had to be placated first). And how could one stage a shoot-out when women kept getting in the line of fire? 'If it were from a man,' he wrote to Mollie about the ladies' letter to the *Enterprise,* 'I would answer it with a challenge.'[28] Indeed, even in the West the women, using the advantage of their sex, could achieve results beyond what a man could do on the field of honor. 'Those ladies have seduced from me what I consider was a sufficient apology,' he wrote to Orion with an interesting choice of verb; 'they got out of me what no *man* would ever have got, & then — well, they are ladies, & I shall not speak harshly of them.'[29]

Shortly after he arrived in San Francisco, he began to work for *The Call.* He and Gillis shared rooms, and in four months changed their lodgings seven times. By 25 September, they were, as he wrote his mother and sister:

very comfortably fixed where we are, now, and have no fault to find with the rooms or with the people — we are the only lodgers in a well-to-do private family, with one grown daughter and a piano in the parlor adjoining our room. But I need a change, and must move again. I have taken rooms further down the street. I shall stay in this little quiet street, because it is full of gardens and shrubbery, and there are none but dwelling houses in it.[30]

Perhaps this image of flowery domesticity, in which two young bachelors are considered safe around a grown daughter and a piano, is a version of his life specially prepared for the women back home, and no doubt Clemens did not spend all his time in San Francisco taking Mrs. J. B. Winters to church. Yet this letter is necessary to provide a context for a very strange letter he wrote to Dan De Quille, shortly after arriving in San Francisco, and which shows, as does no other document of this period, how deeply ambiguous was Mark Twain's sense of himself in the West. Until the second half of the last sentence, the letter seems a good short sketch about the alarming fantasies to which an 'eastern' (in this case, European) lady is subject in the West. Then, at the very end of this extract the tone and apparent point of the anecdote change completely:

> Steve & I have moved our lodgings. Steve did not tell his folks he had moved, & the other day his father went to our room, & finding it locked, he hunted up the old landlady (Frenchwoman) & asked her where those young men were. She didn't know who he was, & she got her gun off without mincing matters. Said she — 'They are gone, thank God — & I hope I may never see them again. I did not know anything about them, or they never should have entered this house. Do you know, Sir, (dropp[ing] her voice to a ghastly confidential tone,) they were a couple of desperate characters from Washoe — gamblers and murderers of the very worst description! . . . . Their room was never vacant long enough to be cleaned up — one of them always went to bed at dark & got up at sunrise, & the other went to bed at sunrise and got up at dark — & if the chamber-man disturbed them they would just set up in bed & level a pistol at him, & tell him to get scarce! They used to bring loads of beer bottles up at midnight, & get drunk, & shout & fire off their pistols in the room, & throw their empty bottles out of the window at the Chinamen below. . . . . They kept a nasty foreign sword & any number of revolvers & bowie knives in their room, & I know that small one must have murdered lots of people. They always had women run[n]ing to their room — sometimes in broad daylight — bless you, they didn't care. They had no respect for God, man, or the devil. Yes, Sir, they are gone, & the good God was kind to me when he sent them away!'
>
> There, now — what in the hell is the use of wearing away a lifetime in building up a good name, if it is to be blown away at a breath by an ignorant foreigner who is ignorant of the pleasant little customs that adorn and beautify a high state of civilization?[31]

Here the narrator's pose is more radically ambiguous than in the traditional western sketch, in which the eastern voice celebrates its acclimatization to the West, while remaining eastern. The greater part of this short sketch implies that Mark Twain and Steve Gillis were living the lives of ordinary young bachelor newspapermen – working shifts, drinking a bit, and perhaps – though this is not clear – displaying a few souvenirs in the form of firearms and knives about their room. Along comes a nervous easterner whose unfamiliarity with the West causes her to inflate these ordinary events into fantasies of drunkenness, sexual riot and frontier outlawry. (As Mark Twain knew, and as he knew Dan De Quille knew, the routine brandishing and firing of revolvers would have been quite out of the question in San Francisco rooming houses in the 1860s.) But the remainder of that last sentence, from 'who is ignorant . . .' to 'high civilization?,' totally and instantly reverses the narrative pose. Now Mark Twain, unable, perhaps, to resist the romantic role into which it seemed, at first, only the hysterical French landlady was casting him, implies that all the events she recounts are literally true, but nothing remarkable out here where men are men, and where 'high civilization' is redefined as drunkenness, murder and sexual licence (neatly summarized by the disorderly flourishing of phallic weaponry). The horrific fantasy of the tenderfoot has become his own fantasy about the 'reality' of the West. Or perhaps it always had been.

To Samuel Clemens the geographical West was preeminently a place without history, with no integral culture, no roots – an absurd physical and social landscape. That is what made his febrile humor possible, and what caused his problem with style in all its senses. It is also what prevented him from writing true satire in the Nevada, if satire can be defined, roughly, as abusive comedy with a consistent, serious moral point. It is true that almost all his sketches brushed up against some contemporary moral or political issue during some stage of their composition or *post facto* justification. The massacre hoax may have been prompted by the feeling that the San Francisco papers were better employed uncovering corruption at home than sniffing it out in Nevada; perhaps even the miscegenation story was prompted by the honest conviction that the funds were going astray somewhere in the East. But something always seemed to throw the narrative voice off: a pointed criticism turned into a sadistic fantasy; a subtle jibe exploded into a wild, irrelevant libel. Why? True satire depends on its author's confidence in the continuity of the community he is addressing: he must certainly comprehend its past, because he wants to portray the present as a falling away from that model; insofar as his critique might be thought to clear the ground for some sort of reform, he must believe in, and apprehend, its future.* But Mark Twain could never quite identify the cultural integrity, let alone the continuity, of the society he was addressing in the West. He played with it, hated it, retreated from it, but did not take it seriously as a culture. Nevada society seemed so detached from its barbaric setting as to be beyond piecemeal reform. 'Society' there seemed merely genteel, and gentility in that context was totally decadent. This is why Mark Twain's social criticism in Nevada so often fails to make moral discriminations and why his opposition to the pretensions of the dances and weddings is so mordant. The Unreliable's mouth opens as a yawning graveyard to swallow the deadly social pieties of Carson City, and Mark Twain fancies the embarrassment, the stripping and finally the racial destruction of the women. What begins as a light-hearted burlesque gets sucked into a black hole of despair about the viability of such a deracinated community.

It would be difficult to overestimate the seriousness of the doubts Clemens felt in the West. He had left a secure profession for a hazardous adventure, had failed utterly to make his fortune, and had had to settle for the initially exciting, but ultimately frustrating life of a Nevada journalist in the 1860s. It is no exaggeration to say that in the West Clemens first looked over the brink, first confronted the possibility that he was, and would be, nothing – that not only he, but perhaps human society itself was, finally 'nothing.'

In the event, he turned away from what he saw as the darkness, back to the lights of the metropolis. He lit out for the States, to a place further East, in both the geographical and social sense than even his first home. In New York and Boston, and later on the journey to Europe and the Holy Land that was to produce *The Innocents Abroad*, he met a number of wealthy easterners who were to change his life. He found, in Mrs Fairbanks, a woman who, though

---

* Of course, some of the greatest satires in the language end without a shred of hope for society, or mankind in general, and one even prophesies the return of universal chaos. But the dark, anarchic visions of Swift and Pope are, so to speak, earned, through long lives and long texts devoted to the passionate examination of social, political, moral and aesthetic issues. Mark Twain's anarchy is disturbing, apart from the obvious reasons, for being so precocious.

respectable and even liable to deplore his slang, was educated, witty and unprudish. In Thomas Beecher, brother of Henry Ward Beecher and Harriet Beecher Stowe, and lifelong pastor of the Langdon family in Elmira, he met, at last, an unsanctimonious preacher. At last, too, he got married. In the East, encouraged by his wife, by his surrogate 'Mother' Fairbanks, and by – above all – a society with enough confidence in its own integrity to deviate occasionally from its social proprieties, he could look back on his life in the West as a sort of holiday; a brief, exciting and circumscribed episode in his career as a writer of increasingly imaginative fiction.

How useful it was for Mark Twain, as an author, to be captured by the East is still a live issue. Van Wyck Brooks was the most famous proponent of what might be called the Pocock school of criticism – that is, those who are resolved to rescue the youth of America from the aesthetic fleshpots of a decadent society. But they will have to explain not only how it is that Mark Twain wrote *Huckleberry Finn* and *Pudd'nhead Wilson* after going East, but (more to the point here) the better parts of *Roughing It* as well. It was Henry Nash Smith who made the important critical distinction between the first half of that book, which 'show[s] a marked advance towards the structural firmness of fiction' and in which 'the management of narrative viewpoint reinforces the meaning Mark Twain had discerned in his material,' and the remainder (most of volume II), for which the author fell back on clippings of his western journalism, in which 'his attitudes are quite unstable' and he oscillates between being 'a spokesman for the offical culture' and burlesquing it.[32] This is surely right. And the reason why the first half of *Roughing It* is at once poised and witty, while the second is inhibited and ambiguous, is that the first was written afresh, in the East, from the vantage point, and for readers who inhabited, a culturally secure environment. Now he could write with real freedom and real energy, and at the same time with comprehending control, of his invaluable experience in the West. If the West gave Mark Twain his seriousness and his exalted fancy, the East taught him how to express it.

And curiously enough, so it did Dan De Quille. For in March, 1875 he got a letter from the celebrated author of *The Innocents Abroad* and *Roughing It,* now ensconsed in his Hartford mansion. In it Clemens suggested that Dan write a history of the Comstock Lode because he, of all the old *Enterprise* hands, best knew 'the strange romantic fortunes & incidents connected with it.' (Clemens also, characteristically, proposed a number of practical details: what royalty to ask for, what size the book should be, how it should be priced, and so forth.[33]) A second letter offered further advice and an invitation to come to Hartford to write the book. They would work in the same room, and Clemens would even lend him money for the trip. 'To write a book felicitously,' he continued, 'a man needs to be delightfully circumstanced & entirely free from cares, interruptions & annoyances. . . . If you write the book out there, it will not be one half as good as it will if you write it here. *Atmosphere* is everything.'[34]

This delightful notion that a western writer needed an eastern mansion as a retreat for his reflections is, of course, a reversal of usual assumptions, and Joe Goodman, for one, was not convinced that the plan would work. 'For downright composition,' he wrote De Quille in April, 'don't trust yourself to any change, however pleasant.'[35] But Dan De Quille did go East, did write the book in Mark Twain's domain, and unlike Joseph Glover Baldwin, who could not complete his serious study of the phenomena he had burlesqued in California, produced the standard *documentary* history of the Nevada silver rush. It is called *The History of the Big Bonanza,* and it is still considered an indispensable source book for the history of Nevada.

7

THE PERENNIAL CRITIQUE AND
THE POEM OF FACT

I THE PERENNIAL CRITIQUE

As far as the intellectuals are concerned, the prophecy that a literature of the West would emerge to liberate America from European
and 'eastern' stereotypes remains unfulfilled to this day. This may
not matter much (editors and reviewers have become much less
defensive about the validity of American culture), yet when it considers the West at all, modern historiography and literary criticism
are still full of laments for what they see as the failure of western
writing to embrace the raw factuality of its setting. The perennial
prophecy has soured into a perennial critique. Symptomatic of this
disappointment is a well-written and influential study of the kind
of non-fiction — or at least the professional non-fiction — surveyed in
this book, Robert Lee's *From West to East*.[1] Lee argues that all the
books about the American West — fiction and non-fiction, novels
and journalism — 'can best be expressed in the image of a Western
man straddling his vast empire in splendour, yet standing with his
back to the West and looking eastward with awe and reverence
toward his superannuated past' (Lee, 1). Like Daniel Boorstin's
tourists at the Grand Canyon, apparently, the inarticulate giant of
western discourse is more interested in stereotypes than in the thing
itself. Lee compares the rough notes and journals of western explorers, travelers, journalists and novelists with the finished accounts
they offered their eastern audiences. One by one they were all nobbled: Washington Irving, Flint, Hall, the Harvard historian Francis
Parkman, Mark Twain of course, even Lewis and Clark. Because
From West to East is at once so neat a summary of the perennial
critique of western writing, so clearly argued, so economical in its
devastating use of primary materials, and at the same time (I think,
because it neglects certain basic premises) so wrong, its thesis needs
to be outlined at some length.

According to Lee, the process by which reports of the western
experience were falsified to suit the expectations of those at home
goes back a long way. It began with the Spanish explorers of North
America. Alvar Nuñez Cabeza de Vaca produced a report of his
discovery 'more literary than real.' The *Rélacion* of the Franciscan
friar Marcos de Niza mentions his having caught sight of the fabulous city of Cibola. Seen from a distant hill, it looked larger than
Mexico City (Lee, 5). The journals of Lewis and Clark went through

three phases, each more 'literary' than the last: their preliminary notes, their own journals, probably written during the expedition, containing romantic passages (especially by Lewis) but retaining much of the rough wonder of their impressions, and the edition begun by Nicholas Biddle and completed by Paul Allen, published in 1814. Biddle, president of the Second Bank of the United States, and its stout defender in the face of the wrath of Andrew Jackson (not to mention Ezra Pound), was also the editor of the Philadelphia literary magazine, *Port Folio*. His version of Lewis and Clark, according to Lee, 'glosses over, smoothes out, leaves out, and . . . wraps the journals in his own "refined" taste' (Lee, 35). He omits touching or pungent vernacular details, and adds 'stylized, rhetorical fluff' (Lee, 36).

As for Flint and Hall, Lee is concerned more with their fiction, finding in the former's *Francis Berrian* a perplexing mixture of Indian life described both in terms of the dull privation Hall actually found among them and noble savagery out of Chateaubriand (Lee, 49–50). Their western magazines, both edited in Cincinnati, turned out to be more 'eastern' than the *United States Literary Gazette* and the *North American Review,* in that they contained little in the way of writing genuinely emanating from the West, and were defensively high-falutin in style.

In Irving and Parkman, two well-educated easterners of independent means, Lee finds the same tendency to comb out the vernacular and inject the picturesque as they revised their journals for eastern publication.* 'When the whole wild landscape, of swelling plains and scattered groves, was softened into a tranquil beauty,' writes Parkman in the version of *The Oregon Trail* serialized in *The Knickerbocker Magazine* in 1847, 'then our encampment presented a striking spactacle. Could Salvator Rosa have transferred it to his canvas, it would have added new renown to his pencil' (quoted in Lee, 80). 'A writer,' adds Lee coldly, 'does not reach to the heights of literature by passing his descriptive problem off in terms of a second-rate

* Lee deals with both Irving and Parkman in the same chapter as characteristic eastern gentlemen on tour in the West. For a full comparison between their journals and the finished product, and for a discussion of their relative merits, see Lee's chapter 4; Mason Wade, ed., *The Journals of Francis Parkman,* 2 vols (New York: Harper, 1947); Howard Doughty, *Francis Parkman* (New York: Macmillan, 1962); and John Francis McDermott, ed., *The Western Journals of Washington Irving* (Norman, Okla.: University of Oklahoma Press, 1944).

painter. . . . The tone is a kind of *Weltschmertz,* the pose of a man who sits on a buffalo skull only to remember New England' (*ibid.*).

Irving's *Tour* is given the lie, not only by the more down-to-earth account kept by Commissioner Ellsworth of the same journey, but by Irving's own rough notes. His preliminary jottings about eating and sleeping in the wilderness provide an interesting contrast with the pastoral moralizing that grew out of them (see above, pp. 23–5). Here are two excerpts from the journal cited by Lee:

Picturesque scene of the camp — some roasting bear's meat and venison — others stretching & dressing skins — some lying on skins in the shade — horses feeding — hunters coming with game — turkeys, &c. — groups relating the morning's exploits — clothes hanging to dry — tent pitched — fine luncheon.

Make my bed under a bog tree on a hillock among long, dry, Prarie grass — a superb couch — sleep soundly sweetly warmly tho a heavy dew fell — Starlight — watch the stars on the prairies as at sea.[2]

'These disjointed phrases,' writes Lee, 'sketch in a complete picture, down to the fine detail of "clothes hanging out to dry," and we are reminded that Irving's *Sketch Book* was written by Geoffrey Crayon, Esq., the "Geoffrey" recalling the story-telling of Chaucer, the "Crayon," the on-the-spot sketching, and the "Esquire" defining a point of view. Beyond this, Irving *colored* his sketches . . . animated them . . . and occasionally . . . tried for the actual sounds of voices' (Lee, 62). By contrast, though, his *Tour* 'is but a pale reflection of his vivacious journals' (Lee, 65). He obscures the truth with literary stereotypes, grievously misrepresenting the guide Antoine Deshertes as a 'Gil Blas of the frontiers,' eliding unsuitable or obscene details of the adventurers' relations with the Indians, omitting or dressing up the vernacular so that an Indian is made to say ' "It seems but three miles distant, yet it perhaps is twenty" ' (Lee, 65–7).

Lee confines his observations on the old debate over the effect on Mark Twain of the eastern embrace to texts that were begun in the West and completed in the East — that is *The Innocents Abroad* and *Roughing It.* He prefers the finished *Innocents* to its first version, Mark Twain's letters to the San Francisco *Alta California,* yet notes in the evolution of the text the 'civilizing process' of Mrs Fairbanks's censorship and a corresponding 'loss of quality' (Lee, 99). Though he reminds his reader that Clemens was not born in the West — not on the frontier, at least — Lee laments the loss in *The Innocents Abroad* of language originating in the West (Lee, 98–9). *Roughing It,* too, is described as a 'washed and weakened version' of earlier fragments appearing first in California periodicals like the Sacramento *Union* (Lee, 109).

The financial and personal security of his marriage, his own success in the sales of *The Innocents Abroad,* the flattering attentions paid him by educated people of the East — all these gave Mark Twain the confidence of an established persona. *Roughing It* is largely written from the pose of a wide-eyed innocent at large in the world for the first time (a thing which at 26, with his river-pilot experience and even a spot of soldiering behind him, Clemens could not have been), and the result, according to Lee (107), was a distortion of the truth. Romance took over from realism — the romance of the West as seen from the eastern drawing room. *Roughing It* is 'so subjective, so exaggerated, so distorted, so jolly, that the West would have to continue to wait for a more honest interpreter. . . . But the West would wait in vain, for the myth of the heroic West is with Twain so firmly established and so widely disseminated that any other treatment will be henceforth reflected' (Lee, 111).

The perennial critique has a good deal of truth in it. Certainly novelists, travelers and explorers alike reacted to their experience in the West by retreating to stylistic poses in which they felt comfortable. But it is odd that Lee, for one, makes no distinction between those writers whose texts are diluted, as it were, against their will or without their knowledge, and those (surely the majority of the cases he cites) who collaborated in preparing their work for an eastern audience. Any comparison between an author's early fumblings and final presentation is bound to produce a contrast as between raw and cooked. It is a symptom of the perennial critique that it neglects to apply a similarly stringent comparison, say, between the notebooks and finished novels of Henry James. The western writers were, mainly, easterners visiting the West, writing books about the experience for other easterners to read. The obvious point needs to be stressed, perhaps, that the process of writing these books was the process of producing them: making rough notes, writing a succession of drafts, each one revised according to the author's sense — and no doubt those of his editor and other 'eastern' advisers — of how best to accommodate the rough impressions of the voyage to the expectations of the readers at home. For purposes of academic study one may well wish to examine the text at various stages of its evolution; criticism, on the other hand, must attend to what the author took his final product to be.*

Since it is true that almost everyone leaving the confines of what he took to be his cultural base felt the anxiety of the cultural void, and responded by asserting more forcefully, perhaps than he would at home, the stylistic conventions he thought represented the culture he had left behind, then this process must be taken, not merely as characteristic of the transmission of the 'western experience' but as part of that experience itself. That is what it comes down to: the experience and its expression are inseparable.

What needs to be insisted on, to return to critical issues, is how much western writing gains by the tension between raw and cooked in what is, after all, a literature mediating between civilization and barbarism. At this point, however, it might be worth underlining the primary distinction in the writing, ignored by the perennial critique but already evident to the reader of this book, between writers who had a sense of their audiences and those who did not. For Flint and Hall, Frémont, most of the forty-niners, and for Mark Twain while he was still in the West, the anxiety of travel in the wilderness was compounded by an uncertainty as to who would read their texts. Flint and Hall were both of and not of the West; writing for the local readers of their journals as well as for the more critical East; Frémont's book, he knew, would be widely circulated by the Government, and would reach all conditions of men; Mark Twain wrote for both home and local markets, and even his Nevada readers were an unpredictable mixture of tastes, interests, degrees of gentility. The forty-niner recording his adventures for his children and grandchildren can hardly have known what kind of reader would eventually pick up his testament. The social and geographical mobility of America, to which his own journey testified so clearly, might produce readers of quite unpredictable levels of sophistication even within his immediate offspring.

On the other hand, Irving, most of the journalists of the Gold

---

* Indeed, that is why the texts I have chosen as examples of the forty-niners' journals are simply what they left as the final word on their experience — for the benefit of their families, their 'posterity' or a prospective publisher — without attempting the (anyway, now impossible) task of separating what they wrote on the trail from anything they may have added or altered on getting home.

Rush (certainly Taylor) and Mark Twain after he went East, all enjoyed the security of an audience that was predominantly sophisticated, hence predictable in its responses. The same is true of Wister and the cowboy romancers. However complex their strategies, their moral and tonal stance was firm. So Mark Twain's various poses (as a canny-naive westerner roaming Europe or as canny-naive greenhorn in the Wild West), far from inhibiting the truth of his experience, allowed the diverse events of his life to coalesce as consistent social satire. They provided the comparative basis on which satire must be mounted. It might be added, though by now it is hardly news, that one of these scenarios he connived in producing was the canard, swallowed whole by the perennial critique, that his pungent genius had been dissipated by his wife, friends, critics, publishers and other agents of eastern and European gentility.[3]

But even the seamless narratives of Irving and Taylor were not without complexity. These men were not just elevated, supercilious visitors to an amusingly bizarre setting. We know that Irving was anxious to establish in the chaos of a new country a source of the 'storied and poetical association' he had found in Europe (and that even Parkman's reference to Salvator Rosa was part of this cultural dialogue). We know that Taylor confronted, and retreated from, the problem of writing about the transcontinental journeys of the forty-niners, in which feats of heroism equal to those recounted in epics of individual enterprise were multiplied a thousand times so as to become commonplace. From Commissioner Ellsworth's letters to his wife we get a different view of Irving's statuesque Indians. 'The squaws were more dirty than the men – both were lousy and some diseased by *VICIOUS* indulgence.' Some of the children 'made water before all the women and even *upon* some of them, laughing heartily to show us how they could.'[4] According to Ellsworth, even Irving found the Osages 'filthy in the extreme.' Not so the Count de Pourtalès, who seems to have mounted every squaw he met from the Mississippi river to Oklahoma, at one point even attempting 'to seduce a young Indian girl at a missionary school' and entering into negotiations with the wife of the missionary to see 'whether the girl c'd be released.'

There were, in other words, instances of disorder that had to be kept outside the stockade of Taylor's and Irving's prose. Even within his text Irving gives the sense of these exclusions, when, after introducing the *dramatis personae* of his adventure and describing the Osages with their 'Roman countenances,' he adds:

Besides these, there was a sprinkling of trappers, hunters, half-breeds, creoles, negroes of every hue; and all that other rabble rout of nondescript beings that keep about the frontiers, between civilized and savage life, as those equivocal birds, the bats, hover about the confines of light and darkness.   (*Tour,* 22)

His text, at least, would avoid such equivocation. But however even in tone, the picturesque and the pastoral are both systems for dealing with the conjunction of nature and culture — the very frontier region which Irving seems to avoid in the paragraph above. In the picturesque composition of artifact and wilderness, does the former tame, or magnify the latter? Is the little temple, gazebo or ancient ruin ennobled or trivialized by its setting? In the pastoral, is civilization what makes us human, or is it a decadent denial of human responsibility? Is instinct just a licence, or an apprehension of the good, superior to book learning? Is to act naturally to act unnaturally?

A romance, after all, can be more than an evasion of the truth. Either it may, as Frank Norris claimed, explore issues larger than a visit to a neighbor's house; because, as Rider Haggard once wrote, 'we have, as it were, macadamized all the roads of life.'[5] Or it may show us the limits of what we know. Henry James read Conrad's obscurity — his narrative refusals, his enveloped story-teller who lapses into melodrama — as a virtue, not a vice:

Mr Conrad's first care . . . is expressly to posit or set up a reciter, a definite responsible intervening first person singular, possessed of infinite sources of references, who immediately proceeds to set up another, to the end that this other may conform again to the practice, and that even at that point the bridge over to the creature, or in other words to the situation or the subject, the thing 'produced', shall, if the fancy takes it, once more and yet once more glory in a gap. It is easy to see how heroic the undertaking of an effective fusion becomes on these terms, fusion between what we are to know and that prodigy of our knowing which is ever half the very beauty of the atmosphere of authenticity.[6]

In James's view, episodes like the melodramatic conclusion to Marlow's journey up the Congo were what made Conrad's novels modern. Indeed, since the modern condition was not to know (and to know it), they were what made his fiction an *accurate* account of our lives. James takes Conrad's narrator as an ironic mask; it is Marlow, not Conrad, who loses his way, who collapses into cliché, and through whom the author dramatizes our ignorance of our own hearts of darkness.

The pastoral also commonly explores the limits of its own presuppositions in another way, by questioning the validity of fiction itself. Fiction, after all, is only another artifact that must be examined along with the products of culture. Somewhere along its course the pastoral story draws attention to its own absurdity, so as to remind its readers or audience that they are witnessing a highly formalized investigation of certain life values, not life itself. Sometimes it is the precarious nature of the setting that is thrown into relief, as when a bear or band of brigands suddenly invades the scene, showing the defenses of the untutored country folk to be inadequate. Sometimes the thematic material is qualified by a satire on its more extreme applications, as when Jacques in *As You Like It* is ridiculed for having moralized the hunting of deer just after Duke Senior has found 'tongues in trees, books in the running brooks,/Sermons in stones, and good in everything.'

Irving's version of this alienation effect centers on a young Osage befriended by Pourtalès:

Such is the glorious independence of man in a savage state. This youth, with his rifle, his blanket, and his horse, was ready at a moment's warning to rove the world; he carried all his worldly effects with him, and in the absence of artificial wants, possessed the great secret of personal freedom. We of society are slaves, not so much to others as to ourselves; our superfluities are the chains that bind us, impeding every movement of our bodies, and thwarting every impulse of our souls. Such, at least, were my speculations at the time, though I am not sure but that they took their tone from the enthusiasm of the young Count, who seemed more enchanted than ever with the wild chivalry of the prairies, and talked of putting on the Indian dress and adopting the Indian habits during the time he hoped to pass with the Osages.

(*Tour*, 34)

Perhaps it was not quite gentlemanly of Irving to pass his exoticism off on the European nobility, commonly thought by Americans to be the richest source of such decadence. Nevertheless, the explicit moral lessons of the *Tour* are ostensibly its most high purpose; so to allow their seriousness to be threatened, even indirectly, shows something of the 'negative capability' of the renaissance pastoral. Irving also demonstrates here that he knows exactly what he is, how he is working, and why. In distinguishing himself from the Count, he not only declares himself an American speaking, primarily, to Americans, but also marks the limits of the European fictions he so assiduously employs in his discourse.

This is not to suggest that Irving did not adopt a role in the *Tour*. He posed as another version of Geoffrey Crayon, the cisatlantic 'Gent.' of *The Sketch Book*. Of course his persona was not exactly him. The real Irving came to maturity by clinging anxiously to the cultural security of Europe, not through the bracing liberations of the American West, and it is doubtful if he really believed the Indians more civilized, because closer to nature, than cultivated white folks from the East. Yet his role was a fiction, not a lie. Through it he not only conveyed the experience of a civilized man confronting the borders of his culture, but also managed to wring historical, pictorial, 'poetical' and moral associations from the American soil. I cannot see how the fragments of his rough journals establish this stance of 'Esquire' better than the finished *Tour*, nor how the complex ironies of the cultivated man speaking about the West to others like himself could have been done better in another form.

The modern editors of Ellsworth's letter to his wife, Stanley Williams and Barbara Simison, would dispute this. For them, Ellsworth's is the 'true record of a memorable adventure,' and Irving's merely an 'elegant narrative.' Irving looked 'through the eyes of a Europeanized romantic; Indian ponies recalled Andalusian steeds; interlaced silhouettes of trees Moorish castles; French villages in Louisiana the old songs of Languedoc; the rangers in camp Robin Hood's merry men.'[7]

This is a significant misreading. What Irving actually wrote about the Indian horses is:

Others are of a low but strong make, and are supposed to be of the Andalusian breed, brought out by the Spanish discoverers. Some fanciful speculatists have seen in them descendents of the Arab stock, brought into Spain from Africa, and thence transferred to this country;   *(Tour,* 117)

The distinction, once again, is between fiction and lie. Where Irving represents a thing as literally true, he supports or qualifies his proposition as required (the 'fancy' belongs, of course, to the 'speculatists,' not to him, though this snippet of zoological archaeology happens to be true); where he speaks in figures, he makes this clear in the customary ways, not excluding irony. The factual content of the *Tour,* indeed, is surprisingly high, much higher than

Ellsworth's letter. There is a good deal of convincing detail about the history and folklore of the country, about the life and manners of Indians, government agents, soldiers and settlers he encountered. As for his elegant pose, the weakest defense of it is that it does not get in the way of his observation — that though he pretends, at times, to a certain distance from his material, he never disdains it. But to put the case more strongly, it might be added that to comment intelligently on social and anthropological detail, or even to recognize it, requires some breadth of experience with different levels of society in various places — the more the better. But last and best, Irving's stance as a cultivated eastern gentleman is a very flexible narrative device. Insofar as he is widely traveled and well read, he is able to comment knowingly on the culture he finds in the West or on the lack of it. Insofar as he plays the part of an easterner in the wilderness, his role is the equivalent of Mark Twain's pose of greenhorn in *Roughing It;* an assumed naivety to dramatize the wonder and excitement of the West. That too is part of the experience.

So beneath the untroubled, exotic surfaces of Irving's *Tour* and Taylor's *Eldorado* there may be more of a dialogue going on than appears at first sight. Yet no one would argue that their books betray that strange fissure between documentary and fantasy that characterizes reports of western travel from Hall through the forty-niners. To understand that more deeply divided discourse, it might help to return briefly to the example of the early Spanish explorers. The *Rélacion* of Alvar Nuñez Cabeca de Vaca (also called the *Naufragios,* or Shipwrecks), is described by Lee as 'more literary than real.' Certainly the story of the small band of men who made their way, after being shipwrecked on the Florida coast, westward by forced march and improvised boats to the coast of Texas, from which they escaped, only after eight years, through New Mexico and Arizona to Mexico, is one of the most astonishing tales of exploration and adventure ever written. It is also maddeningly vague, even by comparison to other contemporary Spanish narratives, about directions and distances. But it also provides an enormous repository of closely observed detail, especially about the various Indian tribes they encountered— their languages, their customs and family conventions, how they hunt, fight, prepare food, and so forth. To take just one example, the diet of the Yguazes Indians is itemized as roots, requiring roasting over two days, spiders, 'the eggs of ants, worms, lizards, salamanders, snakes, and vipers that kill whom they strike . . . the dung of deer, and other things that I omit to mention.'[8]

Of course, as everyone knows who has read Howard Mumford Jones's *O Strange New World,* Europe first imagined America, then discovered it. Before Lee, Mumford Jones also made much of the fictionality of early travel accounts, especially of *De Orbe Novo* (1511 *et seq.;* also called *The Decades of the New World, or West India,* after its first English translation) by the Italian historian to the Spanish court, Peter Martyr of Anghiera. The *Decades* include accounts of explorations by Columbus, de Gama, Cortez, Magellan, Vespucci and others as told to an author who had never been to the lands he was describing. The result is a certain sprinkling of giants, harpies and sea serpents more reminiscent of the medieval *Mandeville's Travels* than of a genuine report of discovery. Also, the American Indians are recuperated within various European types from the classical golden age to the Biblical Paradise, or else described as devils incarnate.[9] Even so, the *Decades* contain much patient description of the physical details of the Indians' appearance, their language and their habits. Occasionally, the unfamiliar was rendered with what seems now a creditable degree of accuracy:

The first time I saw them, I took them for Milanese turnips or huge mushrooms. . . . Their skin is tougher than mushrooms or turnips, and is earth-coloured, while the inside is quite white. . . . When raw, they taste like green chestnuts, but are a little sweeter. (*The Second Decade,* bk IX)[10]

That is a European's first description of the potato. And the following beast is not as fabulous as it sounds:

An extraordinary animal inhabits these trees, of which the muzzle is that of a fox, while the tail resembles that of a marmoset, and the ears those of a bat. Its hands are like a man's, and its feet like those of an ape. This beast carries its young wherever it goes in a sort of exterior pouch, or large bag. (*The First Decade,* bk IX)[11]

Any American would recognize it instantly as a possum.

Texts of this kind, that mix fiction and fact, in which the unfamiliar is sometimes subsumed under European types and at others described in its most minute physical particulars, present a formidable difficulty to the modern reader. The solution of the problem has been to ignore one or the other mode, or to posit a corrupt text, or to insinuate, on the part of the author, a cowardly accommodation to metropolitan taste. The difficulty is especially acute when the conflict seems part of the author's final intention, if not his subject, as in Flint, Hall, Frémont and most of the forty-niners.

In Frémont's case the debate between the picturesque and the scientific has been explained commonly as a collaboration between the rough explorer and his cultivated wife. The most extreme statement of this proposition, in Clive Bush's otherwise excellent book, *The Dream of Reason* (1977), promotes Jessie to the statue of ghostwriter and reduces the explorer to little more than the stooge of his father in law's territorial ambitions: 'The first two expeditions, worked up in sentimental prose on the model of Irving's *Adventures of Captain Bonneville* (1837) by his wife Jesse [*sic*], was put on sale to the public at the father's expense. Benton was the mid-western mouthpiece of Manifest Destiny.'[12]

Frémont's reports form an irresistible type of the perennial critique. Given a text fissured between romantic and realistic expressions of its material, how better to explain it than as the work of two opposing personalities; the one 'western,' male and active, the other 'eastern,' female and passive? But the truth is, as usual, less schematic. Like it or not, we are left with the conflicting styles of western writing – in Frémont, in Bryant, Hall, in most of the forty-niners, even in the early work of Mark Twain – and no theory in which the East is posed as having nobbled the West will explain the fact away. Nor should it be excused. It was a telling symptom of concern about how best to transcribe the West, to convey it to the East. And insofar as that process of transcription involved the act of inscription – insofar, that is, that these writers were imposing their culture upon the nature they found around them – their struggle to find the appropriate style was another version of the dialectic within the holistic pastoral and picturesque typologies of Irving and Taylor.

Yet 'symptom' is too weak a defense. I would like to argue that Flint, Hall and the other writers in this tradition were taking risks with their prose beyond anything attempted by Irving and Taylor. They were trying to deal with a fear that gathered strength as the century progressed, that the West would disappear almost before it could be experienced and described. Irving sensed this too (according to his letter to his brother, it was his reason for making the journey) but the feeling does not impinge on his narrative style. The polymodal discourse, on the other hand, embraces this dilemma, becomes part of its expression. For the search in Flint and Hall for a style appropriate to the West is posed as the question whether the strength of the region lies in the ungoverned profusion of its nature or its susceptibility to culture, now to be imagined but soon to be established in fact. Indeed the prophecy became reality almost as it was uttered. This is why Flint, for all his hopes for the future of western settlement and the conversion of the Indians, could praise the 'magnificent forests' lining the Ohio river because 'the axe has not yet despoiled' them (*Recollections*, 23), and why, in the very midst of his millennial projections of their coming agricultural prosperity, he could speak of the plains being 'vexed' with the plow (*Recollections*, 91). Hall, too, saw and rejoiced that 'All is new. The fertile soil abounds in vegetation. The forest is bright, and rich, and luxurient, as it came from the hands of the Creator' even as he boasted that 'The hundred rivers . . . fill the mind with the visions of the future wealth and greatness of the lands through which they roll' (*Sketches*, 15).

For the transcontinental travelers the sites that most prompted the double style were certainly not about to be overtaken by the march of civilization. Chimney Rock and the Great Salt Desert have yet to be much vexed by the plow, and seem safe for a few years yet. But they too were threatened, or curiously insubstantial; the one was widely (though wrongly) assumed to be wearing away, and was already groaning under a load of description (Independence Rock had been not only over-described but literally inscribed to the point where it became difficult to fit another name onto its bald top after 1850); both areas gave rise to mirages of different kinds. That is why Dr Edward Tompkins (H.FAC 222) described the formations around Chimney Rock as 'the ruins of some of the loftiest and most magnificent pallaces that imagination of man can reach in its most extravagant conceptions' and also as 'an eminence of hard clay and pebbles . . . about 260 feet high and perhaps 300 feet across its base'; because, as he also wrote, 'nature has made such a mockery of the works of art.' 'Nature's mockery' is also why Bryant had to redescribe the 'beautiful villas,' 'edifices,' 'gardens, shaded walks, parks and stately avenues' and other illusions of long-established (indeed, European) cultivation seen in the cruel mirage on the Salt

Desert, as 'a hard crust of saline and alkaline substances combined, from one-fourth to one-half of an inch in thickness, beneath which is a stratum of damp whitish sand and clay intermingled' (*What I Saw*, 174–5).

Nature 'mocked' art; art threatened nature with the plow or the fanciful prose description. Either way, the one spoiled the other, rendered it insubstantial or made it mundane. Why should this produce the double style? Or rather, why should the double style emerge as a method of dealing with the problem? The simple answer is the old principle of rhetoric, that any repetition calls attention to the thing being repeated. By doubling itself, style becomes stylish. The narrative becomes opaque, instead of a transparency through which the reader discerns a substantial subject matter. As the 'matter' dissolves, the manner becomes its own subject, as of course it should in any meditation on 'manners' in nature.

Now since this process of the thickening narrative surface is one of the standard definitions of modernism (appearing, for example, not only in the *nouveau roman* but also in the tendency of the post-impressionists and cubists to abandon perspective and to 'foreground' interest in the painting's surface), it is worth recalling that some literary critics have placed the birth of the modern novel in America at about the middle of the nineteenth century. Frank Kermode, for example, has written of Hawthorne's 'deliberate hesitations,' and 'the manner in which he sought to invent a modern book, mimetic only in the most unstable way, aware of itself, pondering its relation to the past and also the future.'[13]

It is not just Hawthorne's characters who are ambivalent – that is the case with most good novelists – but his narratives. Is Pearl a child of the devil or the natural result of her upbringing as the daughter of a woman cast out from the only society available to her? Do the Pyncheon men die of Maule's curse or of a hereditary circulatory weakness about which Maule knew from the start? This ambivalence does not lie buried, waiting to be mined by clever literary critics; the fussy narrative positively insists on it. When Hester Prynne leaves the house of Governor Bellingham, having been allowed to keep her child, she either meets or does not meet an old woman who may be a witch or just the Governor's 'bitter-tempered sister.' The older woman asks the younger to a coven that night in the woods, and Hester answers, ' "Had they taken her

175

from me, I would willingly have gone with thee into the forest, and signed my name in the Black Man's book too, and that with mine own blood!" ' This is how the chapter ends:

> But here — if we suppose this interview betwixt Mistress Hibbins and Hester Prynne to be authentic, and not a parable — was already an illustration of the young minister's argument against sundering the relation of a fallen mother to the offspring of her frailty. Even thus early had the child saved her from Satan's snare.

The reader is forever being invited to respond either superstitiously or rationally; to scan the text as gothic romance or modern psychological novel, fable or 'authentic' fact.

The Scarlet Letter arrived at mid-century, exactly; *The House of the Seven Gables* came out a year later, the same year as the appearance of *Moby Dick.* Three years after that, in 1854, *Walden* was published, and finally, in 1857, *The Confidence Man.* Edwin Fussell includes Hawthorne, Melville and Thoreau in his book *Frontier: American Literature and the American West* (1965) because they were not only interested in the West but wrote novels, stories and other narratives exploring various borderlines between civilization and the wilderness. It might be added that, as three authors anxious to answer Emerson's call, in 'The American Scholar' (1837), for a national literature, they felt themselves on the frontier of American writing itself, laying out the first plots of an authentic American discourse. Perhaps that is why in all five of the works mentioned above the narrative hesitates between the fantastic and the documentary, mixing the romantic and the realistic in the manner so objectionable to the perennial critics of western writing.

The difference between these authors and most of the forty-niners is one of degrees of consciousness in the deployment of narrative tactics. One has to look only at the first two chapters of *The Confidence Man,* with their insistence on sign-painting and interpretation, their images of cream-laid paper and escritoires, and a fine pastiche of the argument from profusion* to grasp that, for Melville, the problem of inscribing what he calls (in the last paragraph

---

* The convincing suggestion that the 'man in cream colors' (the first avatar of the confidence man and the first inscriber of signs in the story), together with the metaphor of the river boat's 'confidential passages' as 'secret drawers in an escritoire,' amount to a reference to the materials of writing, I owe to my colleague, David Daniell; for Melville's instance of the positive catalogue, see below, pp. 218–19.

of chapter II) 'the dashing and all-fusing spirit of the West' is being mediated consciously.

Walden is particularly instructive in the context of the works of western travel and exploration we have been studying. Though assuredly not in the West, being only a mile or two from the literary fecundity of Concord, Massachusetts, in which Emerson and Hawthorne also lived, Walden Pond provided Thoreau, as he said in *Walden,* with his 'tonic of wildness.' It was a kind of laboratory version of the West, like the setting of the traditional pastoral romance, and his sojourn there a recreation, in experimental conditions, of western discovery. (But then so was the forty-niners' journey, less self-consciously.) Fussell points out that Thoreau thought one had to abjure the actual West for the 'essential' one, and he quotes Thoreau's journal entry to the effect that, 'If I should travel to the prairies, I should much less understand them, and my past life would serve me but ill to describe them. Many a weed here stands for more of life to me than the big trees of California would if I would go there.'[14]

The text of *Walden* shuffles together a good deal of close observation of nature, rendered often in figures and scientific terminology, and the occasional flight of fancy. The combination is reminiscent of Melville in his more playful mood, but it has something in common, too, with Frémont, Bryant and the forty-niners:

There have been many stories told about the bottom, or rather no bottom, of [Walden] pond, which certainly had no foundation for themselves. It is remarkable how long men will believe in the bottomlessness of a pond without taking the trouble to sound it. . . . Many have believed that Walden reached quite through to the other side of the globe. Some who have lain flat on the ice for a long time, looking down through the illusive medium, perchance with watery eyes into the bargain, and driven to hasty conclusions by the fear of catching cold in their breasts, have seen vast holes 'into which a load of hay might be driven,' if there were anyone to drive it, the undoubted source of the Styx and entrance to the Infernal Regions from these parts.

Just as his readers are getting a bit weary of this strenuous demonstration of men's 'vain attempt to fathom their truly immeasurable capacity for marvellousness,' Thoreau breaks off to assure them that:

Walden has a reasonably tight bottom at a not unreasonable, though at an unusual, depth. I fathomed it easily with a cod-line and a stone weighing about a pound and a half, and could tell accurately when the stone left the bottom, by having to pull so much harder before the water got underneath to help me. The greatest depth was exactly one hundred and two feet; to which may be added the five feet which it has risen since, making one hundred and seven.

The more transparent the subject, the more opaque the narrative. The mystery of Walden's depths tempts Thoreau's surface to draw attention, chiefly, to itself. Matter permeates manner, and the bottom of the pond becomes the 'bottom' of his argument. Only a few pages further on, he describes a mysterious harvest:

In the winter of '46–7 there came a hundred men of Hyperborean extraction swoop down on to our pond one morning, with many carloads of ungainly-looking farming tools, – sleds, plows, drill-barrows, turf-knives, spades, saws, rakes, and each man was armed with a double-pointed pike-staff, such as is not described in the New-England Farmer or the Cultivator. . . . They went to work at once, plowing, harrowing, rolling, furrowing, in admirable order . . . but when I was looking sharp to see what kind of seed they dropped into the furrow, a gang of fellows by my side began to hook up the virgin mould itself, with a peculiar jerk, clean down to the sand, or rather the water . . . and haul it away on sleds, and then I guessed that they must be cutting peat in a bog.

What were they actually doing? 'To speak literally, a hundred Irishmen, with Yankee overseers, came from Cambridge every day to get out the ice. They divided it into cakes by methods too well known to require description. . . . They told me that in a good day they could get out a thousand tons . . .' Ice! Surely the least substantial of New England's exports to the gullible South, surpassing even the notorious wooden nutmeg for Yankee cunning, yet in such demand as to require all this effort to get it off the pond. The mysteries of modern commerce, the apparently pointless employment of men and machines interrupting the peace of Walden, sting the author to a defensive reaction. He fights back with words, inventing an outrageous fiction to match the absurdity of the trade. His shimmering figures mime the transience of the commodity, but the conflict between fancy and fact also dramatizes the threat to Walden of technology itself, or what Leo Marx would call the machine in the garden, symbolized by the railroad at the foot of Walden Pond. It is not just the ice that is melting and fragile, but the pastoral setting of Walden, and the pastoral experiment of *Walden* itself.

The question needs to be asked whether this contest in Thoreau and Hawthorne between the fanciful and the scientific, or between the gothic romance and documentary fact, is a genuine dialectic, resolving itself in a synthesis, or merely an endless, undamped oscillation between one mode and the other. For an answer one has only to turn to the chapter called 'Spring' that concludes Thoreau's narrative of his stay at Walden, particularly the remarkable passage about the effect of the heat on the railway cutting. In the new season, the bare sand that marked the rectilinear progress of the hateful railway's interruption, becomes alive; the 'sand begins to flow down the slopes like lava,' taking the form of 'sappy leaves or vines, making heaps of pulpy sprays a foot or more in depth, and resembling . . . the laciniated, lobed, and imbricated thalluses of some lichens; or . . . coral, of leopard's paws or birds' feet, [or] brains or lungs or bowels, and excrements of all kinds.' 'What makes this sand foliage remarkable' (he continues):

is its springing into existence thus suddenly. When I see on the one side the inert bank, – for the sun acts on one side first, – and on the other this luxuriant foliage, the creation of an hour, I am affected as if in a peculiar sense I stood in the laboratory of the Artist who made the world and me, – had come to where he was still at work, sporting on this bank, and with excess of energy strewing his fresh designs about. I feel as if I were nearer to the vitals of the globe, for this sandy overflow is something such a foliaceous mass as the vitals of the animal body. You find thus in the very sands an anticipation of the vegetable leaf.

And so the discourse moves, starting from the language of closely observed nature, through the precise nomenclature of botany, zoology into etymology '(λείβω, *labor, lapsus,* to flow, to slip downwards, a lapsing; λοβός, *globus,* lobe, globe; also lap, flap, and many other words).' It moves into typology too, of course, since the roots of this habit of thought run down through strata of American metaphor like Jonathan Edwards's *Images or Types of Divine Things* to the renaissance doctrine of signatures. And it arrives finally at a self-conscious figuration that renews his perceptions as the spring does the sand, and (paradoxically) the railway does Walden Pond. No one has written so well of this part of *Walden* as Leo Marx:

Thoreau's study of the melting bank is a figurative restoration of the form and unity severed by the mechanized forces of history. Out of the ugly 'cut' in the landscape he fashions an image of a new beginning. Order, form, and meaning are restored, but it is a blatantly, unequivocally figurative restoration. The whole force of the passage arises from its extravagantly metaphoric, poetic, literary character.[15]

Exactly. Nature and technology are synthesized in the figure. And the same process occurs in Hawthorne. It might be argued that the confrontation of superstition with enlightened, progressive, 'psychological' insight would admit of no synthesis. What modern reader, invited to consider Mistress Hibbins either a witch or a lonely, embittered old woman, would choose the former alternative? Yet the last sentence of that chapter reads, 'Even thus early had the child saved her from Satan's snare,' as though the voice of the narrator had settled, finally, on the fabulistic reading. It has not of course — or rather, it now embraces both the rational and the superstitious. After the 'modern' interpretation, 'Satan's snare' can be no more (and no less) than a figure of speech, a measurement of the distance between Hawthorne's contemporary readers and their credulous forebears, yet at the same time a modern insight into the past. In *The House of the Seven Gables* Holgrave is the only character to speak, or write ($\gamma\rho\acute{\alpha}\phi\epsilon\iota\nu$), the whole ($\acute{o}\lambda o\nu$) truth of the Pyncheon's mysterious history. He is not just a daguerreotypist, proficient in the modern technology of superficial delineation, but also a mesmerical seer, capable of recalling hidden truths obscured by false appearances laid down over six generations of Pyncheons. He creates portraits out of light that reveal the dark family history lying behind their subjects. So the physical cause of the Pyncheon family deaths is a hereditary disorder, but the moral cause is Maule's curse. Both explanations are necessary (the latter to uncover obligations hidden too long by the family); neither will stand on its own.

It is in this context of narrative experiment in the prose of major American writers at mid-century that the discourse of western travel must be set, and the odd irony is that it was, for the most part, the work of the least professional — certainly the least proficient — writers in the West that most resembled the writing now taken to be at the classical core of the American canon. The fact is easily explained by the reflection that the one group were self-consciously imitating certain problems of writing, while the other were actually having those problems. But that answer would not serve unless the problems themselves were similar; that is, unless the challenge of writing about the American West was not something like that of writing in and about America as a whole. And of course it was — to the extent that the hopes for a distinctive native literature were transferred to the West as soon as they had been disappointed in the

East. The void of the wilderness was a physical model of the thinness of American cultural deposits so lamented by would-be novelists of the contemporary social scene. And the problem of inscribing on the wilderness plots that were not just copies of the earlier formulae once imposed on the landscape of Europe and the East — the search for forms that respected the natural materials and lineaments of the country without burying it under the mechanism of cliché — this was the very preoccupation of Hawthorne, Melville, Thoreau and Whitman, all of whom were trying to answer Emerson's call for a prose truly native to the American soil.

But if the western travelers provide an insight into the concerns and procedures of these great writers, the same can be said of the other way round. Thoreau concluded his disputation of styles with a discourse drawn from various branches of scientific learning. He did this not to describe what was literally happening on the railway bank, but as a way of expressing the accidental congruity of forms in nature — between lobes of sand and lobes of vegetation, between two similar kinds of motion, two related words, or whatever. His language of science, in other words, is not functional but — in the best sense — rhetorical, an outrageous figure. Thus in metaphor at least, if only there, technology is turned back on itself; the destroyer of the garden is pressed into service as its preserver, perhaps even its restorer.

Now exactly the same thing happens in the debate between the fanciful picturesque and the scientific modes in Hall, Flint, Frémont and the forty-niners. The retreat from the one leads to the adoption of the other, as a rhetoric for the argument from profusion, a way of cataloguing the rich material of the West in a form instantly recognizable and acceptable to the eastern reader. For many the scientific style was the only one they could employ with confidence; so it became, in turn, the basis of a new figure. In Frémont's second *Report* the scientific mode takes over the business of objective landscape description, bringing to the task a vocabulary immensely more powerful than the jargon of the picturesque in its ability to present a verbal diagram:

We continued to travel along to the river, the stream being interspersed with many sand bars (it being the season of low water) and with many islands, and an apparently good navigation. Small willows were the only wood; rock and sand the prominent geological feature. The rock of this section is a very compact and tough basalt, occurring in strata which have the appearance of being broken into fragments, assuming the form of columnar hills, and appearing always in escarpments, with the broken fragments strewed at the base and over the adjoining country. (*Report*, 557)

It is hard to imagine how the visible surroundings, whether 'scene' or geographical 'feature,' could be more precisely rendered. Yet Frémont's passages of scientific description are not cold and barren in the second *Report*. They have a lively rhythm, and can accommodate the ordinary details of everyday anecdote:

May 1 [1844]. – The air is rough, and overcoats pleasant. The sky is blue, and the day bright. Our road was over a plain, towards the foot of the mountain; *zygophyllum Californicum,* now in bloom with a small yellow flower, is characteristic of the country; and *cacti* were very abundant, and in rich fresh bloom which wonderfully ornaments this poor country. (*Report*, 685)

Here the language of botanical description and of human response to the country do not lie frozen, side by side in mutual embarrassment, but form a confident, integrated discourse in which each mode allows the other to do the work it can do best. Whatever Frémont contributed in the history of American geography, whether or not his many specimens and tables really advanced the frontiers of knowledge, his achievement in his *Report* was the gradual development of a style appropriate to the uninhabited wilderness he so wanted to celebrate.

Some of the forty-niners, too, achieved something of this synthesis of subjective and objective analysis. Ezra Bourne went West by pack mule in 1850, so by the 4th of July he was already at the hot springs on the Bear river. His account draws on scientific terminology where it is useful, but does not exclude his joy at the natural curiosities he encountered:

Saw many natural curiosities; passed two extinct volcanoes, their craters were quite visible, lava streams around, large fissures in the rocks which we looked down, but too deep for eye to penetrate. I dropped some fragments of rock into one and could hear the rumbling grow fainter and fainter until it was lost. The soda springs which we came upon issued from a large basin and kept up a continuous effervescence caused by escaping gas. This water tasted like soda, very pleasant taste. Nearby we saw what travelers called Steamboat Spring. Coming from a rock out in the channel of Bear Creek every few minutes it threw up water and spray several feet high, making a puffing noise like the engine of a steamboat. We cooked noon dinner near these springs and celebrated the Fourth by drinking some brandy. (B.C-F 142)

At its best the vocabulary of science extended the writer's range of expression of the facts of his experience. In the passage from Bourne the technical language sets up a framework of objective natural process within which his vernacular 'experiments' (tasting the water, throwing stones down the fissures in the rock) are set off as delighted, childlike reactions. The brief account all but admits to his human frailty in the strange environment of the West, but it does not shrink from the perception, or complain of it. Joseph Wood achieves something of the same effect from the tension between the two modes of description in a passage describing the area between the Humboldt Sink and the Truckee river:

The sun was excessively hot & in many places the roads were extremely rocky & sandy In some places however they ran over the dry bed of the sink & were hard and good. The ground in these places was covered with a saline encrustation which reminded me of walking in a stubble field where a thin sheet of snow had been encrusted over (H.HM 318; August 22, 1849)

Here the vernacular is not afraid to lie down with the technical; indeed the contrast between the two accentuates the natural homeliness of his metaphor, admitting the subjectivity of the individual perception, while leaving the technical language to enrich and clarify the thing encountered.

So if in many of the forty-niners' journals — and especially when it was first employed — the language of science was a kind of defensive jargon, it could come, in time, and with practice, to approximate the strength of Frémont's second *Report* and Bryant's description of the Utah desert. For finally it does not matter if the forty-niners, either, were 'real' scientists 'really' engaged in original exploration, if they could use scientific language to embrace the strange facts of their existence, to widen the range and increase the precision of their narratives while allowing the human response its place in the account. After all, the odd topography, even if it had been surveyed, still had to be described in its quiddity for the benefit of the stay-at-homes. What else, finally, was the journal for?

The most distinguished inheritor of the tradition of describing the western wilderness was John Muir, the Scottish immigrant whose articles on the California Sierra, published in *Harper's, Scribner's* and *The Century* in the 1870s and 1880s, did so much to promote the American National Parks movement. He arrived in America with his family as an eleven-year-old boy in the first year of the California Gold Rush. At the University of Wisconsin he studied botany and geology among many other courses, though, as his prose style makes clear, he was never exclusively a scientist – rather, he used scientific description for special rhetorical purposes. As Herbert Smith writes in his astute critical biography of Muir, 'To be believable, the writings of any idealist must be based on such a solid foundation of fact that the higher flights of his imagination do not shock the reader out of sympathy. Muir's scientific observations serve this purpose for his philosophic observations.'[16]

Muir's prose covers the entire range of western writing, from the most exotic to the most particular. He hated the encroachment of commerce and technology on the wilderness. Like the photographs of Ansel Adams, his landscapes had no people; or if present, the people were turned into things, as in this witty portrait, in *My First Summer in the Sierra* (1911), of a shepherd whose trousers had 'become so adhesive with the mixed fat and resin' from carrying his cooked meat in a pouch at his side and sitting on pitch pine logs,

that pine needles, thin flakes and fibres of bark, hair, mica scales, and minute grains of quartz, horneblende, etc., feathers, seed wings, moth and butterfly wings, legs and antennae of innumerable insects . . . flower petals, pollen dust and indeed bits of all plants, animals and minerals of the region adhere to them and are safely imbedded, so that though far from being a naturalist he collects fragmentary specimens of everything and becomes richer than he knows. . . . Man is a microcosm, at least our shepherd is, or rather his trousers.[17]

Perhaps the shepherd is described in such detail because he is the parodic antimasque to Muir himself. He is less than human because he attracts all these fragments of nature without knowing or caring about them, whereas Muir, though little more a naturalist than the shepherd, used every minute particular he found as part of the foundation of his transcendental ecstasy. As with Thoreau, Hall, Frémont and the forty-niners, Muir was not engaged in functional science so much as in the language of science, a rhetoric to provide the documentary basis for his figurative flights. As examples, one could pick any number of passages in which his joy in the natural surroundings of the West is authenticated by meticulous zoological or geological description, but the following will serve well, because it appeared in one of his earliest publications, and shows something of his mood on first arriving in California:

One magnificent storm from the northwest occurred on the 21st of March; an immense, round-browed cloud came sailing over the flowery hills in most imposing majesty, bestowing water as from a sea. The passionate rain-gush lasted only about one minute, but was nevertheless the most magnificent cataract of the sky mountains that I ever beheld. A portion of calm sky toward the Sierras was brushed with thin, white cloud-tissue, upon which the rain-torrent showed to a great height − a cloud waterfall, which, like those of Yosemite, was neither spray, rain, nor solid water. In the same year the cloudiness of January, omitting rainy days, averaged 0.32; February, 0.13; March 0.20; April, 0.10; May, 0.08. The greater portion of this cloudiness was gathered into a few days leaving the others blocks of solid, universal sunshine in every chink and pore.[18]

By the time he wrote this Muir had already had a good deal of practice in annotating the daily events and conditions of his travels through the countryside. He had not long before completed a walking tour from Indiana to Florida, on which he kept a journal noting details of plants, weather, his impressions of the changing landscape. Though he called his beloved flora 'the plant people,' his account is not without people of the real sort: 'a buxom Tenessee "gal" '; an old farmer convinced that ' "Three kingdoms, England, Ireland, and Russia [had just] declared war against the United States" '; a blacksmith in the Cumberland Mountains, who wonders whether Muir's 'botanizing' is proper work for a man in hard times.

But in California the people drop away as the prose heats up. It is not that he was not capable before this of fanciful, perhaps even sentimental, flights of emotion about nature. 'Oh these forest gardens of our Father! What perfection, what divinity, in their architecture! . . .Who shall read the teaching of these sylvan pages . . .' is a characteristic gush from *A Thousand-Mile Walk* (39). The difference between this and the letter from California is the constantly varying distance between the literal and the figurative. The cloud carries water not only as from a sea, but actually from the Pacific Ocean. The rain may literally 'gush,' though only figuratively passionately. The periphrasis of 'sky−mountains' and 'cloud waterfall' expresses aptly his belief in the interpenetration of the elements of nature, but what keeps the figure from the coyness of 'plant people' is his instance in which all these things may literally become indistinguishable — a mountain waterfall becoming cloud as it drops. The statistics for 'cloudiness' are absolutely right, and in the right place; they carry the motion further toward the factual, authenticating the final figure for sunshine, itself marvellously mixing the 'solid' and the 'universal.'

II THE POEM OF FACT

True 'western realism,' then, was documentary realism. Yet it seldom functioned as documentary. The style was usually copied from another text, and whether it took the form of *réportage,* statistics or scientific description, it rarely added to the store of human knowledge to which it appealed. And it was almost always an alternative statement to a fanciful description of the same phenomenon borrowed from the stereotypes of romance fiction, the picturesque or popular journalism. Whereas in the realistic novel the accuracy of social and 'period' observation bleeds into the fiction and makes it appear a relation of historical events, in western travel writing the two modes are posed as antitheses. They are as separate from one another as the scholarly footnotes in Cooper's *Last of the Mohicans* are from the romance narrative going on above them,* or as the meticulous accuracy of historical costume and setting from the melodrama in a film by James Cruze or John Ford. The documentary is there to ballast the flights of fancy, but in such a way as to make the reader or audience aware of the tension between the two modes. The documentary is both real in itself and a figure of the urgency of the real in a particular moment in history.

In other words, the fact became a fiction in its turn. Or as Wallace Stevens would say, in one of his more famous *Adagia:* 'The exquisite environment of fact. The final poem will be the poem of fact in the language of fact. But it will be the poem of fact not realized before.' This projection for poetry (which means more than the category 'poetry' on a library shelf) is strikingly like Emerson's prediction that 'novels will give way, by and by, to diaries and autobiographies; — captivating books, if only a man knew how to choose among what he calls his experiences that which is really his

---

* The first three words of Cooper's *The Prairie,* beginning the short scientific and historical introduction to that work, are 'The geological formation. . .' Chapter 1 of the narrative proper commences with an epigraph from *As You Like It.*

experience, and how to record truth truly!' The right way to read both pronouncements is to attend not only to their futurity and finality, but to their qualifications as well. Clearly they are talking not about any old fact or experience, but an event which, however common, is made numinous by its approximation to a widely held expectation. This is the language of millennial projection, of the hidden truth emerging at the last days from all the rubbish of accumulated tradition that surrounds it; of the latter-day fact that fulfills obscure prophecies, restores the decadent culture to its primitive values and makes sense of the contemporary moment. It is in this context that the documentary 'facts' of western writing should be read, and against this set of criteria judged as to whether they met or did not meet, Emerson's aspirations for a native American literature.

A sense of the apocalypse is, after all, a common (though not exclusively) American feeling in times of stress. The New England Puritans responded first to the unplotted wilderness with a strenuous assertion of formulae they had left behind. Anne Bradstreet, whose 'heart rose' in dismay, as she wrote in her relation to her children, at the 'new world and new manners,' defied the void with long quaternions ('The Four Elements,' 'The Four Humours,' 'The Four Ages,' 'The Four Seasons' and 'The Four Monarchies') written in the style of Ralegh and Sylvester's Du Bartas, which asserted the cosmological, physiological and historical structures of renaissance Europe. But this recourse came to seem as absurd in seventeenth-century New England as visions of gardens and 'columned edifices' in the Utah desert. The Puritans' second response, not only to their own anxiety but to the scepticism of the metropolis, was the evergreen argument of the provincial. You may have the institutions, the cathedrals, the monuments and other testimonies to a secure culture, but we have the portable household gods (in the Puritans' case the Word) on which all those artifacts are based. We have stolen the kernel and left you, for all your boasting, with an empty husk. We have reformed your culture in the last days and God will favor our beginnings. This essentially millennial claim coincides with the American Puritans' fascination with typology (and corresponding suspicion of metaphor); explains, for example, why Cotton Mather began the *Magnalia Christi Americana,* his great history of the Massachusetts Bay settlement written at a time of particular danger for the colony, with an almost inescapable allusion to the great Latin type of resettlement and renewal, the *Aeneid:* 'I write of the wonders of the Christian religion, flying from the depravations of Europe to the American strand.'* 'The first age was a golden one,' Mather continues; 'to return unto that will make a man a protestant, and I may add, a Puritan. 'Tis possible that our Lord Jesus carried some thousands of reformers into the retirements of an American desert on purpose that . . . he might there, to them first, and then by them, give a specimen of many good things which he would have his churches elsewhere aspire and arise unto.'

' 'Tis possible,' but only possible. For what if New England were to be destroyed by the Indians, or allowed to wither by an unfriendly English establishment, newly crowned after the interregnum? 'But whether New England may live anywhere else or no, it must live in our history!,' wrote Mather only a few lines further on. I wonder if the power of the word has ever, before or since, been so outrageously asserted. He, at any rate, must have doubted the efficacy of this rather rarified New England, for he buttressed the *Magnalia* with statistics, tables, verbatim reports of trials and sermons, and other documentary testimony to the reality and substantiality of Massachusetts life. He also began to send back to London 'specimen[s]† of many good things' existing more than just in the realm of ideas. 'I am collecting some Curiosities, to transmitt unto the Secretary of the *Royal Society* [of which he had had just been made a fellow] by which I hope to make some valuable Accession unto their Treasures,' he wrote in his diary in Dec. & November, 1713. 'But I will use my most exquisite Contrivance, that [full] Testimonies to the Glories of my Saviour may accompany them.'[19]

And so he did. His collected thoughts on American natural philosophy, *The Christian Philosopher; a Collection of the Best Discoveries in Nature, with Religious Improvements* (1721), are close observations of physical events written in the most advanced scientific prose of the day, the plain style of the Royal Society; but for the purpose,

---

* cf. *Aeneid* I, 1–3: 'Arma virumque cano, Troiae qui primus ab oris Italiam fato profugiis Laviniaque venit litora. . .'; 'I sing of arms and the man who first came to Italy and the Lavinian shores, exiled by fate from the coasts of Troy. . .'

† Of course the most likely meaning of Mather's 'specimen' is 'example,' but the OED gives as its primary (and earliest) definition, 'a means of discovering or finding out; an experiment.' The word was used this way as early as 1602.

even in those days not normally associated with scientific description, of documenting supernatural events. If the two polarities of fact and fancy (surely perceived as such, even by the author) fail to come together in this book, there is no doubt that Mather hit upon the argument from profusion, the positive catalogue, as a justification for his newly settled frontier, just as Flint and Hall did 125 years later; that over eighty years before Jefferson (let alone Flint, Hall, Frémont and the forty-niners) he discovered that scientific description offered an unassailable lingua franca through which he could communicate to sceptical metropolitans the experiences of the inexplicable wilderness; and finally that he might try to bring threatening science to the aid of what it threatened, even if, unlike Thoreau and Muir, he would not wholly effect the synthesis.

I believe that what caused such discourses to be written was the millennial conviction that there were very old truths about the environment, or about American society within its environment, that had been overlaid by European conventions and needed to be brought out by a plain, simple statement of what was 'really' there. The new language of science could form one of several modes of treating this old truth, and hence of validating the facts on which the new society sought to base itself. This impulse explains, perhaps, why the apocalyptic preacher (and learned scholar) Jonathan Edwards sought to underpin his affirmation of what he saw as America's threatened native faith, Calvinism, with the latest philosophical and scientific thinking. Here is how he expressed the process of regeneration, being perfectly happy to use the literal heart as a figure of the spiritual:

In the conception of an animal and formation of the embrio, the first thing appearing is the punctum saliens or the heart, which beats as soon as it exists. And from thence the other parts gradually appear, as though they all gradually proceeded and branched forth from that beating point. This is a lively image of the manner of the formation of the new creature. The first thing is a new heart, a new sense and inclination that is a principle of new life, a principle that, however small, is active and has vigour and power, and, as it more beats and struggles, thirsts after holiness, aims at and tends to every thing that belongs to the new creature, and has within it the foundation and source of the whole. It aims at perfection, and from thence are the issues of life.[20]

Authors like Edwards and the Mathers provide a context for Emerson and Thoreau, particularly for their use of the documentary

189

and scientific 'fact not realized before' to render their sense of the American landscape as it really was, and to substantiate their optimistic predictions for its future as the basis for a native American literature. But the same can be said of Flint and Hall, even of Irving, at least as their contemporaries saw them. Reviewing Irving's *Tour,* the *North American Review* puzzled over what kind of book it was. 'It can scarcely be called a book of travels, for there is too much painting of manners, and scenery, and too little statistics; — it is not a novel, for there is no story; and it is not a romance, for it is all true.' What it was, like Flint's *Recollections,* Hall's *Notes,* Emerson's 'The Poet,' Thoreau's *Walden,* and many other such texts, was a species of foundation myth, an attempt to give America back, as Pope would say, the image of its mind. The great value of Irving's *Tour,* according to his contemporaries, was to convert even the most outlandish wilderness (the most unlikely setting for serious history and fiction, according to the old complaint) to something recognizable, even a new form of an old tradition. 'No matter how novel and uncouth the scenery, . . . it is like the village, where we were born,' said the *North American Review.* 'We thank [Mr Irving] for turning these poor barbarous *steppes* into classical land; — and joining his inspiration to that of Cooper, in breathing life and fire into a circle of imagery, which was not known before to exist, for the purposes of the imagination.' It seems a strange compliment now — indeed, it looks very like the grounds on which Irving's work has been generally condemned by modern readers. But another principle of Wallace Stevens's 'fact not realized before' is that it grows old and becomes a cliché in its turn.

A more recent moment of crisis was the decade of the 1960s, when many aesthetic and political institutions seemed on the point of disintegrating. 'The novel seems to be dissolving into its component parts: the essay, the travel book, reporting, on the one hand, and the "pure" fiction of the tale, on the other,'[21] wrote Mary McCarthy in 1960. Interestingly enough, the problem was perceived in terms for which Joseph Glover Baldwin's joke about San Francisco might stand as summary: 'Poetry is out of the question. . . . Fact has displaced fiction.' 'Our daily life becomes incredible to us,' McCarthy continues. 'I remember reading the news of Hiroshima in a little general store on Cape Cod in Massachusetts and saying to myself as I moved up to the counter, "What am I doing buying a loaf of bread?" '[22] A year later Philip Roth echoed this concern when he wrote that 'the actuality is continually outdoing our talents, and the culture tosses up figures almost daily that are the envy of any novelist.'[23] Meanwhile that other great fictive construct, the American Constitution, was not looking too well either. The executive branch of the government, together with its various agencies, had greatly exceeded its power in the tripartite scheme of checks and balances, whether in making war in Vietnam or spying on dissidents at home. Rumors abounded (widely dismissed as paranoid fantasies) of secret files and black lists, even clandestine assassinations. One of the more farfetched notions had it that a gang of robbers, not unconnected with the Mafia and the CIA, and working directly for the President, had broken into a psychiatrist's office to gather damaging personal information on a man who had leaked secrets of the Government's unconstitutional procedures in Vietnam.

The novelists responded to all this much as Mary McCarthy predicted they would. Some of them rediscovered the American fable, or what Robert Scholes, in a now-famous book on the subject published in 1967, called 'fabulation.'[24] No doubt the fabulators (Scholes's category includes Robbe-Grillet, William Golding, Iris Murdoch and Lawrence Durrell along with the Americans Vonnegut, Hawkes, Barth and Terry Southern) were reacting dialectically to a moment in the development of the novel in which traditional realism seemed to have played itself out; and at least the Americans among them, like Wister and even Howells in his Altruian romances, may have been looking for a form in which they could say things more directly than they could in the novel of contemporary manners. But what interests me is not so much the recrudescence of 'pure' fable during the 1960s, as the development of another literary phenomenon alongside it, the emergence of what has come to be called 'fact–fiction' or (to use Norman Mailer's term) 'faction.' This was a hybrid form, in which fiction and documentary were mixed problematically. Its representatives were the 'new' journalists like Tom Wolfe and Hunter Thompson, and novelists turned journalist like Truman Capote (*In Cold Blood,* 1965), and Mailer himself (*Armies of the Night* and *Miami and the Siege of Chi-*

cago, both 1968, and *Of a Fire on the Moon,* 1970), and also writers, like Vonnegut (at least in *Slaughterhouse Five*) and Thomas Pynchon, whose work would still be classified on library shelves as fiction.

In fact the perspective of the late 1970s and early 1980s has widened sufficiently to admit a significant distinction within the category of 'faction' itself. It seems clear now that the new journalists were, and still are, treating facts more conventionally than the novelists. Mailer, Capote and Wolfe were really writing the modern equivalent of the old-fashioned historical novel (*In Cold Blood* and *The Executioner's Song,* 1979, might even be classified as late revivals of the highwayman's confessions so popular in eighteenth-century England) – that is, giving hypothetical motives and characterization, and other such novelistic inventions, to events accepted by them and their readers as historically true. Pynchon and Vonnegut, on the other hand, allowed fantasy and history to encroach on one another's preserve, calling into question the attributes normally ascribed to each. A highly improbable fictional plot would be interrupted by allusions to actual events, such as the very funny tableau in *Gravity's Rainbow* when the hero Slothrop, dressed as Rocketman, catches sight of Micky Rooney at the Potsdam Conference. Or fantasy would invade history, as when the planet Tralfamadore, with its own mad plot about the end of creation, becomes involved with Vonnegut's otherwise largely verifiable account of the bombing of Dresden.

The result of this interference between two modes of narrative was not the same as the historical novel, or not reliably so. History could be enlivened by novelistic character and motive, and fiction could be authenticated by history, but the collaboration could turn out less happily. History could undermine the fictional plot, or the fable trivialize history. In Vonnegut's *The Sirens of Titan* the great (or at least large) monuments of human history are explained as bits of a coded signal from the Tralfamadorians to one of their astronauts stranded on a moon of Saturn. Through impulses from the Universal Will to Become (they move at about three times the speed of light) the Tralfamadorians have influenced the earthlings to build, first Stonehenge, then the Great Wall of China, the Golden House of the Emperor Nero, and finally the Palace of the League of Nations in Geneva. The message, as read from Titan? (1) *'Replacement part being rushed with all possible speed'*; (2) *'Be patient. We havent forgotten about you'*; (3) *'We are doing the best we can'*; and (4) *'Pack up your things and be ready to leave on short notice.'*

Or the two modes could be confused ingeniously, one told in terms of the other. *The Crying of Lot 49* poses a secret, alternative postal service, with a long history extending back into renaissance Europe, tricked out with beguiling references to real historical events hitherto given a more orthodox interpretation, and reinforced with all the apparatus of footnotes and the sceptical analysis of doubtful evidence to be found in an academic history book. The purpose of all this is to break down the generic barriers between fact and fiction. The satirical point is the suggestion that history as we know it is only one of a multiplicity of possible plots of the world in time (other planets, other plots), and usually one constructed to serve the interests of the wealthy and powerful. The aesthetic point is that novels too are a kind of history, that we need to write stories (including history, preferably a version to suit ourselves) to make sense of the world; but also that our plots are double-edged weapons: fresh orderings of reality, images of a higher truth; or paranoid fantasies, or at best clichés overlaying things as they are.

The effect on the reader is of events and stories whose actuality is ambiguous. Did a bizarre American Nazi dressed like Captain America really visit the prisoners in Dresden trying to recruit them to the German Army? Was Mickey Rooney really at Potsdam, and did he actually see Rocketman (another comic-book character caught up in history) crouching in the dark, cradling a twelve-pound bag of hash? In any case, the narrator of *Gravity's Rainbow* says he instantly suppressed all memory of anything so unlikely. Does Oedipa Maas imagine, or is she actually the victim of, an elaborate, secret, electronic assault on her integrity? Did giant industries really influence the bombing in World War II so as to obliterate their outdated plant and spare the factories manufacturing the most advanced weapons for use against their 'own' side? Are there really crocodiles in the New York sewers (to take another instance from Pynchon, this time from his first novel)? Do you remember the fad for baby crocodiles during the 1950s? What did your mother do with yours when you grew bored with it?

All these questions address themselves to the unverifiable. Who knows what secret societies or multinational corporations get up to?

193

Not even their own initiates. Who wants to go down into the sewers? Well, perhaps *someone* knows and does, but not the busy reader. These radical ambiguities are ways of foregrounding the narrative process, drawing the reader's attention to the medium, showing its interdependence on the message. But the hybrid narrative is a particularly American response to anxieties about plotting, quite unlike (for example) Robbe-Grillet's *nouveau roman,* where the events are scrambled so that *no* coherent plot can be synthesized from their particulars. In the American experimental novel (and that genre goes back at least to Hawthorne) the reader is allowed, at least formally, to choose between two versions of the story: the fantastic and the documentary.

Maybe it is only another paranoid plot that brings us back, over this circuitous route, to the 'non-fiction' of the American West. But the anxiety about plotting suffered by the travelers in the wilderness, and the narrative expedients by which they addressed those anxieties, bear a similarity to the modern hybrid novel that seems more than coincidental. And this similarity is most happily illustrated by another 'faction' of the 1960s which dealt with the confusing mixture of the documentary and romance of the West itself. When it appeared in 1964, Thomas Berger's *Little Big Man* was greeted by Orville Prescott in *The New York Times* as 'a superb historical novel about life and warfare on the plains'[25] and it became a good, popular film, starring that representative man of the decade, Dustin Hoffman. Perhaps because the book harmonized so well with contemporary fashion, it has been rather neglected lately. Robert Lee chillingly describes it as 'a satire on Westerns, told with high humor' that is ultimately 'derivative and lifeless' because it borrows so much of its lore from Parkman's *The Oregon Trail.* 'No one pretends it is literature' (Lee, 156). Well, I do, for one, and I would argue further that it is the first western novel to fulfill the prophecies, properly understood, of Emerson, Garland, and even Howells, of a future American fiction set in the Far West.

Little Big Man is reputedly the life story of the 111-year old Jack Crabb, as told to a neurasthenic antiquarian who visits him in an old people's home. That life, apparently, has intersected almost every fact-fanciful event in the history of the West. Brought up by Indians after being kidnapped as a boy from a wagon train, Crabb learns the language and culture of the Cheyenne, before being recaptured by soldiers from Fort Leavenworth and adopted by a childless couple in a small town somewhere in Missouri. From there he lights out to do some prospecting in the Colorado Gold Rush, sets up as a store keeper in Denver, gets married to a Swedish girl and starts a family. Cheated by his business partners, Crabb sets off by stage coach with his wife and son, only to be ambushed by Indians avenging Col. Chivington's massacre of the unarmed Indian village at Sand Creek, Colorado in 1864. The Indians make off with his family, and Crabb trails them with vengeance in his own eye, but to little effect. After a bout of alcoholism, he drives a wagon for contractors building the Union Pacific Railroad, then joins a punitive expedition against Indian hostiles. Here again he is captured, and finally reunited with the band of Cheyenne who adopted him as a boy. He is also 'reunited' with his wife, now the scolding squaw of a Cheyenne brave, and his half-savage son; neither recognizes him. As a result, he gives up his vendetta against their captors, and instead takes an Indian wife of his own. The very morning their first child is born, General Custer attacks and wipes out their camp on the Washita river in the campaign that would make his name. Narrowly escaping from the Battle of the Washita, and having lost his Indian wife and son, Crabb sets out to kill Custer. Disguised as a soldier, he comes within a hair's breadth of his goal, then drifts west to San Francisco and back to Kansas City, where he gambles with, and is taught to shoot by, Wild Bill Hickock, discovers his long-lost niece in a whorehouse and redeems her from her fallen state. After a spell of commercial buffalo hunting, he meets and is in turn 'buffaloed' (that is, pistol-whipped) by Wyatt Earp. Finally, still on Custer's track, he signs up as a teamster in the General's regiment on their way to the Little Big Horn, in which battle he naturally participates, and from which he is naturally rescued by his old friends, the Cheyenne. Meanwhile his sister Caroline is inscribing her own plot across the face of America, falling hopelessly in love with Walt Whitman, fighting with Calamity Jane over Wild Bill Hickock, and finally (like all the pure products of America, according to William Carlos Williams) going mad.

Thus summarized, the story line of *Little Big Man* is a comic super-plot, satirizing the abundance of improbable adventure to be found in romances of the West. It even has the framing narrative of the educated interlocutor, like *The Virginian* and contemporary books of its kind. But not only western romance is pastiched; the conventions of the local-color story and the tall tale are comically extended in Crabb's folksy narrative and his cool exposition of unlikely events. Even the non-fiction documents, the historians' sources, are represented here; for what is Crabb but the oldest 'old timer' of them all, and his story the antitype of all those 'relations' transcribed and collected by Hubert Howe Bancroft, inflated to the most incredible degree?

If *Little Big Man* is a sort of comic compendium of western writing, it also embraces all its possible tones, and both its traditional modes; that is, it is serious as well as comic, romantic as well as satirical, and documentary as well as fanciful. The unlikely tale is authenticated by a hundred details of description and event that seem convincing at the time, whether or not the reader can verify them. Sometimes these are touching insights into the effect of great events on ordinary people. A squaw escaping Custer's army along the icy Washita river stops to bind up her childrens' feet with strips of cloth torn from her own dress. After the battle of the Little Big Horn, the Indians stripping the soldiers' bodies find thousands of dollar bills, which they throw away as so much trash. Crabb sees a little Indian boy with a dollar bill folded as a saddle blanket on a toy horse made of clay. Oddly enough both these vignettes come from a history book,* but here they function as do those imaginative propositions with which historical novelists flesh out their versions of history.

Others of these documentary moments — by far the majority — gain conviction by cancelling the clichés of popular legend, as if to imply: contrary to what you may have seen in the movies, the Old West was really like this. Thus, in Kansas City Crabb goes around with his large revolver in a calf-skin holster, just like thousands of cowboy heroes in pulp fiction. When an (imagined) emergency forces him to a quick draw, he finds that the harder he pulls at the gun, the tighter it is gripped by the holster. Wild Bill Hickock puts him right: "I never," says Hickock, "have held by a holster . . . . Always carry my weapons in the waist. You have to get a tailor to make a real smooth band there, no excess stitching nor

---

* George Bird Grinnell's classic *The Fighting Cheyennes* (New York, 1915), from which Berger seems to have taken much of his Indian lore and most of the details of their battles with the Army. The relevant passages are in Grinnell, pp. 292 and 342.

suspender buttons, and of course your vest ought to be cut so its points don't interfere" (285). 'I learned an awful lot that afternoon,' adds Crabb. 'I had thought I was pretty handy with a gun before reaching K.C., but I was awful raw alongside Wild Bill Hickock' (286). Another revelation is that the Indians, for all their savagery, were not sexually promiscuous. 'That probably comes as a surprise,' says Crabb; 'you may think an Indian goes at it like a jackrabbit, but not the Cheyenne with their own women unless they are married to them, and since the married men always swear off it before going to war, and we were most of the time fighting, the Cheyenne were pretty hard up for tail at any given time' (76). The civilized whites, on the other hand, were relatively careless of their sexual alignments: 'It's peace that is the horny time. Most of them fat merchants in that town was real sex fiends compared to an Indian brave. And them other white boys my age was already slipping into brothels or laying the maids' (113).

By engaging in dialogue with other narratives, moments of this kind attract attention not only to themselves and to the great events they illustrate, but to the multiple possibilities of narrative itself. As in other experimental novels, the medium is no longer a reliable transparency through which 'reality' can be studied, but a reality of its own, with its own history, its own life and its own limitations. And the narrative is thickened further when it begins to play games even with that most unimpeachable of plots, the history of the Old West based on scholarly research sifted through experimental analysis and reinforced by references to actual documents of the period. For there are bound to be places where Jack Crabb's story comes adrift from the story as we think we have it, on good authority, from the academic historians. 'I can certify,' writes the antiquarian in his epilogue, 'that whenever Mr Crabb has given precise dates, places, and names, I have gone to the available references and found him frighteningly accurate – when he can be checked at all.' 'But one name is missing from every index, every roster, every dossier. In my library of three thousand volumes on the Old West, in the hundreds of clippings, letters, magazines, you will search in vain, as I have, for the most fleeting reference to one man . . . I refer, of course, to *Jack Crabb*' (440).

Crabb himself offers credible explanations for his invisibility in the official records. One of them is rather like the reason Mickey

Rooney did not see Slothrop. Shortly before the Battle of the Little Big Horn, Crabb visits Custer at his headquarters trying to sign on as a guide. He says he knows the ways and language of the Cheyenne and might be of some help. Custer dismisses him airily with the reminder that he wiped out all the Cheyenne that amounted to anything down on the Washita eight years before. Crabb, remembering his earlier attempt to kill Custer in revenge for that massacre, says out loud, ' *"You bastard, I should have knifed you when I had the chance."* ' Crabb is 'plumb full of horror once that expression is out,' but Custer either ignores, or does not hear him. Instead, he invites him to sign on as a herder. ' "We need have no doubt of the outcome when even the civilians wish to serve in the van." '

> He returned to his writing, and I left the tent. Custer had not heard my comment, spoke directly to his face! As regards the outside world, he was like a stuffed bird under one of them glass bells. His own opinion sufficed to the degree that he had no equipment for detecting exterior reactions. That's the only way I can explain it.
>
> Anyhow, that's why no roster of the men present at the Battle of the Little Bighorn ever contained my name. Custer thought I was a herder; and the herders and teamsters themselves figured I was an interpreter or guide . . .   (365)

Whether Custer is sealed off from life by his own madness, or Crabb is enclosed within the bell jar of Berger's imagination, there is (almost) no doubt that the two never really met on the same plane of reality. But which plane is the more 'real' is another question. Or, if history and fiction are separate categories, that may be because we insist on putting things into categories. 'The river was just opening up from the winter and I got me a passage on a sternwheeler and rode it as far as Yankton, where I changed to another boat by the name of *Far West*. I did that so I could be at Custer's Last Stand.' 'I'm kidding,' adds Crabb hastily. 'But you know how them things look later' (349). All narratives, fictional as well as historical, are retrospective. It all depends on how you tell the story; the narrative frame you choose imposes its own rules, but you are free to choose the frame. Indeed, the narrator who frames Crabb's story says as much. 'I leave the choice in your capable hands. Jack Crabb was either the most neglected hero in the history of this country or a liar of insane proportions' (440).

Of course, it is not a real choice, any more than is the option to carry on thinking of Mistress Hibbins as a witch, once the narrative of *The Scarlet Letter* has suggested 'modern,' psychological, motives for her strange behavior. But in both books the double reading serves as a rhetorical device for widening the sympathetic and imaginative responses of the reader – that is, at least making him aware of how other people at other times thought and felt – by exploring the boundaries between superstition and reason and dramatizing the amazing human capacity for imposing diverse plots on the same material. For even if there can be little question, after the game is done, of Jack Crabb having really lived in history, the oscillations still resonate between versions of the Old West available to the modern reader. Crabb may be a fictional construct, but his accurate references to historical event, and his countless revelations of the truth underlying the legend, seem to give us back the image of the West as it 'really' was before the plots of romance and popular history overlaid it. But if he is making the whole thing up – that is, if the fictional Jack Crabb is also a liar – then *Little Big Man* remains a convincing expression of the power these events still hold over our imaginations more than a hundred years later.

This is by way of saying that *Little Big Man* is not simply a satire on received notions of western history. True, many old assumptions about Indians and white men are reversed: the former are sensitive, loyal, chaste and keep the letter and spirit of the treaties they make with the Government; the latter are incompetent, rapacious and invariably cheat on their part of the agreements. Moreover (and this has never been much in doubt) the Indians have a rapport with their environment which even extends to the ability to charm buffalo and see visions inaccessible to the white man's rationality, while the Americans seem frenetically bent on destroying all nature around them. Even so, Crabb's movements between white and Indian life give him a perspective on both modes of life (even his language reacts against the experience, becoming more formal among the Indians and more like Huck Finn's in town), so that the reader is never allowed to settle for long into a comfortable, fixed opinion on the comparison. When he first meets the Indians after his adopted adolescence in Missouri, Crabb notices how they stink, and reflects how difficult it is to live without regular, predictable meals. After the Indians kidnap his wife and son, Crabb meets a Cheyenne he knew as a child:

Then I looked close at the scalp he stroked, which was of the silkiest blond. For a moment I was sure it came from Olga's dear head, and reckoned he also had little Gus's fine skull-cover someplace among his filthy effects, the stinking old savage, living out his life of murder, rapine, and squalor, and I almost knifed him before I collected myself and realized the hair was honeyer than my Swedish wife's. (204)

Meanwhile the reputation of the great white heroes is not altogether demolished. Wild Bill Hickock may not, as reported, have put ten shots through the dot of an 'I' on a sign at two hundred yards, but he did get them all within the 'O' at one hundred; and from a handgun, that's good shooting. Custer may have been cruel, incompetent or mad (or all three), but Crabb is moved to admire his courage – even his style – in death. For all his personal and general resentment of Custer, Crabb 'had finally accepted the fact that he was great – and he sure was, don't let anyone tell you different, and if you don't agree, then maybe something is queer about your definition of greatness –' (413).

The greatness of *Little Big Man* lies in its fulness, its willingness to redeem even the objects of its satire, to include all our moods about the West. That is why it belongs to the kind of writing I have been trying to describe in this book, why it more accurately typifies the tradition of western prose than (say) Dee Brown's justly admired *Bury My Heart at Wounded Knee,* which presents only the Indians' side of the story, or Robert Altman's film of Arthur Kopit's *Buffalo Bill and the Indians,* so tediously smitten with the process by which the Dime Novelists romanticized the facts. Crabb's final view of Custer is not just an anxious palinode, or a 'cop out' of his own, harsh perceptions. In a book about the monotony, the violence and the low comedy of life in the American West, it is one of several attempts to explain how we should have come to believe in its heroism and its idealism. Perhaps the West really did have something of this promise; at any rate the romance had become as real as the facts.

NOTES TO THE TEXT

Introduction, pp. 1–14

1 James Fenimore Cooper, *Notions of the Americans,* 2 vols, Philadelphia, 1828, II, 108.
2 'Flint's Valley of the Mississippi,' *North American Review,* XXIII (October, 1826), 362.
3 Ralph Waldo Emerson, 'The Poe,' in *Essays; Second Series* (1844), reprinted in, e.g. Stephen Wicher, ed., *Selections from Ralph Waldo Emerson; an Organic Anthology,* Boston: Houghton Mifflin, 1957, 238.
4 Alexis de Tocqueville, *Democracy in America,* tr. Henry Reeve, ed. Phillips Bradley, 2 vols, New York: Knopf, 1945, vol. II, book i, chap. XVII, p. 80.
5 Walt Whitman, 'The Prairies and an Undeliver'd Speech,' in *Specimen Days and Collect* (1882), *The Prose Works,* I, ed. Floyd Stovall, New York: New York University Press, 1963, 208.
6 W. D. Howells, 'Mark Twain, an Inquiry' (1901), in *Criticism and Fiction,* ed. Clara Marburg Kirk and Rudolf Kirk, New York: New York University Press, 1959, 216–20.
7 Hamlin Garland, 'Provincialism,' in *Crumbling Idols* (1894), ed. Jane Johnson, Cambridge, Mass.: Harvard University Press, 1960, 16.
8 W. D. Howells, 'Mr. Garland's Books,' in *Criticism and Fiction,* 263.
9 *Ibid.* 259.
10 Owen Wister, *Owen Wister out West; his Journals and Letters,* ed. Fanny Kemble Wister, Chicago: University of Chicago Press, 1958; journal entry for June, 1891, p. 118.
11 *Democracy in America,* vol. II, book i, chap. XVII, p. 81.
12 W. H. Gilman, ed., *The Journals and Miscellaneous Notebooks of Ralph Waldo Emerson,* 13 vols, Cambridge, Mass.: Harvard University Press, 1960 *et seq.,* VII, 418–19.

Chapter 1, pp. 15–36

1 Daniel Boorstin, *The Image; or, What Happened to the American Dream,* New York: Athenaeum, 1962, 250.
2 See Christopher Hussey, *The Picturesque,* London: G. P. Putnam's Sons, 1972, 107. The British traveler Capt. Basil Hall, whose *Travels in North America in the Years 1827 and 1828* (3 vols, Edinburgh and London, 1829) was almost as widely read as Mrs Trollope's *Domestic Manners of the Americans,* used a more sophisticated device called the *camera lucida,* as his version of the Claude glass. He writes (*Travels,* III,

172): 'The Camera Lucida accomplishes both light and shade, with so much ease and certainty, that I have often wondered why it is not more used. It has always appeared to me that the fullest correct markings, as they are called, of any distant place, are far more satisfactory to look at, than the most highly finished drawing, in the composition of which, the fancy of the artist has had some share.' The device used a prism and mirrors to throw a reduced image on a surface on which the outline could be traced and the shading added.

3   Nathaniel Parker Willis, *American Scenery,* 2 vols, London: George Virtue, 1840, I, 2.

4   'Speech at the Irving Dinner,' *New York Mirror,* June 9, 1832; cited in Stanley Williams, *The Life of Washington Irving,* 2 vols, New York: Oxford University Press, 1935, II, 27n.

5   *Ibid.* II, 24.

6   Cited in Washington Irving, *A Tour on the Prairies,* ed. John Francis McDermott, Norman, Okla.: University of Oklahoma Press, 1956, xvii. In a footnote to this page, McDermott gives the provenance of the letter as follows: 'Washington City, December 18, 1832. Originally published in the London *Athenaeum* (1833), 137–38; reprinted in the New York *Commercial Advertiser,* and copied from the latter by the *Arkansas Gazette,* June 26, 1833.'

7   'A Tour on the Prairies,' *North American Review,* XLI, 88 (July, 1835), 14. Although the review is anonymous, A. B. Cushing (*Index to the North American Review,* Cambridge: John Wilson & Son, 1878, 55) gives the author as Edward Everett, sometime editor of the *North American Review* and Professor of Greek at Harvard, and (when he wrote this) U.S. Congressman for Massachusetts. He later served as the State's Governor, Minister to England and President of Harvard.

8   Wayne Franklin, *Discoverers, Explorers, Settlers; the Diligent Writers of Early America,* Chicago: University of Chicago Press, 1979, 60.

9   See Gary Wills, *Inventing America,* New York: Random House, 1978, 259–72.

10 Thomas Jefferson, *Life and Selected Writings,* ed. Adrienne Koch and William Peden, New York: Modern Library, 1944, 186.

Chapter 2, pp. 37–50

1   Allan Nevins, *Frémont – the West's Greatest Adventurer,* 2 vols, New York: Harper, I, 127.

2   Jessie Benton Frémont, MSS, cited in Nevins, *ibid.*

3   Ferol Egan, *Frémont; Explorer for a Restless Nation,* New York: Doubleday, 1977, 120.

4   See Donald Jackson and Mary Lee Spence, eds., *The Expeditions of John Charles Frémont,* 3 vols, Urbana: University of Illinois Press, 1970 *et seq.,* I, 168–9.

5   *Ibid.* I, 250n.

Chapter 3, pp. 51–83

1   House Executive Document 1, 30th Congress, 2nd Session, 51–2; collected in Robert Richmond and Robert Nordock, eds., *A Nation Moving West,* Lincoln: University of Nebraska Press, 1966, 196.

2 *A Compilation of the Messages and Papers of the Presidents,* New York: Bureau of National Literature, Inc., 1897, VI, 2486.

3 Alonzo Delano, *Alonzo Delano's California Correspondence,* ed. Irving McKee, Sacramento: Sacramento Book Collectors Club, 1952, 22.

4 See George Stewart, *The California Trail,* New York: McGraw-Hill, 1962, 232.

5 *Ibid.* 220.

6 See, for example, Ray Billington, *America's Frontier Heritage,* New York: Holt, Rinehart and Winston, 1966, 26–9.

7 See Merril Mattes, *The Great Platte River Road; the Covered Wagon Mainline via Fort Kearny to Fort Laramie* (n.p.: Nebraska State Historical Society, 1969), 378–420, for a description of Chimney Rock and a full survey of things written about it in the diaries.

8 *Ibid.* 379–80.

9 See especially his chapter in *The Image,* 'From Traveler to Tourist; the Lost Art of Travel,' pp. 77–117, which, I think, poses a false distinction, implied in the title.

Chapter 5, pp. 104–128

1 Cited in *The Shirley Letters from the California Mines,* ed. Carl Wheat, New York: Knopf, 1949, v. The editor of *The Pioneer* was Ferdinand Ewer.

2 Constance Rourke, *American Humor,* New York: Doubleday, 1931; Doubleday Anchor Books, 1953, 103–7.

3 Kevin Starr, *Americans and the California Dream,* New York: Oxford University Press, 1973, 375.

Chapter 6, pp. 129–160

1 *Mark Twain's Autobiography,* (edited and) with an introduction by Albert Bigelow Paine, 2 vols, New York: Harper & Brothers, 1924, I, 7.

2 The guide book was *Philadelphia As It Is in 1852,* by R. A. Smith, Philadelphia: Lindsay & Blakiston, 1852. See Fred Lorch, 'Mark Twain's Philadelphia Letters in the Muscatine *Journal,*' *American Literature,* XVII (1946).

3 Samuel Langhorne Clemens (SLC) to Orion Clemens, Philadelphia, 26 Oct., 1853; Webster Collection; typescript in Mark Twain Papers, Bancroft Library, University of California, Berkeley (MTP). Other parts of this letter are published in *Mark Twain's Letters (MTL),* ed. A. B. Paine, 2 vols, New York: 1917.

4 SLC to his family, New Orleans, probably February 11, 1859; Moffett Collection, MTP; previously unpublished.

5 SLC to Pamela Moffett, Carson City, October 25, 1861; Samuel C. Webster Collection, MTP; published, with omissions, in *MTL.*

6 SLC to Pamela Moffett, Esmeralda, California, August 15, 1862; published in *MTL,* I, 85; original unknown.

7 SLC to Jane Clemens and Pamela Moffett, Carson City, February 8, 1862; published, with omissions, in *MTL,* I, 63–8.

8 SLC to Pamela Moffett, August 15, 1862; *MTL,* I, 85.

9 SLC to Jane Clemens, Carson City, October 25, 1861; Webster Collection, *MTP;* previously unpublished. This letter and another now lost were probably sent by Mrs

Clemens to the Keokuk *Gate City,* and a sketch edited from both letters was published in that paper on November 20, 1861.

10 William Wright to J. M. Benjamin, Omega, Nevada, January 26, 1860; William Wright Papers, Bancroft Library, University of California, Berkeley (WWP).

11 Dan de Quille (William Wright), 'Salad Days of Mark Twain,' *San Francisco Examiner,* January 22, 1893; reprinted in Oscar Lewis, ed., *The Life and Times of the Virginia City Territorial Enterprise,* Ashland, Oregon: University of Oregon Press, 1971.

12 Keokuk *Gate City,* November 20, 1861.

13 Keokuk *Saturday Post,* 1 Nov., 1856; Keokuk *Daily Post,* 29 Nov., 1856 and 10 April, 1857. The Snodgrass Letters are reprinted as *The Adventures of Thomas Jefferson Snodgrass,* ed. Charles Honce, Chicago, 1928.

14 SLC to Jane Clemens and Pamela Moffett, San Francisco, 4 June, 1863; Moffett Collection, MTP; previously unpublished.

15 'The Pioneers' Ball,' *Virginia City Territorial Enterprise* (VCTE), possibly 19 or 21 Nov., 1865.

16 William Wright to Lou Benjamin, Virginia City, 23 Aug., 1874; WWP.

17 William Wright to Lou Benjamin, Virginia City, 29 Nov., 1874; WWP.

18 Lou Benjamin to William Wright, Cedar Falls, Iowa, 10 Dec., 1874, WWP.

19 Dan de Quille reviewed the response to the hoax in *VCTE* for 30 Aug., 1874, citing the *Daily Telegraph* for 3 Aug., 1874. See also *Comstock Bonanza,* ed. Duncan Emrich, New York, 1950, 244–9, where the original story and de Quille's later review are both reprinted in full.

20 Mark Twain, 'A Couple of Sad Experiences,' *The Galaxy,* IX (June, 1870); reprinted in *Mark Twain's Contributions to the Galaxy,* ed. Bruce McElderry, Jr, Gainsville: Scholars' Facsimiles and Reprints, 1961.

21 Sacramento *Daily Union,* 31 Oct., 1863; typescript in the Horace Grant Smith Papers, Bancroft Library, University of California, Berkeley.

22 See, for example, Henry Nash Smith and Frederick Anderson, eds., *Mark Twain of the Enterprise,* Berkeley: University of California Press, 1957, 24–30, which reprints contemporary letters relating to the controversy; also Paul Fatout, *Mark Twain in Virginia City,* Bloomington: University of Indiana Press, 1964, 196–213.

23 Mark Twain, *Roughing It,* ed. Franklin Rogers and Paul Baender, Berkeley; University of California Press, 1972, 356–9.

24 *Mark Twain's Autobiography,* I, 354–61.

25 Cited in Fatout, *Mark Twain in Virginia City,* 209.

26 Mariposa, California, *Weekly Mariposa Gazette,* 4 June, 1864.

27 'Hoity! Toity!!,' Gold Hill, Nevada, *Evening News,* 24 May, 1864; reprinted in *Mark Twain of the Enterprise,* 190.

28 SLC to Mollie Clemens, Virginia City, 20 May, 1864; reprinted in *ibid.* 190.

29 SLC to Orion Clemens, Virginia City, 25 May, 1864; MTP; reprinted in *ibid.* 201–2.

30 SLC to Jane Clemens and Pamela Moffett, Webster Collection, MTP; reprinted, with omissions, in *MTL,* I, 99–100.

31 SLC to Dan de Quille (William Wright), San Francisco, probably 15 July, 1864; WWP.

32 Henry Nash Smith, *Mark Twain; the Development of a Writer,* Cambridge: Harvard University Press, 1962.

33 SLC to Dan de Quille, Hartford, Conn., 24 March, 1875; WWP.
34 SLC to Dan de Quille, Hartford, Conn., 4 April, 1875; WWP.
35 Joseph Goodman to Dan de Quille, n.p., 16 April [1875]; WWP.

Chapter 7, pp. 161–200

1   Robert Edson Lee, *From West to East; Studies in the Literature of the American West*, Urbana: University of Illinois Press, 1966.
2   John Francis McDermott, ed., *The Western Journals of Washington Irving*, Norman: University of Oklahoma Press, 1944; cited in Lee, *From West to East*, 61–2.
3   The case against the canard is argued most convincingly in Justin Kaplan's *Mr Clemens and Mark Twain*, London: Cape, 1967 and Dennis Welland's *Mark Twain in England*, London: Chatto and Windus, 1978.
4   Henry Leavitt Ellsworth, *Washington Irving on the Prairie, or a Narrative of a Tour of the Southwest in the Year 1832*, ed. Stanley Williams and Barbara Simison, New York: American Book Co., 1937, 17; other citations here, in order of their appearance, from pp. 6 and 14.
5   Frank Norris's famous attack on the realistic novel came in his essay, 'A Plea for Romantic Fiction,' reprinted in his *The Responsibilities of the Novelist* (1903): 'Realism is minute; it is the drama of a broken teacup, the tragedy of a walk down the block, the excitement of an after noon call, the adventure of an invitation to dinner. It is the visit to my neighbor's house, a formal visit from which I may draw no conclusions.' Rider Haggard's remarks along the same lines appear in his 'About Fiction,' *Contemporary Review*, LI, 172–80 (Feb., 1887), 174.
6   Henry James, 'The New Novel,' *Times Literary Supplement*, no. 635 (10 March, 1914), 133–4, and no. 637 (2 April, 1914), 157–8; reprinted in Henry James, *Selected Literary Criticism*, ed. Morris Shapira, London: Heinemann, 1963; Harmondsworth: Penguin, 1968, 381.
7   Ellsworth, *Irving on the Prairie*, viii.
8   Alvar Nuñez Cabeca de Vaca, 'The Narrative,' in *Spanish Explorers in the Southern United States, 1528–1543*, ed. Frederick Hodge, New York: Scribner's, 1907, 65.
9   Howard Mumford Jones, *O Strange New World*, New York: Viking, 1964, 17–18.
10 Peter Martyr of Anghiera, *De Orbe Novo; the Great Decades*, tr. and ed., Francis Augustus McNutt, 2 vols, New York: Putnam, 1912, I, 263.
11 *Ibid.* I, 164.
12 Clive Bush, *The Dream of Reason*, London: Edward Arnold, 1977, 223.
13 Frank Kermode, *The Classic*, London: Faber & Faber, 1965, 111.
14 *The Journal of Henry David Thoreau*, ed. Bradford Torrey and Francis Allen, 14 vols, Boston: Houghton Mifflin, 1949, X, 190–1; cited in Edwin Fussell, *Frontier; American Literature and the American West*, Princeton: Princeton University Press, 1965, 194.
15 Leo Marx, *The Machine in the Garden*, New York: Oxford University Press, 1964, 262.
16 Herbert Smith, *John Muir*, New York: Twayne, 1965, 124. A more leisurely, ample and conventionally descriptive biography of John Muir can be found in William Frederick Badé, *Life and Letters of John Muir*, 2 vols, Boston: Houghton Mifflin, 1924.
17 John Muir, *My First Summer in the Sierra*, Boston: Houghton Mifflin, 1911, 172–3.

This book, and his *A Thousand-Mile Walk to the Gulf* (Boston: Houghton Mifflin, 1916) are a good introduction to the works of John Muir. See also the anthology, *The Wilderness World of John Muir*, edited by Edwin Way Teale (Boston: Houghton Mifflin, 1954) and Linnie Marsh Wolfe's edition of *John of the Mountains; the Unpublished Journals of John Muir* (Boston: Houghton Mifflin, 1938). William Badé has edited the published works in a series of ten volumes, of which his own *Life and Letters* forms the last two (Boston: Houghton Mifflin, 1915–24). To get an idea of Muir's vigorous advocacy of wilderness conservation, see his 'two brilliant articles' that 'turned the tide of public sentiment' in favor of the National Parks Movement (according to Badé in the *Dictionary of American Biography*, XIII, 1934, 316), 'Forest Reservation and National Parks,' *Harper's Weekly*, June 5, 1897, and 'The American Forests,' *Atlantic Monthly*, LXXX (Aug., 1897). See also Holway Jones, *John Muir and the Sierra Club; the Battle for Yosemite*, San Francisco: The Sierra Club, 1965.

18   The article, called 'Twenty Hill Hollow,' was first published in *The Overland Monthly* for July, 1872, and is described by Herbert Smith (*John Muir*, p. 53) as 'a self-conscious literary travelogue,' quite different from the personal journal Muir kept at the same time at which 'Twenty Hill Hollow' is set – that is, 1868, Muir's first year in California. The journal version can be found in *John of the Mountains*, pp. 1–33. A slightly revised version of the 'Twenty Hill Hollow' essay is published at the end of William Badé's edition of *A Thousand-Mile Walk to the Gulf* as a letter Muir wrote to Ezra Carr from the vicinity of Twenty Hill Hollow, in the Sierra foothills near the mouth of the Merced river, July, 1868. This excerpt is cited from Badé's edition, pp. 205–6.

19   Cotton Mather, *Diary*, 2 vols, New York: Frederick Ungar, 1957, II, 265–6. Mather made this entry within days after the death by measles of his second wife, their new-born twins and his beloved infant daughter, Jerusha. *The Christian Philosopher; a Collection of the best Discoveries in Nature, with Religious Improvements* has been reprinted in facsimile, edited by Josephine Piercy (Gainsville: Scholar's Facsimiles and Reprints, 1968).

20   Jonathan Edwards, *Images or Shadows of Divine Things*, ed. Perry Miller, New Haven: Yale University Press, 1948, 127.

21   Mary McCarthy, 'The Fact in Fiction,' *Partisan Review*, XXVII (Summer, 1960), 438–58, reprinted in her *On the Contrary*, New York: Farrar, Straus and Cudahay, 1961, 270.

22   *Ibid.* 267.

23   Philip Roth, 'Writing American Fiction,' *Commentary*, XXXI (March, 1961), 224; cited in John Hollowell, *Fact and Fiction; the New Journalism and the Nonfiction Novel*, Chapel Hill: University of North Caroline Press, 1977, 5.

24   Robert Scholes, *The Fabulators*, New York: Oxford University Press, 1967. Scholes deals with the recrudescence of 'pure' fable in Durrell, Vonnegut, Hawkes, Barth, Terry Southern and Iris Murdoch. Hollowell's *Fact and Fiction* is a workmanlike study of the new journalists, especially Capote, Mailer and Tom Wolfe.

     A more general study of fact–fiction, not related to America in the 1960s, is *The Literature of Fact; Selected Papers from the English Institute*, ed. Angus Fletcher, New York: Columbia University Press, 1976. The book collects papers from two sessions of the Institute held in 1974 and 1975, by Northrop Frye, Hayden White, Victor Turner, Jerome Mazzaro, David Hackett Fischer and Edward Said. On the general sense of crisis in the novel in English during the 1960s, see the title essay in David Lodge, *The Novelist at the Crossroads,* London: Routledge and Kegan Paul, 1971.

25 Orville Prescott, 'Jack Crabb, Survivor of the Little Bighorn,' *New York Times,* 9 Oct., 1964, 37.

PRIMARY TEXTS CITED AT LENGTH

This is a list of primary texts examined in detail in the body of the book. In the case of published works, my principle has been to use the best edition readily available to the reader. This means the standard scholarly text, where there is one, or the first edition where not. I have taken some pains to distinguish between printed and unprinted overland journals, even in the brief citations, because whether or not the manuscript has attracted the interest of a prospective editor tells something about the manuscript itself, and something else about the changing fashions of academic taste. I have cited printed versions where available, with two exceptions: the diaries of H. M. T. Powell and Mary Stuart Bailey. In these cases the printed versions contained errors of transcription sufficient to warrant returning to the manuscripts.

Manuscripts

Algeline Ashley (Jackson), Diary . . . crossing the plains in 1852 [from Hanesville, Ohio? to California by way of Salt Lake City]
   typescript
   (H) HM 16773
Mary Stuart Bailey, Journal of the overland trip from Ohio to Calif. [April 13 – Nov. 8, 1852]
   (H) HM 2018
Ezra Bourne, Diary of an overland journey [from Oxford, Ohio] to California in 1850
   typescript by Prue Bourne
   (B) C-F 142
Solomon Gorgas, Diary of an overland journey from St Joseph, Mo., to Placerville, Calif., by way of Ft Laramie; also return voyage to New York via the Isthmus of Panama [April 28, 1850 – April 8, 1851]
   (H) HM 651
Elijah Howell, Crossing the plains, May–Sept., 1849
   typescript of the original Ms in possession of the State Historical Society of Missouri
   (B) C-F 121

James Mason Hutchings, Diaries, May 1848–Oct. 1849 [Liverpool–New York–
New Orleans–California]
typescript by Gertrude Hutchings Mills
(B) 69/80 C

Silas Newcomb, Journal [of trip from Darien Wisconsin to] California and Oregon [by way of] St Joseph, Mo., and Salt Lake City [April 1, 1850–March
31, 1851]
photostat of original in the W. R. Coe collection, Yale University
(H) FAC 4

H. M. T. Powell [Journal and Sketchbook, 1849–52; 2 vols; vol. 1, Notes on
California; Diary, April 3, 1849–March 14, 1852, of Journey to California
via the Santa Fe Trail]
(B) C-F 115, vol. 1

Niles Searls [Diary, May 9–Oct. 1, 1849]
(B) C-F 46

D.[avid] P. Staples, Memorandum book on the journey to Calif. [April 16–
Sept. 1, 1849]
(B) C-F 165

Henry Sturdivant [Journal of a Voyage to California via the Isthmus of Panama
and return trip via Nicaragua, Dec. 9, 1849–Jan. 11, 1852]
(H) HM 261

[Dr Thomas], Journal of Dr. T, 1849
copied by George Johnson, in his [Notes, Reminiscences, etc. Chiefly Concerning Coloma, Calif. and its Inhabitants, 1849–1942]
(B) C-B 383:1

[Edward Alexander Tompkins] [Diary of an] Expedition to California [via] St.
Louis, Independence, Salt Lake, Humboldt River, Carson's Valley and Fre-
mont's south pass of the Sierra Nevada, [April 2–Sept. 20, 1850]
Facsimile copy
(H) FAC 222

Allen Varner, [Letter] to Elias Varner, Independence, Mo., April 29, 1849
Xerox copy of an original owned by the Jackson County Historical Society,
Independence, Mo.
(H) FAC 685
[8 letters] to David Varner, Independence, Mo., Rector's Bar, Calif., and San
Francisco, Calif., 1849–1853
(H) HM 39978–39985

Mary Eliza Warner, Diary of Mary Eliza Warner written at the age of fifteen
covering the trip by wagon train of her family to California in 1864
Bancroft Library typescript
(B) C-F 66 A & B

Joseph Warren Wood, Diary [of an expedition to California via Sublette Cutoff,

Ft Hall, and Truckee river; life in the mines; return east (1852) via Nicaragua . . . May 6, 1849–April 4, 1853]

(H) HM 318

Printed books

Mary Stuart Bailey, 'A Journal . . . from Ohio to California, April–October, 1852,' in Sandra Myres, ed., *Ho for California! Women's Overland Diaries from the Huntington Library*, San Marino: The Huntington Library, 1980.

Joseph Glover Baldwin, 'California Flush Times, by the Author of the Flush Times of Alabama, Letter from an Emigrant' and ['Ebb Tide'], edited by Richard Amacher and George Polhemus as *The Flush Times of California*, Athens, Ga.: University of Georgia Press, 1966.

Thomas Berger, *Little Big Man*, New York: The Dial Press, 1964.

J. D. Borthwick, *Three Years in California*, with eight illustrations by the author, Edinburgh: W. Blackwood & Sons, 1857.

Edwin Bryant, *What I Saw in California*, New York: D. Appleton & Co., 1848.

Louise Amelia Knapp Smith Clappe (Dame Shirley), *The Shirley Letters . . . from the California Mines, 1851–1852*, edited by Carl Wheat, New York: Knopf, 1949.

Timothy Flint, *Recollections of the Last Ten Years in the Valley of the Mississippi*, edited with an introduction by George Brooks, foreword by John Francis McDermott, Carbondale and Edwardsville: Southern Illinois University Press; London and Amsterdam: Feffer & Simons, 1966.

John Charles Frémont, *The Expeditions of John Charles Frémont*, edited by Donald Jackson and Mary Lee Spence, vol. I (*Travels from 1838 to 1844*), Urbana: University of Illinois Press, 1970.

Charles Glass Gray, *Off at Sunrise; the Overland Journal of Charles Glass Gray*, edited by Thomas Clark, San Marino: The Huntington Library, 1976.

James Hall, *Notes on the Western States, Containing Descriptive Sketches of their Soil, Climate, Resources and Scenery*, Philadelphia: Harrison Hall, 1838.

Sketches of History, Life, and Manners in the West Philadelphia: Harrison Hall, 2 vols, 1835.

Sallie Hester, 'The Diary of a Pioneer Girl; the Adventures of Sallie Hester, Aged Twelve, in a Trip Overland in 1849,' *The Argonaut*, XCVII, 2528, p. 3; 2529, pp. 3–4; 2530, p. 3; 2531, p. 3; 2532, p. 3; 2533, pp. 3–4; 2534, pp. 3–4 (Sept. 12–Oct. 24, 1925).

Washington Irving, *The Adventures of Captain Bonneville*, edited by Robert Rees and Alan Sandy; *The Complete Works of Washington Irving*, vol. XVI, Boston: Twayne, 1977.

'A Tour on the Prairies,' edited with an introductory essay by John Francis McDermott, Norman: The University of Oklahoma Press, 1956.

Thomas Jefferson, *Notes on the State of Virginia,* in *The Life and Selected Writings of Thomas Jefferson,* edited, and with an introduction by Adrienne Koch and William Peden, New York: Random House, 1944.

Overton Johnson, *Route Across the Rocky Mountains, with a Description of Oregon and California . . . ,* edited by Carl Cannon, Princeton: Princeton University Press, 1932.

Leonard Kip, *California Sketches, with Recollections of the Gold Mines,* introduced by Lyle Wright, Los Angeles: Kovach, 1946.

Mary Jane Megquier, *Apron Full of Gold; Letters from San Francisco, 1849–1856,* edited by Robert Cleland, San Marino: the Huntington Library, 1949.

Hiram Pierce, *A Forty-Niner Speaks; A Chronological Record of the Observations and Experiences of a New Yorker . . . in California . . . March, 1849 to January, 1851,* introduced by Sarah Wiswell Meyer, Oakland: Keystone Inglett Printing Co., 1930.

H. M. T. Powell, *The Santa Fe Trail to California, 1849–1852; the Journal and Drawings of H. M. T. Powell,* edited by Douglas Watson, San Francisco: the Grabhorn Press for the Book Club of California, 1931.

Sarah Royce, *A Frontier Lady; Recollections of the Gold Rush and Early California,* edited by Ralph Henry Gabriel, with a foreword by Katherine Royce, Lincoln: University of Nebraska Press, 1932.

J. M. Shively, *Route and Distances to Oregon and California, with a Description of Watering Places, Crossings, Dangerous Indians, &c, &c,* Washington, D.C.: Wm Greer, 1846.

Bayard Taylor, *Eldorado, or Adventures in the Path of Empire,* introduction by Robert Glass Cleland, New York: Knopf, 1949.

Mark Twain, *Early Tales and Sketches,* vol. 1: *1851–1864,* edited by Edgar Branch, Robert Hirst and Harriet Smith, Berkeley: the University of California Press for the Iowa Center for Textual Studies, 1979. (vol. 15 of *The Works of Mark Twain*)

John Wood, *Journal of John Wood,* Columbus, Ohio: Nevins and Myers, 1871.

AN ESSAY ON FURTHER READING

This guide is for the general reader with access to a good library in a fair-sized city or university. So it includes a certain amount of information, too cumbersome for the main narrative but useful to the non-specialist as background or context. For the same reason printed books only are listed here, and for the most part paperbacks and other ephemera excluded too, unless the book specified appears only in that form. Manuscripts cited in this study appear in the preceding section and in individual notes, but a summary of the more important collections consulted would include: at the Bancroft Library, University of California at Berkeley: the Mark Twain Papers, the William Wright ('Dan de Quille') Papers (P-g 246), the Grant Horace Smith Papers (P-g 244) and the Bancroft collection of memoirs, diaries and letters relating to Nevada and California, and to overland journeys to the Pacific; at the Huntington Library, San Marino, California: diaries and letters relating to overland journeys to the Pacific and to journeys around the Horn and via the Isthmus of Panama, and the Huntington collection of letter sheets and other memorabilia of the California Gold Rush. To the staff of these libraries, and to the personnel of other libraries I have used for this work – particularly the British Museum and Senate House, London, the Coe Library at Berkeley and the new Green Library at Stanford – I extend my warmest thanks for their suggestions, their patient instruction and a thousand other acts of kindness for which a paragraph like this can never be sufficient recompense.

Finally, I have no suggestions for 'further reading' relating to chapter 7, because that is mainly an occasion for reconsidering authors and subjects discussed earlier in the book. Where new material is introduced, the slack has been taken up in the endnotes.

The historical context

Since so much of this book has to do with travelers' impressions of the trail from Missouri to the Pacific, the reader who is not a specialist in American western history might appreciate a brief account of how the trails westward came to be discovered, explored and publicized. The first major explorations west of the Mississippi were those of Meriwether Lewis and William Clark (1803–6) and Zebulon Pike (1806). Both were government-sponsored investigations of the vast Louisiana Purchase, bought from France in 1803. President Jefferson sent Lewis and Clark to explore the northern half of the Purchase, and then to trace the portages between the sources of the Missouri and the rivers leading to the Pacific Ocean. They followed the Missouri from its junction with the Mississippi all the way to its headwaters in what is now Montana, thence west to the Snake river and down the Columbia to the Ocean at the point now dividing Oregon from Washington State. A somewhat watered-down account of this expedition, edited by Nicholas Biddle and Paul Allen from the journals of Lewis and Clark, was published in 1814 under the title *History of the Expedition to the Sources of the Missouri, across the Rocky Mountains and Down the Columbia to the Pacific*. The full text of the Journals, plus other manuscript material drawn from notebooks, letters and other sources, was edited by Reuben Thwaites in eight volumes (1904–5). A modern historical study with important implications beyond its immediate topic, is J. L. Allen's *Passage through the Garden; Lewis and Clark and the Image of the American Northwest* (1975).

Pike's expedition took a route across the middle of the Louisiana Purchase, from St Louis north to the Republican river, west along the Arkansas past Pike's Peak in what is now Colorado. His *An Account of Expeditions to the Sources of the Mississippi and through the Western Parts of Louisiana* was published in 1810, and later edited by Elliott Coues (1895). Donald Jackson has edited Pike's *Journals, with Letters and Related Documents* (1966).

In 1811 John Jacob Astor sent Wilson P. Hunt at the head of an overland expedition to establish a Pacific trading post for his fur company. Hunt followed the path of Lewis and Clark up the Missouri, but cut across the Snake via a more southerly route. An arresting account of this journey is included in a popular book about the fur trade, *Astoria* (1836), written by Washington Irving and his nephew, Pierre. A year later Robert Stuart led a return expedition eastwards along the Columbia and Snake rivers, but cut further south even than Hunt, crossing the Continental Divide at the South Pass between the Wind river and Sweetwater mountain ranges (now in Wyoming). From there he headed down the Sweetwater river to where it joins the North Platte, then down the Platte to the Missouri. This route formed the basis of the Oregon Trail, the main way West for emigrants to the Pacific Northwest, and the path followed by parties heading for California, until they left it in what is now southeastern Idaho and cut down into Utah and Nevada. Stuart's expedition is also described in *Astoria*, and a modern edition of his own account appears in *The Discovery of the Oregon Trail; Robert Stuart's Narratives* (1935), edited by P. A. Rollins. Kenneth Spaulding has edited Stuart's journal as *On the Oregon Trail* (1953).

More Southern expeditions westward include that of Jedediah Smith, who went southwest in 1826 from the Great Salt Lake, down the Sevier and Virgin rivers, into southern California, north up the San Joaquin valley, and back to Salt Lake across the Nevada and Utah deserts. His journals, kept between 1822 and 1829, are included in *The Travels of Jedediah Smith*, edited by M. S. Sulivan (1934), and in H. C. Dale, ed., *The Ashley–Smith Explorations* (revised ed, 1941). James O. Pattie and his father Sylvester blazed the yet more southerly Gila Trail between 1827 and 1829, south from Santa Fe to the Gila river (now in southern

Arizona), thence west past the Colorado river to San Diego in present California. James Pattie's *Personal Narrative* (1831), heavily edited by James Flint, was published in 1831, and later in Reuben Thwaites's *Early Western Travels*, vol. 18 (1905).

The California Road, the portion of the overland route from the Oregon Trail to California, was discovered by James Walker in 1833. As a guide on Major Benjamin de Bonneville's excursion to investigate possibilities in the fur trade, Walker left de Bonneville's camp in the Rockies, headed south to the Great Salt Lake, thence west across the Utah desert until he picked up the Humboldt river. This he followed until it disappeared into the sand at the Humboldt Sink, at which point he turned straight west for California. Irving's *The Adventures of Captain Bonneville, U.S.A.* (1837) describes the voyage. A year after Walker's expedition, Nathaniel Wyeth set out on a journey to establish a trading company in Oregon. Wyeth followed Stuart's route up the Missouri to the Platte, the Sweetwater, South Pass, the Snake and the Columbia, to Fort Vancouver and the Willamette valley, now in Oregon. Contemporary accounts appeared in books by Wyeth's companions on the voyage, John B. Wyeth (*Oregon, or a Short History of a Long Journey*, 1833), and John Kirk Townsend (*Narrative of a Journey . . . to the Columbia River*, 1839), and Wyeth's exploits also figure in Irving's *Bonneville*. His own *Correspondence and Journals* were published by the Oregon Historical Society in 1899.

Wyeth's and Walker's routes West became the two great transcontinental tracks for emigrants to the Pacific Coast, the Oregon Trail and the California Road respectively. Famous later excursions, like John Charles Frémont's official exploration of the route to the Rocky Mountains (1842) and the great Mormon trek to the Salt Lake (1846 and following) kept to the Platte–Sweetwater line, except that the Mormons took the north banks of both rivers to avoid encountering other emigrant parties. Frémont's description, published by the U.S. Government as *Report of the Exploring Expedition to the Rocky Mountains* (1843) is discussed at length elsewhere in this book. The authoritative text is included in the three-volume edition of Frémont's work by Donald Jackson and Mary Lee Spence (1970 *et seq.*).

Explorers and mountain men were not the only people to describe the trails West and the life lived along them. Father Pierre de Smet, the Belgian Jesuit missionary to the Indians of the Northwest, published four books about his experiences, *Letters and Sketches* (1843), *Oregon Missions and Travels* (1847), *Western Missions and Missionaries* (1859) and *New Indian Sketches* (1863). The first and second of these are included in volumes 27 and 29 of Thwaites's *Early Western Travels* (1906). Much slighter than the work of de Smet, but a lively account of the California Trail and of life in California, widely read by the forty-niners, was Edwin Bryant's *What I Saw in California* (1848), frequently reprinted as *Rocky Mountain Adventures*. Finally, Francis Parkman's *The California and Oregon Trail* (1849), first serialized as 'The Oregon Trail' in *The Knickerbocker Magazine* in 1847 and subsequently reprinted under that title, has become a classic of American literature, needing no further description here, except the reminder that it was the first book by the major historian. Modern editions of Parkman's papers include his *Journals*, edited by Mason Wade (1947) and *Letters*, edited by Wilbur Jacobs (1960).

As for modern guides to the discovery, exploration and expansion of the American West, one might mention three handy, inexpensive paperbacks published by the University of Nebraska Press at Lincoln, Nebraska. *American Expansion; a Book of Maps*, by Randall Sale and Edwin Karn (1962) provides a colored map for every decade between 1790 and 1900, showing the movement west of the frontier, the development of the prominent trails, the location of land offices, and so on. A brief descriptive text accompanies each map. Nelson Klose's *A Concise Study Guide to the American Frontier* (1964) is just what its title claims for it: a brief history of the subject, with paragraphs outlining treaties, acts and other historical events, and a useful bibliography. *A Nation Moving West; Readings in the History of the American Frontier* (1966) is a full and well-edited anthology of contemporary accounts of travel and expeditions, diaries and letters, compiled by Robert Mardock and Robert Richmond. A similar collection, even more eclectic and densely packed, has been edited by Bayrd Still, *The West; Contemporary Records of America's Expansion Across the Continent: 1607–1890* (New York: Capricorn Books, 1961).

As for full-scale history books, the standard studies include John Hawgood's *America's Western Frontiers; Exploration and Settlement of the Trans-Mississippi West* (1967), Carl Wheat's five-volume *Mapping the Transmississippi West, 1540–1861* (1957–63) and the work of Ray Billington, which goes far beyond descriptive history, into economics, sociology and behaviorial study, in an attempt to analyze the motives and means of the westward impulse itself. See his *America's Frontier Heritage* (1966) and his classic study, *Westward Expansion; a History of the American Frontier* (4th ed, 1974).

For further reading, consult the substantial bibliographies in the books listed here, or a standard guide to study like *The Harvard Guide to American History*, edited by Frank Freidel (1974), especially Section 13 ('Westward Expansion and the Frontier,' I, 324–6) and Section 9 ('Travels and Description . . . 1790–1865,' I, 141–50).

Introduction

The negative catalogue of forms and conventions missing from American society was a common trope in descriptions of the country, especially for travelers whose point of view was culturally to the 'east' of the field of observation. A brief selection arranged chronologically would include, in addition to that already cited by Fenimore Cooper in *Notions of the Americans* (1828), the following instances, beginning with this in Alexis de Tocqueville's beautiful account of 'A Fortnight in the Wilds,' a journey he made in 1831: 'Whichever way you looked, the eye would never find the spire of a gothic belfry, a wooden cross marking the way, or the moss covered threshold of a presbytery. None of these venerable relics of old Christian civilization have been transported into the wilderness; nothing there awakens thoughts of the past or of the future. One does not even find sanctuaries sacred to those who are no more. . . . Here man seems furtively to enter upon life. There is no meeting around his cradle of several generations to express hopes. . . . His name is not inscribed on the registers of the city. None of the touching solemnities of religion are mingled with the family's solicitude' (*Journey to America* [1860], translated by George Lawrence, edited by J. P. Mayer, 1959). Frances Trollope also thought of the formal religious observances missing from the experience of the backwoods pioneer family: 'These people were indeed independent, Robinson Crusoe was hardly more so . . . but yet it seemed to me that there was something awful and almost unnatural in their loneliness. No village bell summoned them to prayer, where they might meet the friendly greeting of their fellow-men. When they die, no spot sacred by ancient reverence will receive their bones – Religion will not breathe her sweet and solemn farewell upon their grave . . . and the wind that whispers through the boughs will be their only requiem. But then they pay neither taxes nor tithes, are never expected to pull off a hat or to make a curtsy, and will live and die without hearing or uttering the dreadful words, "God save the king" ' (*Domestic Manners of the Americans,* 1832).

It was not long before Cooper returned to the subject. This is from his preface to *Home as Found* (1838): '[The people of America] possess no standard for opinion, manners, social maxims, or even language.' Dame Shirley's variation on the theme ('no churches, lectures, concerts or theatres; no fresh books, no shopping, calling nor gossiping little tea-drinkings; no parties, no balls, no picnics . . . no promenades, no rides nor drives . . . no *nothing*') is cited and discussed briefly in chapter 5. The point to note there is that she ends her catalogue on a surprising up-beat: 'Now I expect to be very happy here. . . . As for churches, "the groves were God's first temples" ' (see Louise A. K. S. Clappe [Dame Shirley], *The Shirley Letters . . . from the California Mines, 1851–1852,* edited by Carl Wheat, 1949). Nathaniel Hawthorne's complaint in his preface to *The Marble Faun* (1860) is briefer and better known: 'No author, without a trial, can conceive of the difficulty of writing a romance about a country where there is no shadow, no antiquity, no mystery, no picturesque and gloomy wrong, no anything but a commonplace prosperity, in broad and simple daylight, as is happily the case with my dear land.' Again, a sort-of palinode to his criticism, achieved through the timely, strategically placed 'happily.' Examples like this make James's even more celebrated negative catalogue, applied (as it happens) to the creative environment inhabited by Hawthorne himself, look more conventional. The famous list ends, almost auto-destructively, with a joke: 'No sovereign, no court, no personal loyalty, no aristocracy, no church, no clergy, no army, no diplomatic service, no country gentlemen, no palaces, no castles, nor manors, nor old country-houses, no parsonages, nor thatched cottages; no great Universities nor public schools – no Oxford, nor Eton, nor Harrow; no literature, no novels, no

216

museums, no political society, no sporting classes – no Epsom nor Ascot!' And James too consolidates his up-beat ending, not this time by a joke, but simply by the statement that a joke of some kind, exists mysteriously somewhere in the comparison: 'The natural remark, . . . would be that if these things are left out, everything is left out. The American knows that a good deal remains; what it is that remains – that is his secret, his joke, as one might say' (*Hawthorne*, 1879). Even the twentieth century has its version of the trope. This example, from John Cheever's novel *Falconer* (1975), is not about America, but it is about prison as an extended metaphor for America, and travel in an alien land as an image for prison: 'He bathed in strange and rusty water, wiped his ass on strange and barbarous toilet paper and climbed down unfamiliar stairs to be served a strange and profoundly offensive breakfast. That was travel. It was the same here. Everything he saw, touched, smelled and dreamed was cruelly alien, but this continent or nation in which he might spend the rest of his living days had no flag, no anthem, no monarch, president, taxes, boundaries or graves.'

The lesser-known response to the negative catalogue was an alternative list, either of the abundant matter to be found in America (an answer, as it were, to the lack of manner) or of newly discovered types awaiting exploitation by writers still to come. An early example is found in William Wood's *New Englands Prospect* (1634, see the modern edition by Alden Vaughan, 1977), where lists of trees, birds and other things are set in verse to make them more impressive:

> Trees both in hills and plains in plenty be,
> The long-lived oak and mournful cypress tree,
> Sky-towering pines, and chestnuts coated rough,
> The lasting cedar, with the walnut tough;
> The rosin-dropping fir for masts in use,
> The boatmen seek for oars light, neat-grown spruce, . . .
>
> The princely eagle, and the soaring hawk,
> Whom in their unknown ways there's none can chalk:
> The humbird for some queen's rich cage more fit,
> Than in the vacant wilderness to sit.
> The swift-winged swallow sweeping to and fro,
> As swift as arrow from Tartarian bow. . . .

According to Ernst Curtius (*European Literature and the Latin Middle Ages*, translated by Willard Trask, 1953, p. 195) the catalogue 'is a fundamental poetic form that goes back to Homer and Hesiod.' Wood's immediate source may have been the list of trees in Book 1 of Spenser's *Faerie Queene*, but even this derives from a similar catalogue in Chaucer's *Parlement of Foules*, and the catalogue was such a widespread trope in medieval and renaissance descriptions of nature that specific source hunting is probably futile.

In the introduction to *The Sketch Book*, just before his famous complaint that America lacked the 'charms of storied and poetical association' that made Europe so attractive a field for the novelist and historian, Washington Irving goes to some lengths to insist on the material richness of the natural setting in America: 'on no country have the charms of nature been more prodigally lavished. Her mighty lakes, like oceans of liquid silver; her mountains, with their bright aerial tints; her valleys, teeming with wild fertility; her tremendous cataracts, thundering in their solitudes; her boundless plains, waving with spontaneous verdure; her broad, deep rivers, rolling in solemn silence to the ocean; her trackless forests . . . no, never need an American look beyond his own country for the sublime and beautiful of natural scenery' ('The Author's Account of Himself,' *The Sketch Book*, 1820). This 'argument from profusion' was also employed by Flint and Hall as a defense of the physical and social environment of the West against what they saw as the scepticism of eastern periodicals about the stability of society in such a formless landscape (see chapter 1, pp. 28–30). But at least one New England magazine responded warmly to Flint's advocacy of the Mississippi valley, because the notice in *The North American Review* (vol. XXXIII, 53, 1826) of his *Recollections of the Last Ten Years* (1826) lists western types to be discerned in that book ('The preachers, the lawyers . . . the Indian, the negro, the fanatic') that may well have given Emerson the idea for his 'fisheries . . . Negroes . . . Indians . . . boats . . . repudiations . . . trade . . . planting . . . clearing . . . Oregon and Texas' in 'The Poet' (1844). It may have been his hostile attention to Emerson's work, or just his familiarity with Hall's *Sketches* (from which he took most of the two chapters in *The Confidence-Man* on the backwoodsman's hatred of the Indian) that prompted Melville to something approaching a parody, in the second chapter of that novel, of the positive catalogue of life in America (or in the world? or only in the West? the range of reference expands and contracts):

'As among Chaucer's Canterbury pilgrims, or those oriental ones crossing the Red Sea towards Mecca in the festival month, there was no lack of variety. Natives of all sorts, and foreigners; men of business and men of pleasure; parlor men and backwoodsmen; farm-hunters and fame-hunters; heiress-hunters, gold-hunters, buffalo-hunters, bee-hunters, happiness-hunters, truth-hunters, and still keener hunters after all these hunters. Fine ladies in slippers, and moccasined squaws; Northern speculators and Eastern philosophers; English, Irish, German, Scotch, Danes; Santa Fe traders in striped blankets, and Broadway bucks in cravats of cloth of gold; fine-looking Kentucky boatmen, and Japanese-looking Mississippi cotton-planters; Quakers in full drab, and United States soldiers in full regimentals; slaves, black, mulatto, quadroon; modish young Spanish Creoles, and old-fashioned French Jews; Mormons and Papists; Dives and Lazarus; jesters and mourners, teetotalers and convivialists, deacons and blacklegs; hard-shell Baptists and clay-eaters; grinning negroes, and Sioux chiefs solemn as high-priests. In short, a piebald parliament, an Anacharsis Cloots congress of all kinds of that multiform pilgrim species, man.

'As pine, beech, birch, ash, hackmatack, hemlock, spruce, bass-wood, maple, interweave their foliage in the natural wood, so these varieties of mortals blended their varieties of visage and garb. A Tarter-like picturesqueness; a sort of pagan abandonment and assurance. Here reigned the dashing and all-fusing spirit of the

West, whose type is the Mississippi itself, which, uniting the streams of the most distant and opposite zones, pours them along, helter-skelter, in one cosmopolitan and confident tide.'

Other lists of American types still to be developed in fiction include the letter from Mark Twain discussed in chapter 6, p. 137, numerous instances in Whitman's *Leaves of Grass* (1855, *et seq.*) and *Specimen Days and Collect* (1882), and even this late example in an essay by Mary McCarthy, expressed, typically, as an outgrowth of natural processes peculiar to America: 'There are more people than ever before, at least in the sense of mutations in our national botany, and this is probably due to mobility – cross-fertilization. Take as an example a gangster who was in the slot-machine racket, decided to go straight and became a laundromat king, sent his daughter to Bennington, where she married a poet-in-residence or a professor of modern linguistic philosophy. There are three characters already sketched out in that sentence and all of them brand-new: the father, the daughter, and the son-in-law. Imagine what one of the old writers might have made of the wedding and the reception afterward at the 21 Club. . . . People speak of the lack of tradition or of manners as having a bad effect on the American novel, but that self-made man is a far richer figure, from the novelist's point of view, than the man of inherited wealth, who is likely to be a mannered shadow' ('Characters in Fiction,' in *On The Contrary,* 1961).

W. D. Howells's association with the West, even the fact that he could call himself a westerner, was enormously important to his career. Kenneth Lynn's intelligent biography of Howells (*William Dean Howells; an American Life,* 1971) suggests that the combination of his western origins and his four years' service as American Consul in Venice (a political favor awarded him for his campaign biography of Abraham Lincoln) made Howells irresistible to the Boston–Cambridge cultural establishment when they were looking for new blood to transfuse into the *Atlantic Monthly.* Lynn also shows how assiduously Howells encouraged writers whom he took to be western. For an idea of Howells's literary criticism, including his views on the western promise for literature and his admiration for Mark Twain, see his *Criticism and Fiction* (first published, 1891, modern edition by Clara and Rudolf Kirk, 1959). Edwin Cady has also provided an excellent sampler of Howells's criticism in his edition of *W. D. Howells as Critic* (1973). Hamlin Garland's testimony to the encouragement he received from Howells can be found in his *Diaries,* edited by Donald Pizer (1968). Howells's theory of realism and his struggle against the recrudescence of romance in England and America are amply documented in Edwin Cady's two-volume biography. *The Road to Realism; the Early Years, 1837–1885,* and *The Realist at War; the Mature Years* (1956 and 1958).

For a history of the growth of popular fiction set in the West, the reader should start with Richard Slotkin's *Regeneration Through Violence; the Mythology of the American Frontier* (1973). Slotkin begins his study by describing the various stereotypes through which Europeans 'invented' America, then explores various American narrative encounters with the wilderness, from early accounts of captivity by Indians through the novels of Fenimore Cooper. Henry Nash Smith's classic *Virgin Land; the American West as Symbol and Myth* (1950) explores the West as a topic for popular literature from Cooper through the dime novels. John Cawelti's *The Six Gun Mystique* (1971) is about the conventions of cowboy fiction and how they were translated into film. A new study of the greatest interest in fixing critical and generic standards for the huge body of writing that has been loosely characterized as western fiction is *The Novel of the American West* (1980), in which John Milton develops the theory that the relative newness of culture in the West left a nearly blank screen on which the eastern romancer could project, with impunity, whatever mythic models he wished. The wider topic of popular fiction in America is covered by John Cawelti's *Adventure, Mystery, Romance* (1976) in chapters on literary formulae, genres, archetypes, crime novels, detective stories, westerns and social melodrama. Also on the subject of popular fiction are Frank Mott's *Golden Multitudes* (1947) and James Hart's *The Popular Book; A History of Literary Taste* (1950).

To sample popular fiction set in the American West, the reader might begin with the Davy Crockett Almanacks of 'Wild Sports in the West,' naively illustrated collections of tales of impossible exploits on the frontier. Number 1 (1835) has been reprinted in Franklin Meine's edition of *The Crockett Almanacks, Nashville Series* (1955), and James Thorpe of the Huntington Library has edited and introduced a full-color facsimile of number 3 (1971, first published 1837). For a good idea of the stages by which Cooper's Leather-Stocking Tales came to be transformed in the popular Dime Novels, the reader might compare *The Last of the Mohicans* (1826) with James Hall's short story 'The Backwoodsman' in his *Legends of the West* (1832), Robert Montgomery Bird's *Nick of the Woods; or the Jibbenainosay* (1837), and Edward Ellis's dime novel, *Seth Jones; or, the Captives of the Frontier* (1860). The last named is available in a modern volume in which it is paired with Edward Wheeler's *Deadwood Dick on Deck*, edited by Philip Durham (1966). See also E. F. Bleiler, ed., *Eight Dime Novels* (*Old King Brady, Frank James, Nick Carter, Deadwood Dick, Buffalo Bill, The Steam Man, Frank Merriwell, Horatio Alger*), 1974.

Though *The Virginian* (1902) was widely read, and loaned its story line to a thousand movies, Owen Wister and his successors among the cowboy romancers cannot be said to have produced popular formula fiction under the shadow of Fenimore Cooper. *The Virginian* like Eugene Manlove Rhodes's *Bransford in Arcadia* (1914), *The Throwback* (1906), by Alfred Henry Lewis, and Emerson Hough's *North of 36* (1923), was self-consciously pastoral and articulate with the Social Darwinism of Herbert Spencer and William Graham Sumner. These were westerns for thinking men, the sort of American idealists concerned about Manifest Destiny and Kipling's 'White Man's Burden.' Wister and Theodore Roosevelt (who corresponded with Kipling too) were good friends. See Wister's account of their relationship in *Roosevelt; the Story of a Friendship, 1880–1919* (1930). Roosevelt's own interest in the West as a proving ground for the American values of self-reliance and democracy was developed in *The Winning of the West* (1889–96), a fascinating account, in four volumes of dashing prose, of the social and geographical forces behind American expansion westward in the eighteenth century. The study was admired by no less a western historian than Frederick Jackson Turner. On a more intimate scale, Roosevelt wrote accounts of life on and around his own ranch in Dakota Territory, and these eventuated in three volumes about ranch life, nature and hunting, of which the most interesting (for detailed descriptions of life on a cattle ranch) is the second, *Ranch Life and the Cattle Trail* (1888). This first appeared serially in *The Century Magazine* (vol.xxxv, 4, February, 1888 *et seq.*) illustrated by Frederic Remington. Remington was a friend of Wister's too, and their letters have been edited by Ben Vorpahl as *My Dear Wister; the Frederic Remington – Owen Wister Letters* (1972). G. Edward White's *The Eastern Establishment and the Western Experience; the West of Frederic Remington, Theodore Roosevelt and Owen Wister* (1968) studies the relationship of the three men in the context of their shared ideology.

Emerson's ideas on autobiography, and his rather special practice of it in the *Journals,* has aroused considerable interest lately. It is now a commonplace that the 'I' of his own autobiography is more widely representative than is the case in European personal narrative. See, for example, Erik Thurin, *The Universal Autobiography of Ralph Waldo Emerson* (1974). In his *The Puritan Origins of the American self* (1975) Sacvan Bercovitch traces Emerson's split between the public and private to the 'Puritan concept of intermediate identity.' G. Thomas Couser's *American Autobiography; the Prophetic Mode* (1979) extends Bercovitch's theme into specific cases, like those of Benjamin Franklin, Thoreau, Whitman, Gertrude Stein and Norman Mailer. A general study of considerable interest is James Olney's *Metaphors of Self* (1972), which begins with a theory of autobiography, by no means simple but clearly expressed without jargon; and then considers autobiographies of ascending degrees of complexity, from Montaigne to Eliot's *The Four Quartets.*

Chapter 1: The West and the man of letters

The idea of the sublime and the beautiful in natural landscape can be traced through the writings of English authors often cited as harbingers of the romantic movement, such as Joseph Addison's essay in *The Spectator,* nos. 411–422 (1717), called *On the Pleasures of the Imagination,* Mark Akenside's long poem, *The Pleasures of Imagination* (1744) and Edward Young's *Night Thoughts* (1740). The standard work on the subject is Edmund Burke's *A Philosophical Enquiry into the Origins of our Ideas of the Sublime and Beautiful* (1756–7). There is a modern edition (1958) by J. T. Boulton. Sir Uvedale Price (*Essays on the Picturesque,* 1794) offered a third category to Burke's two, taking as his model not French landscape painting but the Dutch landscapes popular in his time. Modern treatments of the subject include Marjorie Hope Nicholson's essay 'Sublime in External Nature' in vol. 4 of the *Dictionary of the History of Ideas* (1973) and Christopher Hussey's *The Picturesque* (1927).

Biographers of Andrew Jackson are understandably reticent about his Indian removal policy, but Edward Pessen, in *Jacksonian America; Society, Personality and Politics* (1969), does not mince words, and John William Ward's *Andrew Jackson; Symbol for an Age* (1962) has a few balanced pages on the subject. See also Mary Young, 'Indian Removal and Land Allotment; the Civilized Tribes and Jacksonian Justice,' *American Historical Review*, LXIV (1958) and Grant Foreman, *Indian Removal; the Emigration of the Five Civilized Tribes of Indians* (1953).

The standard biography of Washington Irving is still Stanley William's *Life of Washington Irving* (1935). A more recent, less hostile account of Irving's life until his return to America can be found in William Hedges, *Washington Irving; an American Study, 1802–1832* (1965). An attractive book about the author in his setting, and packed with information about the cultural struggle between Europe and America, is Van Wyck Brooks, *The World of Washington Irving* (1944). Irving's own journal of his western tour can be found in the three-volume edition of his *Journals and Notebooks*, edited by Nathalia Wright and Walter Reichert, part of the *Complete Works of Washington Irving* emerging under the general editorship of Henry Pochmann. Another description of the same voyage appears in Commissioner Henry Ellsworth's *Washington Irving on the Prairie, or a Narrative of a Tour of the Southwest in the Year 1832*, edited by Stanley Williams and Barbara Simison (1937), and both of Irving's European companions left accounts of the tour as well. The journal and letters of Albert, Count von Pourtalès have been edited by George Spaulding and translated by Seymour Feiler as *On Western Tour with Washington Irving* (1968). C. J. Latrobe's *The Rambler in North America, 1832–33*, which includes his version of the Irving tour, was published in 1835.

Flint and Hall have aroused less interest than Irving, but James K. Folsom has written a clear and lively account of Flint's life and work in the Twayne United States Authors Series (*Timothy Flint*, 1965) and Randolph Randall a biography of Hall (*James Hall, Spokesman of the New West*, 1964). John T. Flanagan's *James Hall, Literary Pioneer of the Ohio Valley* (1941) is a critic's assessment of Hall's writing.

For Jefferson's ideas about geography, natural history and anthropology see Daniel Boorstin's *The Lost World of Thomas Jefferson* (1948). Gary Wills's scholarly and stimulating *Inventing America* (1978) demonstrates how thoroughly Jefferson shared contemporary European and American scientific ideas, including the assumption that complex emotional states could be quantified. Early explorers and travelers in America with a genuine scientific bent include Gonzalo Fernandez de Oviedo y Valdes, *Historia Natural y General de las Indias* (1935 *et seq.*), Andre Thevet *Les Singularitez de la France Antartique* (1558), translated by Thomas Hacket and published in the same year as *The New Found Worlde, or Antarticke . . .* , Thomas Hariot, *A Briefe and True Report of the New Found Land of Virginia* (1558) also reprinted in Hakluyt's *The Voyages of the English Nation to America*, vol. II (1889), William Strachey, *The Historie and Travaile into Virginia Britannia* (written 1612, published 1849), William Wood, *New England's Pros-*

pect (1634), Mark Catesby, *The Natural History of Carolina, Florida, and the Bahama Islands* (1754), John Bartram, *Observations on the Inhabitants, Climate, Soil, Rivers, Productions, Animals, and Other Matters . . . In . . . Travels from Pennsylvania to Onondage, Oswego, and the Lake Ontario, in Canada . . .* (1751) and *A Description of East Florida . . .* (1766), and finally John's son, William Bartram, *Travels Through North and South Carolina, Georgia, East and West Florida . . .* (1791). The Oviedo has been translated and edited by Sterling Stoudemire (1959), the Strachey by Louis Wright and Virginia Freund (1953), the Wood by Alden Vaughan (1977), and William Bartram's *Travels* by Francis Harper (1958). The other texts are available in modern facsimile editions. An anthology of early English reports of the New World is *The Elizabethans' America*, edited by Louis Wright (1965). Wayne Franklin's *Discoverers, Explorers, Settlers; the Diligent Writers of Early America* (1979) treats some of these authors to a close stylistic analysis too subtle to be paraphrased here. A more general account of the European image of early America is Howard Mumford Jones's seminal *O Strange New World: American Culture, the Formative Years* (1967). See also Edmundo O' Gorman, *The Invention of America* (1961), and Percy Adams, *Travel and Travel Liars, 1660–1800* (1962).

Chapter 2: Frémont and the humble bee

The standard edition of Frémont's explorations is now *The Expeditions of John Charles Frémont*, edited by Donald Jackson and Mary Lee Spence. Volume one (1970) contains Frémont's expedition to the Rockies which terminated at the South Pass in 1842 and the journey to Oregon and California in 1843–4, plus relevant letters and other documents. Volume two (1973) contains his expeditions to the Central Rockies and the California Sierra, his involvement with the Bear Flag Revolt, his service as civil governor of California, and his two exploring trips to search out a route for a transcontinental railroad. A supplement to volume two presents the documents relating to his court martial, following his refusal to recognize the authority of Stephen Kearny, Commander of the Army of the West, on the latter's arrival in California. A third volume will cover his *Travels from 1848 to 1854.*

For another, less reverent account of Frémont's expedition to the Rocky Mountains in 1842 see the diaries of his German cartographer, Charles Preuss, *Exploring with Frémont*, translated and edited by Erwin and Elizabeth Gudde (1958). As for biographies, Allan Nevin's *Frémont; the West's Greatest Adventurer* (1928) reissued (1939) as *Frémont; Pathmarker of the West*, third edition, 1955, can still be read for its verve and narrative sweep, but it has been all but superceded by Ferol Egan's new *Frémont; Explorer for a Restless Nation* (1977), which takes account of many sources not available to Nevins, and is also written with considerable tact and liveliness.

Chapter 3: The forty-niners

The standard history of California is John Caughey's *California; a Remarkable State's Life* (1940, 3rd edn, 1970). A recent study of the social, intellectual and literary history is the learned and immensely readable, *Americans and the California Dream* (1973), by Kevin Starr. Further reading on the history of the California Gold Rush should begin with Rodman Paul, *California Gold; the Beginnings of Mining in the Far West, 1848–1880* (1947). An attractive compilation of information about the Gold Rush, excerpts from diaries, pictures, maps and other graphics can be found in the volume in the Time–Life Old West Series on *The Forty Niners* (1974, text by William Weber). For information about life and conditions on the Overland Trail, turn first to Merril Mattes, *The Great Platte River Road: the Covered Wagon Mainline Via Fort Kearney to Fort Laramie* (1969). Though, as the title makes clear, his book deals mainly with the trail in Nebraska (and includes material on emigrants to Oregon as well as to California), Mattes provides the most authoritative and complete account of the geography, conditions and statistics of that part of the route about which the forty-niners wrote most, and he appends a most useful bibliography of diary and journal accounts of overland travel, both printed and in manuscript. John Unruh's *The Plains Across; the Overland Emigrants and the Trans-Mississippi West, 1849–1860* (1979) is a clearly written, massively documented study of the overland emigrants – their motives for going, their fears and expectations, and their actual experience on the journey.

For a history of the California Road alone, with individual chapters devoted to the conditions, major events and statistics of each year of the emigration, see George Stewart, *The California Trail; an Epic with Many Heroes* (1962), which not only provides the facts and figures in a readable prose style, but also analyzes human behavior with considerable tact. Anyone interested in following the California Trail today, at least as far as southeastern Idaho, where it divides off from the Oregon Trail, might like to own a copy of Gregory Franzwa's paperback, *The Oregon Trail Revisited* (2nd edn, 1978), a detailed guide to the trail today, where it can be found and how followed. The book includes maps, photographs of historical sites as they look now, a brief history and bibliography. Less practical but more beautiful is *Ghost Trails to California* (1974), by Thomas Hunt and Robert Adams, a picture book of full-color landscapes and close-up photographs of hot springs, desert alkali and wagon ruts through rocky passes, that richly evokes the physical conditions of the trail through Utah, Nevada and the California Sierra. Excerpts from emigrants' diaries are cut into the descriptive text accompanying the pictures.

Further exploration of the diaries and letters of overland emigrants might begin with one or more of the annotated collections, like Dale Morgan, ed., *Overland in 1846; Diaries and Letters of the California–Oregon Trail* (1963), or Walker Wyman, ed., *California Emigrant Letters* (1952). Of the rather special conditions, feelings and responses of the forty-niners on the overland route to

California, no single book gives a better idea than J. S. Holliday's superb annotated anthology of forty-niners' letters and diaries, *The World Rushed In* (1981), of which this author saw a manuscript version. At the centre of Holliday's compilation is the diary and letters of William Swain, who went overland from Michigan to California in 1849, but he also uses 512 other diaries and letters from which he cuts in excerpts relevant to experiences, or geographical features recorded by Swain. The story is followed into the diggings themselves and continues with journal entries and letters describing the return of the forty-niners via the Isthmus of Panama to the East Coast. Letters to the miners from their families are included also, to give an idea of the stress felt by those left behind. Nothing in print documents so clearly as does this long-awaited book that the forty-niners were on a kind of excursion that nevertheless changed their lives profoundly, and that most of them went, in the first instance at least, with the intention of returning home, and without their families – in other words, that they were neither emigrants nor pioneers, but something else for which popular western historiography has yet to find a category.

A selective list of individual forty-niners' diaries in printed form might begin with *The Overland Diary of James A. Pritchard from Kentucky to California in 1849* . . . (1959), edited by Dale Morgan with an excellent introduction surveying the history of the forty-niners and a useful bibliography. The monumental *Gold Rush; the Journals, Drawings and other Papers of J. Goldsborough Bruff, April 2, 1849–July 20, 1851*, edited by Georgia Willis Read and Ruth Gaines (1949) also contains considerable lore and information about the Gold Rush beyond the already substantial writings of Bruff himself, plus a good bibliography. Other published forty-niners' diaries of particular interest not treated or listed elsewhere in this book include Alonzo Delano's *Across the Plains and Among the Diggings* (first edn, 1854, reprinted in 1936), Lorenzo Saywer's *Way Sketches, Including Incidents of Travel Across the Plains from St. Joseph to California in 1850* . . . , edited by Edward Eberstadt (1926), and John Steele's *Across the Plains in 1850*, edited by Joseph Schafer (1930). See also Steele's *In Camp and Cabin*, included in Milo Quaife's edition of John Bidwell's *Echoes of the Past about California* (1928). For a bibliography of printed books of transcontinental travel, see Henry Wagner and Charles Camp, *The Plains and the Rockies; a Bibliography of Original Narratives of Travel and Adventure* (revised and extended 4th edn, 1973).

Chapter 4: The unofficial Gold Rush

The most widely used practical guides to the various trails overland were William Clayton, *The Latter-Day Saints' Emigrants' Guide* (1848), Lansford Hastings, *The Emigrants' Guide to Oregon and California* (1845, modern facsimile edited by Charles Henry Carey, 1932), Overton Johnson and William Winter, *Route Across the Rocky Mountains* (1846, reprinted in 1932, edited by Carl Cannon), John Shively, *Route and Distances to Oregon and California* (1846, reprinted in Dale Morgan, ed., *Diaries and Letters of the California Trail*, 1963), and Joseph Ware,

The Emigrants' Guide to California (1849, modern edition by John Caughey, 1932).

Lawrence Cremin's *American Education* is becoming established as the standard history of the subject. Volume one (*The Colonial Experience, 1607–1783*) appeared in 1970, and volume two (*The National Experience, 1783–1876*) in 1980. For a lively introduction to the question of women's education in the early nineteenth century, and their efforts to remedy their disadvantage, see the relevant sections of Andrew Sinclair's *The Better Half; the Emancipation of American Women* (1965).

Book-length studies of women in the West include Nancy Ross, *Westward the Women* (1944), Dee Brown, *Gentle Tamers; Women of the Old West* (1958) and Glenda Riley, *Women on the American Frontier* (1977). Sandra Myres's new collection, *Ho for California! Women's Overland Diaries from the Huntington Library* (1980) includes the journal of Mary Stuart Bailey treated in chapter 4; it is amply annotated and handsomely produced. Clifford Drury has edited another collection of diaries, letters and biographical sketches in his *First White Women Over the Rockies* (1966). This includes the narratives of Mrs Mary Richardson Walker, who crossed in 1838 (originally published in 1931) and Narcissa Whitman, the first woman to travel the Oregon Trail when she went west with her husband Marcus, the Congregationalist missionary in 1836. There are few women's accounts of the journey across in 1849–50, but the following list provides a sample of published women's diaries and letters of the transcontinental experience, mainly at other times: Mrs Luella Dickenson, *Reminiscences of a Trip Across the Plains in 1846 and Early Days in California* (1904), Mrs Lodisa Frizzell, *Across the Plains to California in 1852*, edited by Victor Paltsits (1915), Margaret Ann Frink, *Journal of the Adventures of a Party of California Gold Seekers . . .* (1897), Mrs Phoebe Newton Judson, *A Pioneer's Search for an Ideal Home* (1925) and Mrs Lavinia Honeyman Porter, *By Ox Team to California . . . in 1860* (1910). Finally, one should mention another primary source which, though not about the Gold Rush or the Overland Trail, is a moving testament to the predicament of an educated woman on various western frontiers, Rodman Paul's meticulous and beautifully produced edition of *A Victorian Gentlewoman in the Far West; the Reminiscences of Mary Hallock Foote* (1972). Mrs Foote, a talented illustrator for Scribner's and *The Century* and the wife of the civil engineer Arthur de Wint Foote, followed her husband on his various surveying and building assignments in the West, keeping a careful record of her experiences and sending over 500 letters to her old friend Helena Gilder and her husband Richard Watson Gilder, editor of *The Century* until 1909. Working mainly from her letters, the California author Wallace Stegner based his historical novel *Angle of Repose* (1971) on her experience in the West.

Chapter 5: The journalists' California

The four journalists treated at length in chapter 5 have prompted little in the way of scholarly study, still less literary criticism. Taylor alone has earned a biography, Richmond Beatty's *Bayard Taylor, Laureate of the Gilded Age* (1936), and a volume in the Twayne United States Authors Series (Paul Wermuth, *Bayard Taylor*, 1973). Other Taylor titles include his collected *Poems* (1868), his *Dramatic Works* (1880), *A Journey to Central Africa* (1859) and *At Home and Abroad* (1862). Like Irving and Mark Twain, Taylor first established his *bona fides* as an American writer by 'covering' Europe as a travel correspondent. His first book of prose, for which he was made literary editor of the New York *Tribune,* was *Views A-Foot; or, Europe seen with Knapsack and Staff* (1846).

Besides his *California Sketches* and eleven short sketches published in the *Overland Monthly* between 1869 and 1874, Leonard Kip wrote a number of historical romances, among which were *Aenone, a Tale of Slave Life in Rome* (1866), *Hannibal's Man* (1873) and *Through the Great Siege* (1893). John Borthwick's journalism for *Blackwood's* can be sampled in his 'Nicaragua and the Filibusters,' *Blackwood's Edinburgh Magazine,* LXXIX, March, 1856. His superb engravings accompany his text of *Three Years in California* and also appeared, according to the short biographical note in *Who Was Who in America,* (historical volume, 1607–1896), in the *Illustrated London News.* Contributions to that journal then were anonymous, but the illustrations appearing in the issue for Saturday, 9 August, 1851 may be Borthwick's. *Three Years in California* was reprinted in 1917 as *The Gold Hunters.*

Louise Clappe first used the pseudonym 'Dame Shirley' for some poems and rather flowery sketches published in the *Marysville* [California] *Herald* for 8 April and 1 May, 1851. *The Shirley Letters from the California Mines* first appeared serially in *The* [San Francisco] *Pioneer* from January, 1854 through December, 1855. Rodman Paul has discovered most of what is known about her life (see his 'In Search of "Dame Shirley," ' *Pacific Historical Review,* May, 1964), but as far as I know, the text of the original letters has never been found, nor the identity of the sister in Massachusetts, whom she calls 'Molly,' positively established. This means, as I take it, that the letters may never have been real letters at all, let alone written on the dates assigned to them.

To get an idea of how the San Francisco establishment saw itself and the city at mid-century, see *The Annals of San Francisco* (1855), or Theodore Augustus Barry and B. A. Patten, *Men and Memories of San Francisco in the Spring of '50* (1873). For a more detached view, see Kevin Starr, *Americans and the California Dream* (1973), *passim* or one of the standard histories of the city, like Oscar Lewis, *San Francisco; Mission to Metropolis* (1966).

For a sense of the reportorial genres in which each of the four California journalists worked, see (for Taylor) any of the exotic, *soi-disant* accounts written by travelers in the West, like Irving's *Tour* or Bryant's *What I Saw,* cited elsewhere in this study; and (for Dame Shirley) any English epistolary novel from Fielding's *Pamela* (1740–1) onwards, not overlooking later adaptations of the device, such as in Jane Austen's *Sense and Sensibility* (1811) or (nearly contemporary with the publication of Dame Shirley's *Letters*) Esther Summerson's narrative in Dickens's *Bleak House,* first published serially in 1852–3.

Of travel accounts by British writers in America, the tradition in which Borthwick worked, there is a plethora. The best known and most influential (in America, anyway) were Captain Basil Hall's *Travels in North America in the Years 1827 and 1828* (1829), Frances Trollope's *Domestic Manners of the Americans* (1832), Captain Frederick Marryat's *A Diary in America, with Remarks on its Institutions* (1839) and Charles Dickens's *American Notes for General Circulation* (1842). Of these, Dickens is the most favorable, Trollope less so but more intelligent, and Marryat the least of either. For good samplers of English travelers in America see the anthologies by Edith Coomb (*America Visited*, n.d.) and Allan Nevins (*American Social History as Recorded by British Travellers*, 1931). Robert Athearn has edited a collection of travel writings by British travelers in the American West, called *Westward the Briton* (1962). A recent study of the British traveler in America is Peter Conrad's *Imagining America* (1980).

For an idea of the macaronic travel sketch and other newspaper burlesques, the tradition in which Kip worked his *California Sketches*, see the work of the various pseudonymous humorists like Artemus Ward (Charles Farrar Browne), Petroleum V. Nasby (David Ross Locke) and Mark Twain (Samuel Langhorne Clemens). The early sketches and letters of Mark Twain are discussed elsewhere in this book. Albert Nock has made a selection of Artemus Ward's work (1924, reissued 1970). 'Nasby' can be sampled in *Andy's Trip to the West, Together With a Life of its Hero, by Petroleum V. Nasby, a Dimmicrat of Thirty Years Standing, and who Allus tuk his Licker Straight* (1866); and *Nasby in Exile; or, Six Months of Travel in England, Ireland, Scotland, France, Germany, Switzerland and Belgium* (1882). Earlier and closer to home were the humorous *Pen Knife Sketches, or Chips of the Old Block* (1853) and *Old Block's Sketch Book; or, Tales of California Life* (1856) by Alonzo Delano. See also George Hunter Derby, *Phoenixiana; or Sketches and Burlesques by John Phoenix* (1856). The essential introduction to the subject is Constance Rourke's classic, *American Humor: a Study of the National Character* (1931), and a more recent study of considerable interest also for its ramifications into American literature of the nineteenth and twentieth centuries is Richard Bridgman's *The Colloquial Style in America* (1966).

The subject of the precociousness of western historiography, especially in California, is discussed in Starr, *American and the California Dream*, in his chapter IV, 'A Rapid, Monstrous Maturity.' Starr cites the characteristic cases of John Frost's *History of California*, which emerged in 1850, the year in which the state was admitted to the Union, and *The Annals of San Francisco* written by three journalists, Frank Soulé, John Gihon and James Nisbet, and published just five years later. Hubert Howe Bancroft, the San Francisco publisher, book collector and historian of California and the West must also be cited as perhaps the most distinguished exemplar of the industriousness and enthusiasm of early California historians. A study of his life and work is J. W. Caughey's *Hubert Howe Bancroft; Historian of the West* (1946). Two books with chapters on American historiography of the West are Michael Kraus's *A History of American History* (1937) and John Higham's *The Reconstruction of American History* (1963).

Finally, Joseph Glover Baldwin's 'The Flush Times of Alabama and Mississippi,' a collection of sketches – some humorous and some serious – about the legal profession in the Old Southwest, was first published as a series of essays in *The Southern Literary Messenger* (Jan., 1853 *et seq.*), then as a book at the end of the same year. 'California Flush Times,' now edited by Richard Amacher and George Polhemus (1966) first appeared in *The Southern Literary Messenger* for November, 1853. The uncompleted manuscript, which his modern editors have titled 'Ebb Tide,' appears in the modern volume. Baldwin was also the author of a serious study of Jefferson, Hamilton, Jackson, Clay and Randolph, called *Party Leaders* (1855). A short biographical sketch is included in the modern edition of *California Flush Times*.

Chapter 6: Mark Twain's West

Since chapter 6 was written, Mark Twain's *Early Tales and Sketches, 1851–1864* has appeared in the Iowa–California edition of *The Works of Mark Twain*, edited by Edgar Branch, Robert Hirst and Harriet Smith (vol. 15 of the Iowa–California Twain, 1979), but a systematic edition of Clemens's letters relating to this period is still awaited. Where relevant, citations from the early journalism have been altered to conform to the *Early Tales* pagination. Good books abound on this stage of Mark Twain's career. E. M. Mack's *Mark Twain in Nevada* gives a good idea of the social and intellectual milieu of Virginia City, including a lively account of Artemus Ward's visit to the town and his early friendship with Mark Twain. Paul Fatout's *Mark Twain in Virginia City* (1964) is especially valuable for its account of the duel that was never fought. Useful for the sense of mood and tone it conveys of Virginia City in the 1860s, is Dan de Quille (William Wright), 'Salad Days of Mark Twain,' in *The Life and Times of the Enterprise* (1971), edited by Oscar Lewis. The book contains a valuable bibliography of other *Enterprise* authors. *Mark Twain of the Enterprise* (1957), edited by Henry Nash Smith and Frederick Anderson, is a selection of Mark Twain's *Enterprise* pieces amply fleshed out with valuable biographical and bibliographical notes. Edgar Branch performed the same service with Mark Twain's journalism in the San Francisco *Call* in his edition of *Clemens of the Call* (1969). His *The Literary Apprenticeship of Mark Twain* (1950) studies the development of the writer from his earliest journalism in Hannibal through his western period.

Readers wishing to get another fix on the importance of the West to Mark Twain's development should triangulate from his *The Celebrated Jumping Frog of Calaveras County, and Other Sketches* (1867), *The Innocents Abroad* (1869) and *Roughing It* (1872). These, his first three books, represent something written while his life in the West was still fresh in his experience, an extended travel sketch on Europe and the older civilizations of Egypt and the Holy Land, and a retrospective look at his adventures in the West. The best accompaniment to this reading would be Henry Nash Smith's sensitive and scholarly *Mark Twain; the Development of a Writer* (1962).

The debate on whether Mark Twain sold out to the East is represented by (for the motion) Van Wyck Brooks's *The Ordeal of Mark Twain* (1920), and (against) Bernard de Voto's *Mark Twain's America* (1932). The best general studies are Justin Kaplan's critical biography, *Mr. Clemens and Mark Twain* (1966) and James Cox's subtle and thoughtful *Mark Twain; the Fate of Humor* (1966).

Dan de Quille's *The Big Bonanza* was first published by Mark Twain's own publishers, The American Publishing Company, in 1876. A modern edition with an introduction by Oscar Lewis (1947) includes excerpts from the letters between Mark Twain and Dan de Quille about the project. De Quille also wrote a shorter, less colorful history of the Nevada Silver Rush, called *A History of the Comstick Lode & Mines, Nevada and the Great Basin Region, Lake Tahoe and the High Sierras* (1889). This was reprinted in facsimile in 1973, and is still in print today.

INDEX